The Dinka:
A Nilotic Lifecycle

Francis Mading Deng

The publisher wishes to acknowledge and thank Dr. Douglas H. Johnson for his invaluable help and support for Africa World Books and its mission of preserving and promoting African cultural and literary traditions and history. Dr. Johnson and fellow historians have been instrumental in ensuring that African people remain connected to their past and their identity. Africa World Books is proud to carry on this mission.

The Sudan Cultural Development Project, involving the reproduction of books and their translation into Arabic and making them widely available, is made possible by the generous support of the Swiss Agency for Development and Cooperation which the author and publisher gratefully acknowledge.

First published in 1972 as 'The Dinka of Sudan'
Reissued in 1984 and updated in 1986.
Reissued and updated in 2022 as 'The Dinka: A Nilotic Lifecycle'

ISBN (Softcover): 978-0-6455229-0-7
ISBN (Hardcover): 978-0-6454529-0-7

Cover design, typesetting and layout : Africa World Books
Unit 3, 57 Frobisher St, Osborne Park, WA 6017
P.O. Box 1106 Osbourne Park, WA 6916

Africa
World Books
Pty Ltd

Dedication

To the memory of my brother, Chief Abdalla Monyyak de Deng, who, on September 17, 1970, with our brothers Lino Chan and Abugaber Bulabek and our uncles Arob Mahdi, Col Guiny, and Kiir Jal, fell dead before a firing squad of assassins.

May this book be a modest symbol of the cause for which they died.

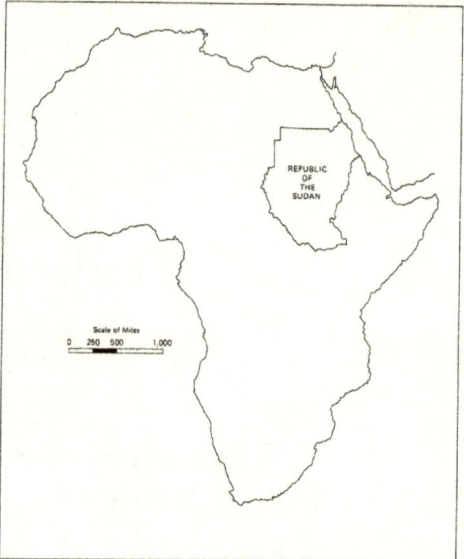

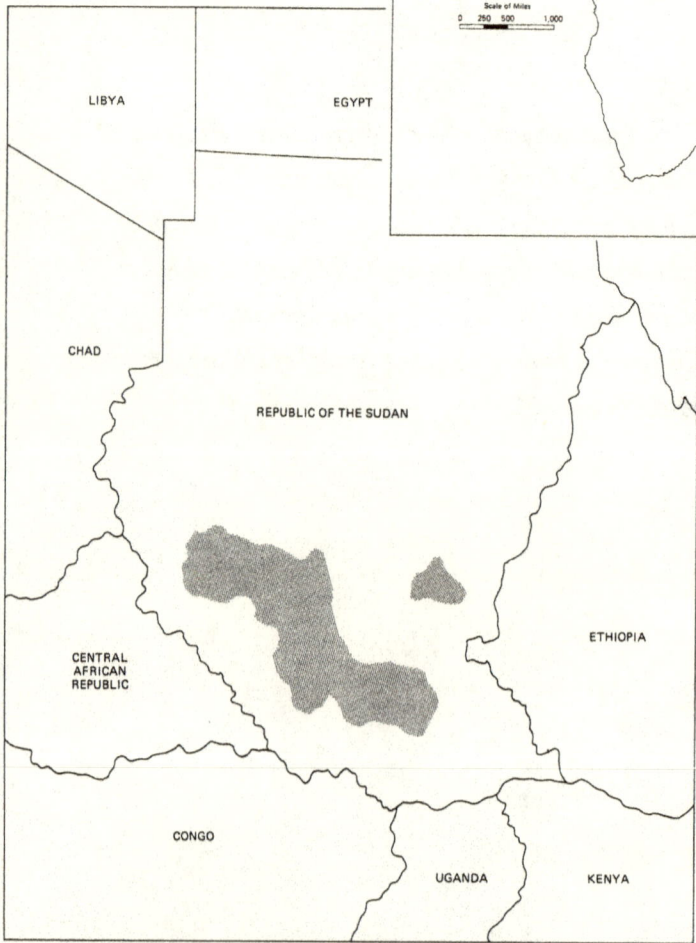

THE DINKA OF THE SUDAN

Contents

Updated Preface

The Dinka: A Nilotic Lifecycle

The Dinka of the Sudan has been reproduced in three versions and used as a reference in anthropology courses in universities abroad for decades. I wrote a substantial postscript to the third edition in 1986 in which I discussed the substantial transformation the Dinka had undergone since the book was first published in 1972 and 1984.

Significant changes have occurred since the book was reissued in 1986, especially with the armed struggle that was staged by the Sudan People's Liberation Movement and its military wing, the Sudan People's Liberation Army (SPLM/SPLA) in 1983 and lasted for 22 years. The 2005 Comprehensive Peace Agreement provided for the exercise of self-determination in the South which led to the independence of South Sudan on July 9, 2011.

In this updated preface, I comment very briefly on five issues:

- A brief overview of the changes the Dinka have experienced since 1986, of which the partition of the Sudan and its consequences is a defining factor;

- The dilemma of studying the culture of one ethnic group by a member of that group in a country of ethnic and cultural diversity;
- The commonality of fundamental values across ethnic and cultural divides and the search for a unifying normative framework of universal human dignity;
- The need for studying different cultures to discern similarities and differences, with the view to fostering a shared national identity and value system; and
- The paradoxes of self-determination, and the challenge of resolving internal conflicts through inter-state cooperation.

Overview on Transformative Developments

From the time the second civil war that was championed by the Sudan People's Liberation Movement and its Army, SPLM/A, broke out in 1983, the world of the Dinka has been fundamentally transformed. The premise this transformation is that the SPLM/A, unlike the previous liberation movements in the South, which had secession as their stated objective, stipulated a vision of a New Sudan of full equality without any discrimination based on race, ethnicity, religion, culture or gender. That vision began to inspire the marginalized ethnic groups in Northern Sudan in a way that significantly transcended the North-South divide. Freedom fighters from the Nuba Mountains of Southern Kordofan and the Angassana Hills in the Blue Nile, and later Darfur, began to join the liberation struggle. Even the Nubians of the far North began to voice their pride in their ancient Nubian identity and civilization and disavow the distorted vision of the country as Arab, with politicized Islam as its inter-ethnic glue.

The strategy of the leader of the movement, Dr. John Garang de Mabior, a friend with whom I worked very closely, was however more complex than one of unwavering commitment to unity in a

New Sudan. It is true that Garang believed in the unity of a transformed Sudan of full equality, but he also saw that as a pragmatic
tactical way of pursuing the alternative goal of secession. His view
was that independence for South Sudan could not be obtained by
shouting out ideals from the mountain top, but by fighting for it on
the ground. Fighting for such a transformative goal however requires
a vision that unites and wins support rather than one that alienates
and divides, with increased opposition to the vision. Calling for unity
in equality was a winning strategy, while secession was antithetical to
the overriding principle of preserving colonial borders that African
leaders stipulated from the beginning of the independence movement, and endorsed and supported by the international community.
If the widely shared goal of full equality could not be achieved within
unity, then secession must be a justified fallback option. If on the
other hand the vision of a New Sudan could be achieved, then why
insist on secession within a much smaller territorial space, instead
of sharing the bigger pie on equal footing?

In the end, the vision of a New Sudan of full equality could not
be achieved through armed struggle, and self-determination that
led to the independence of South Sudan became the only viable
alternative. This is why the title of this book had to change to *The
Dinka A Framework of Lifecycle*. But the vision of a New Sudan of
full equality had already infected the whole country, including the
North. Sudan could no longer be the same. In any case, full equality
without discrimination is a universal principle from which no country
is immune. Even with independence, South Sudan continued to be
challenged by the quest for equality among its various ethnicities.
The question for inclusivity and equality is both horizontal across
the country and vertical at all levels, from national down to local.

As a result of the unresolved challenges of an inter-ethnic and
inter-communal quest for equality, South Sudan after independence
has become a country torn apart by internal conflicts across the

country and at all levels. Rampant insecurity has permeated the countryside and frustrated farming and self-sustaining agricultural productivity. This has rendered a country endowed with vast arable land, with plentiful sources of water, largely dependent on foreign food aid. Populations have been massively displaced and migration to urban centers has resulted in acute poverty that has created unprecedented class structures in a previously egalitarian society. The strategy of the SPLM of taking towns to the rural areas, using oil to fuel the engine of agriculture, and building a network of roads, has remained a relic slogan on paper.

The people I have described in the book, who were widely known for their pride and dignity, are tragically being severely negatively impacted. There is therefore an urgent call for cultural revival and renaissance and the adoption and implementation of the strategy of transitional integration which I proposed and expounded in my doctoral dissertation and published in 1971 as *Tradition and Modernization: A Challenge for Law Among the Dinka of the Sudan*, of which *The Dinka of the Sudan* was a byproduct. Transitional integration requires approaching development as a concept of self-enhancement from within, building on indigenous values and institutions. In the case of the Dinka, these cultural values are outlined and elaborated in *The Dinka of the Sudan*.

For the strategy of transitional integration to be successfully pursued, peace and security must first be credibly and sustainably established. Sudan and South Sudan have increasingly become twinned countries suffering from intertwined crises that require cooperative strategies across the board within and between the two countries. As Sudan was about to be divided, I wrote a small book, *Sudan at the Brink: Self-Determination and National Unity*, in which I saw the independence of the South as a foregone conclusion, but argued that unity and separation were degrees of ongoing relations that could be strengthened or weakened according to the will of the people and their leaders. After the independence of South Sudan, I pursued that argument in another book, *Bound by Conflict: Dilemma of Two Sudans,* in which argued that despite their partition, the two countries remained united by conflicts that crossed their borders through their mutual support for each other's rebel groups and tribal militias. What was needed was cooperation between them to resolve their internal conflicts in a way that could improve their bilateral relations and foster close partnership.

With the recent developments in which Sudan was a lead member of the countries that mediated the peace agreements in South Sudan and South Sudan's facilitation of Sudanese negotiations for peace within the country, that goal is being promisingly pursued. More efforts with enhanced sustainable results are however still needed.

The Dilemma of Ethnic Studies

In studying Dinka culture, I have always been acutely aware of the risks involved in studying and documenting the culture and values of one's own ethnic group. These risks are multiple. One is the assumption of bias associated with what is perceived as essentially self-reflection and projection. The other is the tendency of members of the group studied to take what is documented as known to them because it is about them. The third is a dismissal of the study by rival groups on competitive grounds. And, of course, there is the well-known biased view that indigenous cultures are primitive and outmoded relics of fading social order, not worthy of modern attention. I was often criticized by colleagues in the national government for writing on the Dinka, which they considered parochial. These comments were not only racist but grossly misguided and unstatesmanlike. What is required is patriotic civility, objectivity, and sensitivity to the demands of constructive equitable management of diversity.

As *The Dinka of the Sudan* was first published abroad and used in foreign universities, I have been very much impressed by conflicting responses from readers. There were those who placed emphasis on the differences they saw between their Western culture and the remote indigenous culture of the Dinka, to which they could hardly relate. And there were those who saw similarities and were also impressed by the differences and comparative merits of Dinka culture. Some readers, of whom the editors of this book are an example, admired the Dinka values described by the book. The overriding values of *Cieng baai* embodying the ideals of unity and harmony, and *Dheeng*, which comprises principles of individual and collective dignity, had a particular appeal.

Unfortunately, our people take these values for granted, which poses the risk of losing them, especially among our young generations. I have heard members of my own Dinka community, especially those in my age group, say that they of course know whatever I write about the Dinka. One reacted to my book, *The Dinka and Their Songs*, which was acclaimed by literary reviewers for its poetic merits, by wondering whether they really represented our Dinka poetry or my own invention. Fellow Northern Sudanese ministers, who came to my house in Khartoum and to which I played the records of Dinka songs produced by Folkways company in New York in long-playing albums, could not believe that the Dinka had songs of the quality that merited such modern production. Of course, technology has now become widely available and Dinka songs, some in modernized forms, are being widely recorded and disseminated. But the richness of our indigenous cultures remains obscure and hardly appreciated, even by our people. When I give talks to our young people, many of whom grew up outside their cultural environment, eyes open wide, and deep appreciation glows on their faces, as they sense some affinity to what I describe, but view it as a barely recognizable dying culture. This trend must be reversed.

The Search for Commonality in Diversity

I am of course aware that my pride in the culture I describe may be offensive to members of other cultures who are equally proud of their own cultural value systems and see exhalting another culture as a denigration of their own culture. During the South Sudan National Dialogue in which I was Deputy Reporteur and Spokesman and also charged with quality control of the documentation of the process, there was a strong resentment from some members about what they saw as a chauvinistic attitude on the part of the dominant ethnic groups, whom they accused of dominating the country on the basis of their cultural values and the assumption of cultural vacuums in other ethnic groups. This was at best an exaggeration, if not entirely false. But perceptions are as real and consequential as facts. Perceptions of gross inequality in diversity must therefore be corrected through remedial measures.

Interestingly enough, apart from the varied responses from Western readers which I alluded to earlier, *The Dinka of the Sudan* generated favorable comparisons within our country and the wider region. A scholar from one of the Equatorian communities told me that the culture described in the book is almost identical to that of his own ethnic group. Another scholar from Somalia told me that on reading the book, he felt that if the adjective 'Dinka' were replaced by 'Somali,' the book would be almost entirely on Somali culture and worldview.

The dilemma is that while we must study our individual cultures, doing so may have the unintended negative consequence of entrenching the differences, not to mention the competitive dismissal of the results. In an attempt to remedy this situation, I recently initiated a project with several objectives. The first is to document every one of our component South Sudanese cultures. The second is to discern the similarities and differences among them. And the third is to develop a unified framework based on complementarities and synergies. The outcome could be incorporated into our educational curriculum at all levels of the system and be used in developing a culturally oriented normative framework of governance and constitutionalism as well as guiding principles for our international relations. Work on that project is ongoing.

From Bound by Conflicts to Bonded by Solutions

As noted earlier, unity and separation are degrees of ongoing relations and though separated, the two Sudans remained bound by conflicts, though their recent cooperation is now getting them bonded by their joint efforts to resolve their internal conflicts that spill over their borders. The crisis of identity that had torn the old Sudan apart remains a challenge to both countries. Sudan, which expected the secession of the South to leave their residual country united behind an Arab-Islamic agenda, is finding that the vision of a New Sudan which the South had ironically stipulated and championed, is still a popular call that is threatening the survival of their old public order.

South Sudan itself is not immune from the identity crisis that had torn the Sudan apart. Diversity is a relative phenomenon reflected at all levels, who's is why internal conflicts that are identity-related filter down to the level of local communities. While the differences between the Arab-Islamic North and the African Secular South might have been more pronounced, the ethnic differences that characterize South Sudan also pose a serious challenge to the unity of the country. This calls for constructive management of identity through inclusivity and various forms and degrees of equitable unity in diversity.

Countries challenged by diversity are faced with a choice from three alternatives. The first and the best option is to create a framework with which all groups could identify as equal citizens. The second is to formulate a system of coexisting differently, but equitably. The third, a residual option, is to accept an unavoidable partition if neither of the two options is mutually accepted. The two Sudans still confront these choices. It is difficult to see how Sudan can be further divided and fragmented. And of course, breaking up South Sudan is not an option that any of the ethnic groups can pursue as a viable option. Managing diversity constructively to ensure inclusivity and equality remains the desirable and achievable alternative for both countries. And cooperation toward that objective is not only a mutually beneficial strategy but one whose positive outcome would significantly facilitate close bilateral ties between the two countries.

Between two independent states, there are border communities whose inter-communal relations and potential conflicts require the cooperation of the two states to manage constructively. Sovereign control over these communities may be contested by the states concerned. Resolving these contesting claims may require granting the communities a degree of internal self-determination or self-administration that makes them autonomous, but still linked to the two neighboring states. In a sense, this modifies the sovereignty of the two concerned states over the border states.

Concluding Word on Book

The Dinka of the Sudan, now given the new title of The Dinka: A Framework of Lifecycle, has been in print for fifty years and has been extensively used as a resource in social anthropology by universities abroad. I am exceedingly glad that it is now coming back to its roots at home in Africa and more accessible to our readers in South Sudan.

My objective in documenting Dinka culture in the sixties is even more pertinent today as we face the challenge of statecraft and nation-building in our own independent South Sudan. But my objective is not limited to the Dinka but to our fellow South Sudanese and beyond. This requires that we understand our individual cultures and develop a shared framework of national identity and cultural values, to inform our educational system, formulate principles of governance and constitutionalism, and stipulate guidelines for our diplomacy and international relations.

I want to end by expressing my deep appreciation and gratitude to Africa World Books, and particularly to its founder and publisher, Peter Lual Reech Deng, for the historic and challenging venture of documenting the culture, history, and the multi-faceted struggle of our people at this critical juncture in building the nation. I hope our people will reinforce Peter Deng's vision and endeavors by becoming responsive and supportive readers. I would also like to express my deep appreciation for the editorial contribution of Dr. Sara Maher. She has significantly enriched the volume with meticulous attention to contextual details in light of the changes Dinka society has undergone since the book was first published.

Francis Mading Deng
Woodstock, N.Y.
July 8, 2022

Foreword

About the Author

Francis Mading Deng was born in 1938 at Noong, near Abyei, the administrative center of the Ngok Dinka of which his father was Paramount Chief. He attended elementary and intermediate schools in the Southern Sudan and received his secondary education in Khor Taggat in the Northern part of the country. Afterward, he entered Khartoum University where he graduated with LL.B. (Honors) in 1962 and was appointed to the Academic Staff of the Faculty of Law. He then proceeded to England and the United States for graduate studies, obtaining the LL.M. and the J.S.D. degrees from Yale University in 1965 and 1967 consecutively, after which he joined the United Nations Secretariat in New York in the Division of Human Rights. During his period at the United Nations, Dr. Deng also taught Legal Anthropology at New York University and African Law at Columbia Law School. In 1971, he took a leave of absence from the United Nations to undertake a post-doctoral research project with the Yale Programme of Law and Modernization. A year later, he joined his country's foreign service and served consecutively as Ambassador to the Scandinavian countries, Ambassador to the United States of America, Minister of State for Foreign Affairs, and Ambassador to Canada in the status of Minister of State. After leaving the foreign service in 1983, Dr. Deng was Guest Scholar at the Woodrow Wilson International Center for Scholars in Washington D.C. for a brief period and was subsequently appointed the first Distinguished Fellow of the Rockefeller Brothers Fund in New York.

Other books by Dr. Deng include the award-winning *Tradition and Modernization: A Challenge for Law Among the Dinka of the Sudan*; *Dynamics of Identification: A Basis for National Integration in the Sudan*; *The Dinka and Their Songs*; *Dinka Folktales*; *Africans of Two Worlds: The Dinka in Afro-Arab Sudan*; *Dinka Cosmology. Recollections of Babo Nimir*, and *the British in the Sudan*, were co-edited with Professor Robert O. Collins of the University of California, Santa Barbara.

About the Book

This case study is written by Francis Mading Deng, son of the late Paramount Chief of the Ngok Dinka. That fact in itself suggests that the reader is in for an unusual experience as he or she reads this case study. There are many passages in this book where we are privileged to enter the cultural system with the insider's view and with his interpretations. This, by itself, is not a guarantee of good ethnography, for the perspective of the outsider to the system is essential as well. But Dr. Deng also provides us with this other perspective. He holds a Doctorate in Law from Yale University and has been closely associated with the work of Dr. Godfrey Lienhardt, Oxford University anthropologist, for whom Dinka ethnography has been a major professional concern.

This case study has a strategy. It starts with the life goals of the Dinka, then lays out the major points in the life cycle of individuals in Dinka society, pursuing the meaning of events in these periods out into the whole of the cultural system. From this strategy we acquire a rich and well-balanced view of Dinka life, but at the same time, find personal experience within it. The reader learns of the structure of society, sex roles, courtship, kinship, age-sets and rivalries, the family, property, mores, law, religion, philosophy, poetry, and dance.

While reading this book we experience the rich qualities of Dinka life and at the same time the intellectual gratification of conceptual analysis. Dinka life has a quality that beguiles and stirs the reader. The gentlemanly qualities subsumed by the term *dheeng*, apparent in pride and manners, are of high importance. For instance, men must eat fastidiously, talk elegantly, and stand and walk with poise. Yet there is much raw violence in Dinka life. This violence is most striking among the unrestrained youth, but it dominates much of the life and behavior of Dinka men. There are other paradoxical qualities in Dinka culture. Like many of the world's peoples the Dinka think of themselves as superior people and yet they are subservient to their cattle. Young men identify with their "personality" oxen, decorated with tassels and worked leather and wearing a bell that clanks rhythmically as the young men and their oxen walk about to be admired, particularly by the girls. This identification with the cattle is a phenomenon that is quite alien to the Westerner, so an attempt to understand it will move us closer to the heart of Dinka culture, and to other African cultures where the famed "cattle complex" is, or was, significant.

The author uses effective techniques of communication, allowing, for example, his own experiences as a Dinka youth to enter into the description. Another unusual feature of this case study is the use of songs, composed in free verse, to give us the Dinka flavor to events such as courtship, loss of pride, displays of temper or aggression, mocking of rivals, or announcement of events. From these songs we can at least dimly sense the real qualitative differences between Western and Dinka patterns of thought and expression; and at the same time, we can sense the common human quality of the emotions and motivations involved.

In the last chapter, the author discusses the devastating North-South conflict—the 16-year-old civil war in which, it is estimated, over a million people have died and many more have been displaced. This conflict is seen as running much deeper than political differences alone. It is a matter of ethnic differences between the Arabic North and the Negroid South, of religious-cultural differences between Islam and Christianity, and of the differences between urban national and traditional tribal segments. This war is one of the tragedies of today's Africa where not only tribal and cultural loyalties determine rivalries and wars, but in addition legacies from the colonial past create seemingly unresolvable rifts resulting in savage civil conflicts. And the situation for the Dinka, as well as for other peoples in Africa, is compounded by the fact that not only the European powers built empires there, but also the Arabs and in many areas Negroid peoples created state societies from conquests over each other. Nevertheless, Dr. Deng is optimistic that these conflicts will ultimately be resolved, although at incredible human costs, and that the Dinka will find their way into a position of peaceful interaction with the other elements of the Sudanese nation, at the same time preserving many of the characteristics of traditional Dinka culture that have made his people unique.

- George and Louise Spindler

Acknowledgments

The idea for this book first originated in 1963 when the editors of this series invited Dr. Godfrey Lienhardt to prepare a case study on the Dinka, and he suggested me as a co-author. Although our plans did not materialize, I have benefited a great deal from Dr. Lienhardt. He is both a friend and the leading authority on the Dinka. I am very grateful to Professor John Middleton who recommended to the editors of this series that plans for the Dinka study be resumed. For many years now my dear friend, Jane Glassman, has been a close assistant in my writings, and without her editorial help and constructive criticism this book would not be what it is.

To my Dinka informants and to the composers and singers, I hope the book is a worthy tribute.

- F. M.D.

The Dinka:
A Nilotic Lifecycle

The author, 1971. (Courtesy of Pach Brothers, N.Y.)

Chapter One:

Introduction

The Dinka are a Nilotic people in the Republic of the Sudan. With a population of nearly two million in a country of only fifteen million people and over five hundred tribes, they are by far the most numerous ethnic group in the Sudan. Also striking is their vast territory covering about a tenth of the nearly one million square miles that make the Sudan the largest country in Africa.

To the nineteenth and even the mid-twentieth century travelers, the Dinka were better known as "giants about seven feet tall who, like the Nile cranes, stand on one foot in the river for hours looking for fish." [1] The word "giant" should not conceal the slimness of the Dinka. Another observer writes:

> *If you can picture to yourself a race of long-legged, well-built people so tall that a seven-foot man is no uncommon sight, so slim that a white man cannot fit his hand into their shield-grips or his body into their canoes (indeed, I cannot recall even*

---

1   Confidential Report to the United Nations on the Anglo-Egyptian Sudan, 1947.

*having seen a fat Dinka); and if you can picture these people
clad in nothing but beads and an expansive, cheery grin, you
are at least visualizing the bare outlines of the portrait I am
attempting to paint.* [2]

These are, indeed, bare outlines: They do not say, for instance,
that the one leg is assisted by a shafted spear; that fishing is only
supplementary to cattle herding and agriculture; that women do not
go naked; and that tall and slender as the Dinka are, the degree falls
short of the description. But things have changed. As the Dinka have
become more accessible to the world, exotic descriptions are giving
way to more accurate information.

The land of the Dinka is in the rich savannah, segmented by the
waters of the Nile and its tributaries. Large in numbers, widespread
in settlement, and divided by many rivers, some are unaware of one
another as fellow Dinka. A congeries of about twenty-five mutually
independent tribal groups, they are united by their physical characteristics, their ethnocentric pride, and their striking cultural uniformity.
Today, the vast majority of Dinka tribes fall under the administration
of Bahr-el-Ghazal and the Upper Nile, two of the Sudan's three
southern provinces, but one group, the Ngok Dinka, fall under the
authority of Kordofan, one of the six provinces of the North.

In racial and cultural terms the Ngok are Southerners. The anomaly
of their administration results from the fact that their chiefs signed
allegiance to both the Turko-Egyptian and the Anglo-Egyptian colonial governments in El Obeid, the capital of Kordofan. For centuries
prior to the advent of colonialism, the Ngok had been in contact
with the Arab tribes farther north. The close diplomatic relations
and cross-cultural influences between their leaders resulted in the
centralized and hierarchal political system of the Ngok which sharply

2   Major C. Court Treatt, *Out of the Beaten Track*, New York: E. P. Dutton &
     Co., Inc (1931), p.112.

contrasts with the "acephalous," uncentralized nature of traditional Dinka society. The Ngok have always had divine chiefs, although their power was diffused into the lineage system. In most aspects of their culture, the Ngok have been little affected by their contacts with the Arabs. In view of their relative isolation from the bulk of the Dinka and close contacts with the Arabs, the extent to which the Ngok have retained their Dinka culture is remarkable.

The cultural continuity of the Dinka is often ascribed to their pride and ethnocentrism, which are conspicuous in their own name for themselves. They do not call themselves "Dinka" but Monyjang, which means "The Man [or the husband] of Meri." This denotes that they see themselves as the standard of what is normal for the dignity of man and asserts their superiority to "the others" or "foreigners" (the juur: singular, jur).

While viewing themselves as "Lords of Men" the Dinka are loving slaves of cattle and they will gladly admit this. In the spirit of a devout slave, a Dinka will kill and even risk his life for a single cow. They have a myth that explains their involvement with, and suffering for, cattle: The Dinka went hunting and killed the mother of the buffalo and the cow. Both, bereft and provoked, vowed to take vengeance against man. The buffalo chose to remain in the forest and attack man whenever he laid eyes on him. (To this day, the buffalo is one of the few animals that will charge against man without provocation.) The cow on the other hand ingeniously preferred to fight man within man's own system: to be domesticated to make man slave for her; to play man off against man; and to cause him to fight and kill for ownership, possession, or protection of her.

But, if the cow is subtle, the Dinka too has his reasons for being allured into her trap. Cattle provide him with much of his worldly needs. Cows provide dairy products that the Dinka consider not only the best, but also the most noble, food. While they deplore killing the animal out of craving for meat and will do so only in sacrifice to God, spirits, and their ancestors - and sometimes in honor of guests, or for special feasts - almost every animal is eventually destined for the fire or the pot, since every animal is eaten whatever the cause of its death. Through dedication and sacrifice, cattle protect the Dinka against the evil forces of illness and death. Their payment as "bridewealth" guarantees the continuation of the Dinka race, and the distribution of the bridewealth among a wide circle of relatives cements the network of human ties so highly regarded by the Dinka. Cattle are also paid as blood wealth in homicide and in compensation for a variety of other wrongs. Their dried dung provides the Dinka with fuel and fertilizer, their urine with disinfectant, their hides with bedding skins, and their horns with snuff boxes, trumpets, and spoons. So important for the welfare of the Dinka and so honored by them are their cattle that the Dinka speak of the cow or the bull as the "creator." With bridewealth sometimes going as high as 200 cows, the Dinka are probably the richest cattle-owners on the continent of Africa and certainly in the Sudan. They also keep sheep and goats. But to these animals they afford only a fraction of their devotion to cattle.

Less known is the fact that the Dinka are cultivators, although their production is generally on the subsistence level and sometimes below it. This is partly because of their lavish hospitality, extravagant festivity, and resentment of saving as miserly. Much, however, has to do with their rudimentary implements and the adverse climate both of which limit the size of the land they can till and the amount they can produce. So irregular are the rains that they may fall and people plant, then stop, and crops die, or soak the fields and drown the crops. While their land is full of all-season rivers, the Dinka do not use irrigation except on their small plots of tobacco which are cultivated during the dry season. Worms, locusts, birds, and a variety of animals are additional threats at all stages of cultivation.

For human beings and animals there is much discomfort in Dinkaland. The blazing sun of the dry season kills the grass and

A dry season landscape in Malual Dinka country with sleeping huts built on stilts. There are no cattle byres in the photograph. (Courtesy of the United Nations)

deceives the traveler with moving mirages of rivers and lakes. The soil dries up, forming wide and deep cracks into which humans and animals fall. The ground and trees are covered with sturdy thorns. Swarms of restless flies torment both men and herds. Armies of mosquitoes necessitate exhaustive fanning or escaping into the smoky and stuffy huts. The wet season comes with heavy and stormy rains that may fall for days, leveling the tall grass and impeding even milking and cooking. Thunder and lightning leave behind fallen trees, burning huts, and sometimes dead relatives: tragedies that for the Dinka are divine manifestations calling for dedication and sacrifice. The Nile and its tributaries overflow, leaving floods, swamps, and mud. Lions, leopards, hyenas, wild dogs, rhinos, buffaloes, hippos, crocodiles, snakes, and scorpions are a continuous threat - so much more real than travelers' tales can tell.

Although the Dinka is always in direct contact with a hostile environment, he loves his country. He is self-sufficient in a way not easily explained by the simplicity of his desires. As he sees it, God has been most generous to him. He has cattle, sheep, and goats and he grows a wide variety of crops. His rivers and lagoons teem with fish just as his land is covered with animals. There are also many kinds of wild crops, vegetables, and fruits to satisfy his craving. Honey is in plenty. Depending on the season, his skies and pools are marvelously decorated with birds of every color, shape, and size. His fields and home sway with butterflies. The land is flat, changing from dark clay to white sand; from desert-like openness to jungle-like forests. The greenness of infant grass carpeting the land after the early rains, the reflections of the sun through falling rains, and the bright rainbow linking opposite ends of his horizon are only examples of the beauties. The rainy season the cattle returning to graze near the homes and bellowing to their tethered calves, the calves lowing to their mothers - near but unreachable, a boy singing as he starts a fire and tethers the cattle, the smoke from the fire mingling with the rays of

A yet incomplete cattle byre. Contrast the thatching with that of the huts on the facing page. Either can be used for sleeping huts or cattle byres. The latter are usually about four times the size of sleeping huts and are never

the setting sun, and the sweet smell of the dried, smoking cow dung make a dry-season dusk.

Because the country is flat, vision goes far; and in the evenings when fires are lit in distant cattle-camps, one sees a beacon of orange, pink, and yellow rising bright into the sky to spotlight the camps for a Dinka traveler. The sounds of distant drums, of bellowing herds, of howling boys, of singing birds, all combine to produce the harmonious tunes of the slow rhythm of tribal life. At night, the high-pitched sounds of crickets, the cries of frogs, of a mother singing any song as a lullaby at the peak of her voice while jiggling an accompanying gourd, of a gentleman's singing of his favorite ox, while the ox bellows with gratification are a pleasant break to the stillness of rural nights.

Moon-lit nights attract children to play for long hours when they would otherwise be asleep and young men to travel long distances to visit their girlfriends and to sit all night in the open air conversing until dawn.

Against the dangers of his hostile environment, the Dinka builds huts for himself and cattle byres for his herds. His walls of wood and mud and his roofs of rafters and grass have won great admiration from many a visitor. The length and firmness of the roof grass and the slimness and the straightness of the tall trees from which he curs his rafters and make his thatch remarkably smooth. Dinka buildings can last for well over ten years, and in a country of rudimentary technology where termites and other pests threaten timber, this is no easy feat.

To a Dinka, his country, with all its deprivations and troubles, is the best in the world. Until very recently, going to a foreign land was not only a rarity but a shame. For a Dinka to threaten his relatives with leaving Dinkaland was seen as little short of suicide. What a lot to give up, and for what!

In character, the Dinka is a socially conscious yet individualistic person, gentle and humorous, but sensitive, temperamental, and prone to violent reaction when his sense of pride and dignity is hurt - and that may not take much. Dinka society is an exceedingly violent society, and from very early age one of the central values in a boy's education is valor and physical strength. Determination and readiness to fight for one's honor and right against anyone of whatever strength merit high esteem in children and youth. Fighting with clubs between individuals and local groups leaves many a Dinka with scars on the head; and fighting with spears between tribal segments leaves many a feud to continue in perpetuity.

In sharp contrast with the violent disposition of militant youth, who provoke wars that are fought by all, is the emphasis on "ideal" human relations and on the attributes of unity, harmony, and persuasion. The chiefs and elders are largely persuasive, even though they admire the coercive character of their youth. Valor is institutionalized by means of organized warrior age-sets, and every Dinka joins one upon his initiation into adulthood. But this nurtured valor is ideally to be used against the aggressor and not for aggression. In fact, the Dinka never admit to being the aggressors. In their war-songs, they exalt themselves as ferocious resisters of aggression; but for the youth, any slight provocation is sufficient to incite a fight. Aside from repelling aggression, the violent disposition of youth is sublimated by directing it toward the protection of society against wild animals, herding in hostile land, cultivating the fields of the chiefs, building their homes, and taking preventive action against the violation of certain norms by members of the age-set. But there are other ways of sublimating the aggressive disposition of youth. Singing and dancing are typical institutions which augment Dinka youth's inner pride and outward dignity.

Proud and ethnocentric as the Dinka are, they are nevertheless hospitable and friendly to all visitors. Their high moral standards and sense of personal dignity and integrity prevent their taking advantage of foreigners. But once they are given a reason for disrespect by the misconduct of a foreigner, that foreigner barely qualifies as a human being. The Dinka are then prone to use their wits against him without the least feeling of guilt.

While the Dinka now form part of modern Sudan, they remain among the least touched by modernization. Their pride and ethnocentrism has always been given as an important factor in their conservatism and resistance to change. Postcolonial trends now indicate that this explanation is a partial truth. Colonial policies kept the tribes in isolation and tried to preserve traditional cultures. The abandonment of these policies have now led to intensive cross-cultural interaction. As a result of this interaction and of modern education, the Dinka are demonstrating an adaptability to change that was never predicted. But the strains and the pains of change are grave. The most obvious tragedy is that it is turning a dignified and independent people into an insecure, "inferior," and even subservient people whose lot so far seems to be a disintegration of the old order without an adequate substitution of a new one. While individuals have with varying success integrated themselves at various levels of the modern Sudanese social strata, for most of the Dinka the experience is harsh, the cost is high, the profit is low, and the future is dim. For others, the change is only a vacillation in pursuit of the material values of the town as a means of obtaining those traditional values which can now be bought with cash. It is increasingly common for Dinka youth to labor in towns in order to earn money with which to buy oxen for esthetic display or cattle for marriage. In this to-and-fro migration, much change for the worse takes place in both worlds. The filthy shacks they live in, their diet of little but bread and local beer, and their low social standing are examples.

The tragedy of change is aggravated by the political crisis between the Negroid South and the Arab North, the hostilities of which predate independence. As in all modern wars, many innocent people become victims of terrorism and of brutal death from both sides. Southerners paradoxically find more security in Northern towns, where some standards of public order are still observed with respect to all. Scores of thousands have also fled the country for refuge abroad and, as is true of refugees in general, they fall into an inferior level of the new society. To quell the insurgence, or otherwise solve the problem, many governments have come, failed, and gone.

The Dinka speak of the period of the nineteenth-century hostilities with Arab slavers as the time when the world was spoiled; today they speak of their world as spoiled. Yet, wittingly or unwittingly, they are coming to grips with the crisis and are bound to exert greater influence on the national level. If only because of their numbers, the Dinka will be of pivotal importance in the future of the Sudan.

The traditional society I have described here will of course wither away in the course of time, but the Dinka will take with them into the mainstream of modern Sudanese and world communities those values, sentiments, and characteristics which they hold dear or cannot otherwise shed. In a sense then, I am writing about what was, what is, and what will be.

I am also writing as a Dinka observer and naturally, there is much that can be said for and against this standpoint. The obvious danger is distortion in both directions. One may be too defensive about one's society and overstate. Or one may be too cautious about the dangers of involvement and understate. Being a Dinka, and a son of the Ngok Paramount Chief, I come from a family into which information on the society flows every day. To the Dinka, the home of the Chief is the central meeting place. Since Dinkaland is a land of equality even among unequals, interaction between us and those who converged on us was never restricted. As a child I grew up like any Dinka child, interacting freely with other children and without social barriers. The major exception is that I was one of the first few who went to school and became exposed to change. As I grew up going to school far away from home, my interests in Dinka traditions sharpened and focused. While studying law at Khartoum University, I came to a point where I wanted to bridge the gulf between the law I had always seen functioning at home and the law I was studying in the University. There was no official interest in customary law in the University, but some of the expatriate members of the faculty were quite interested. They encouraged me and unofficially cooperated. Under their guidance, I spent my vacations studying Dinka customary law, sitting in my father's Court, examining court cases back to my grandfather's records, and interviewing chiefs and elders. Some faculty members even persuaded the expatriate dean to have the faculty commission one lecturer and a senior student to go home with me to carry out further investigations and to check my data.

Since customary law cannot be studied in isolation, my work on the Dinka broadened. My collection even included several hundred tape-recorded songs which I later transcribed and translated. Abroad, I continued my work on the Dinka with lawyers and anthropologists. I have given this rather detailed account to emphasize that in my interest in the Dinka and in my investigation about them, I have tried to be an objective student while benefiting from my insider's view.

Perhaps I should point out that the name "Deng," when encountered, does not always refer to my family. Deng is a common name among the Dinka. It is used in honor of the deity Deng, a complex spirit second only to God in importance.

Now a word about the format and the methodology of the book. My main objective is to describe the Dinka, and my theoretical orientation is a broad one which does not in any way impede this objective. I am interested in writing about the Dinka not just as a collective whole, but as participants in a social process which I see as people seeking values through institutions by using resources. "People" includes individuals, groups, and mythical entities. "Values" is a rough conceptualization of everyday preferences, material and spiritual and not just a formulation of ideals commonly associated with the word "value." By an "institution" I mean all the established patterns of practices specialized to the pursuit of a value or an aspect of it. Resources are both material and human. This conception of the social process implies that, while society aims at the ideals, ordinary life involves competition, conflict, and failure in varying degrees. It is, however, important to present these processes and variations within a total "system" with an "inner logic" and a hierarchy of values and norms which provide the yardstick for measuring and evaluating behavior. Except in those areas in which I indicate the contrary, my description pertains to the present. Some of the things I experienced or observed in my youth may have changed, but without concrete evidence to the contrary.

I describe them as part of the present.

First, I present the overriding goals which condition the system. These are procreation, concepts of ideal human relations, and the value of human dignity. To describe the life of the Dinka in concrete terms, I then follow a life-cycle approach highlighted by birth, infancy, childhood, youth, adulthood, aging, and death. As Dinkaland is now undergoing conspicuous changes, the last chapter is "Change" and describes both its cultural aspects and the individuals affected by it. The conclusion summarizes the book and raises some issues concerning the future of the Dinka in the context of the problems now confronting them.

Chapter Two: Goals

Procreation

For a Dinka, where he comes from and where he goes to are points in the cycle of life revitalized and continued through procreation. Despite the anxieties birth provokes, it is a cause for joy; but death is an end from which procreational immortality is the only salvation.

Every Dinka fears dying without a son "to stand his head": to continue his name and revitalize his influence in this world. From the time a boy is born, he is prepared for this role; and from the time he becomes of age to the time he enters the grave, the main concern is that he himself begets children to do for him what he has done for those before him. A poor man of age who has no cattle with which to marry, a young man whose relatives are reluctant to arrange his marriage, or a man who for whatever reasons cannot fulfill this prime objective, is the truly mortal being in the eyes of the Dinka. When a man dies leaving children behind, people mourn but are quick to add that his is not "the bad death." But a man who dies without issue is truly dead. Another word for death is "perishing" (*riar*); to stir a man against a relative who is reluctant to arrange his marriage or to motivate a poor man to search for bridewealth, the usual threat is "Your head will perish" or simply, "You will perish." Should a man die without issue, he leaves behind an obligation for his kinsmen to select one relative to beget children for him with the widow he leaves behind or with a wife the chosen relative marries for his "ghost." These are the institutions of the "levirate" and the "ghost marriage." Since resources are not always sufficient, not every man is availed of this remedy: Some die and their lines disappear.

Immortality through procreation is more than child-bearing and child-rearing. The expression "standing the head" (*kooc e nhom*) has much greater social implications than the usual word for "birth" (*dhieth*). It is not uncommon to hear a parent complain "I have not given birth," or to invoke his lineage against the child by saying, "This is not our birth" or "This is not our kind." These are expressions of disappointment, shame, or lack of pride in the child who has failed to reflect the good in the parent or in the lineage. "Birth" in this sense is synonymous with procreation.

But the biological and social dimensions of immortality are more evident in "standing the head" than in "birth." Procreational immortality is an extension of this life into the hereafter or of the hereafter into this life through the memory of the dead. The closer the dead are to the living, biologically and socially, the greater the memory. Hence, one's biological child is the best way to procreational immortality.

A child who is handsome, courageous, courteous, intelligent, wise, well-spoken, or otherwise worthy of praise gives his parents the joy of seeing themselves immortalized in virtue. So identified are children with their parents and other relatives that the Dinka see it as self-praise and in bad taste to praise their own children or relatives. Indeed, they do not - except in songs when people may brag of themselves, their kinsmen, and their friends, or in certain circumstances where candid opinion is necessary. Children are praised and shown much affection but in subtle ways. A Dinka will even deprecate his child in terms all Dinkas understand as modesty - albeit false. Every Dinka is likely to have an idealized image of himself and his lineage. Unless the evidence is abundant, a defect in a child is denied or attributed to some origin outside the heredity of the parent concerned. I have heard a father say in disapproval of a son's conduct, "You never know the heart of a woman [meaning the son's mother]; who knows where she might have brought this birth [meaning the son]. None of our kind behaves like that." Ironically, the father was reputed to have had in his childhood and youth, the obstinacy and the tough-headedness, which his son was at that time demonstrating against him.

What a Dinka father wants is the perfection of his lineage through his posterity. The more children a man has, and from as many wives as he can afford, the more they complement and complete this idealized image. Among them will be men of distinguished physical attraction, warriors of renowned bravery, courtiers of intelligence and wisdom, men of excelling courtesy and social consciousness, and such other attributes as his genes or luck may bring. It is desired that a child, especially a son, should reflect his father's attributes. There is no greater joy for a Dinka son than to hear that he resembles his father. Conversely, it hurts a man to hear that he does not resemble his father or that he resembles his mother. This indicates the intense patriarchal nature of Dinka society. Women receive great attention and deference, but only as a special breed of junior partners and - one may say - as agents of male-oriented goals. This does not mean that procreational immortality is exclusively male-oriented; it means that the hierarchy of sex extends into immortality. A man may be very proud of his mother and her kin and may even love her more than his father, but objectively the male line remains dominant. Women reinforce this sex stratification. A mother is delighted to see and hear that her child, especially a son, resembles his father; she is offended to hear (if not to know) that he resembles her. Since the Dinka naming system is based on the father's line, the mother is insulted if her child should be called with reference to her, except when the child is within the confines of her own agnatic group. A mother is quick to see the attributes of her husband or his lineage in her child, whether they be positive or negative; and she will readily speak with false modesty on the "good" and joke about the "bad" (which is never really bad so long as it is agnatic heritage). She almost never admits, even if she sees, her contributions or that of her kinsmen unless for some reason they are exceptionally important.

Immortality through posterity is one of the foundations of Dinka cultural continuity. The better the dead are remembered and represented, the more conditions remain as they left them, and vice versa. For to abandon a tradition would mean to deny the existence of the ancestors and their contributions to the culture of their progeny. A suggestion for the abolition of an outmoded custom is often quickly answered with, "Your words are true, but it is the custom of our forefathers from the distant past." That is supposed to give it unquestionable validity and application. In Dinka legends and folklore, and especially in songs, accounts about ancestors' long-gone are recited and traced to explain present conditions even when the evidence is shaded with myths and miracles that no longer hold. The premise that the more one achieves, the greater the share of living memory one receives, leads to the conclusion that the ancestors who lived longer and did more are greater than the ordinary dead. The intensity of lifetime relationships is a crucial determinant. For this reason, and because procreation normally implies marital ties, the family is the primary means to procreational immortality.

By stressing the continuance of one's identity and influence in this world, the Dinka do not imply that there is no other form of existence after death. But their belief on this matter is admittedly complex and unclear. They categorically discard the Christian concept of life - hereafter as introduced by missionaries. Traditionalists would listen to young Christian converts telling their newly acquired wisdom with enthusiasm, and then laugh as if to say that the children were too young to make sense or were being taught fantasies out of touch with the world of sanity. They would assert that once a man was dead, he could never rise to be judged in another world. The Dinka have no illusions about the perishability of the human flesh. Both on the ground and in the sky, there are animals and birds of prey that will fight over dead animals and unburied humans. Even when a carcass has been buried, other agents of consumption lie in wait. A rather cynical way of referring to the dead is that they are "eaten by ants and termites" (*aci boot*). But, while the Dinka believe that the dead cease to exist in an organic way (making some allowance for the bones), they seem to believe in some form of spiritual existence. The dead continue to communicate demands to the living through dreams or divinations. If these are not met, they may punish the living to the point of death. The person killed is not always the person punished. This is not only because the death of one relative is seen as punishment for other relatives but also because a dead person may cause the death of a relative out of love and a desire for the survivor's companionship in the next world. The Dinka often explain the illness and the death of children whose mothers are dead in terms of the mother's being angered by how the living have mistreated her child and being desirous of taking the child away from them to join her among the dead. She may be appeased and reconciled, or she may be adamant and kill her beloved child.

In addition to communications supposed initiated by the dead, the Dinka pray to their dead to beg God, lesser deities, or other dead to forgive their wrongs and even to stop being whimsical against man. An old man whose age-mates are mostly dead may express disapproval of the living by wishing he would join them. This is much more than the usual "I wish I were dead." A person may threaten to inform his dead relatives of how things have changed for the worse.

He may even acknowledge virtue by undertaking to "tell your father when we meet in the earth." It is rather paradoxical that ancestors who are believed to keep a keen eye on the conditions of the living need to be informed. But on the other hand, to the Dinka, the notion of coming fresh from the scene of life gives empirical dimension and emphasis to the divine enlightenment of one's ancestors.

By emphasizing the survival of every individual through a lineage, the concept of procreational immortality gives vitality to both individual and group identities. Every individual is thus more directly concerned about founding his own lineage. Although his concern in this regard would seem to imply group interest, the two by no means always agree - in fact, they often clash. The usual point of conflict is marriage. The father or an elder brother may want the cattle to multiply before a son or a younger brother may marry.

The significance of every individual in the family line is given impetus by the fact that from an early age a Dinka child learns to recite his father's genealogy to the most distant ancestor traceable. The ability to do so is one of the earliest ways of testing the child's intelligence, and every mother tries to make her son impressive. As the child's cognitive capacity grows, the biography of his (or her) ancestors, the myths of their origin, the legends of their deeds, and their status in the society they once lived in are recounted to explain the position now occupied by the family. If the reality of today fails to reflect the glory of yesterday, and this is usually the case since the Dinka exaggerate their ancestral heritage, the story must explain the points of divergence. As every ancestor is venerated, the fall is better explained in terms of misfortune than of shortcoming. Or the blame goes to the moral weakness of contemporary generations, which renders man incapable of greater deeds. Dinka may take pride in a rise from a low status, but more often they glory in the heritage of a high status or lament their fall. In most cases, the identity and the status of the family line is the totality of the positive identities and achievements of all its individual members from the founder down to the present-day father. In a society of fundamental equality, a low point is rarely reached. Although certain families tend to maintain their status and give continuity to the basic structure, a great deal of restructuring is continuously occurring, with the poor getting richer - for instance because many daughters have brought in much bridewealth - and the richer getting poorer, for instance because of lack of daughters or female relatives. Otherwise, social importance is relative and subjective. Most Dinka take pride in something and feel important for something. The family being an important element in this, Dinka do not hesitate to distort history and enhance their lineage. This to the Dinka is not undesirable, if it is conceived as a lie at all.

The communal aspect of the concept of lineal continuity is equally striking, if not more so. Immortality can be made effective only through a chain of descendants seen as a collective whole. People trace their genealogies through individuals, but the descent group is collectively designated by possessive reference to its head. By viewing the group as an integration of mutually interdependent - and yet mutually exclusive - entities in which the role of the individual remains vital, a foundation is laid for understanding the cooperative, the competitive, and even the conflicting interests of individuals and groups.

Unity and Harmony

Dinka concepts of unity and harmony are expressed in *cieng* which, as a verb, means "to live together," "to look after," "to order or put in order," "to inhabit," and "to treat [a person]." As a noun, it means "morals," "behavior," "habit," "conduct," "nature of," "custom," "rule," "law," "way of life," or "culture." And these last ten are in addition to the noun forms of the verbs above. As these words indicate, *cieng* may be used in purely descriptive terms, but more often its usage is normative and implies a judgment of values. To emphasize such judgment, the Dinka add appropriate adjectives and adverbs: "bad *cieng*," "good *cieng*," "to *cieng* well," or "to *cieng* badly." To say that "this is *cieng*" or "that a person knows *cieng*" is to evaluate positively; to say that "it is not *cieng*" or that a person "does not know *cieng*" is a negative judgment.

Although some of these meanings may not show it clearly, *cieng* is a concept of human relations. It puts "human" values like dignity and integrity, honor and respect, loyalty and piety, and the power of persuasiveness at its core. Material values are dependent on human values even though they are used to express moral sentiments. Thus, traditional education, rather than emphasizing knowledge for its own sake, aims at promoting that which makes for good human relations. In Dinka economy, *cieng* lays stress on sharing produce and providing for the needy rather than on increasing production beyond subsistence. Cooperation in production is important, but the objective is more human than economic. When a man holds a feast and invites his age-mates, friends, and neighbors to work in his field, their aim is to help him produce his normal yield, not to increase production for its own sake.

Cieng does not merely advocate unity and harmony through attuning individual interests to the interests of others; it requires assisting one's fellowmen. Despite the violent nature of Dinka society, good *cieng* is opposed to coercion and violence: for solidarity, harmony, and mutual cooperation are more fittingly achieved voluntarily and by persuasion.

Cieng has the sanctity of a moral order not only inherited from the ancestors who had in turn received it from God, but also fortified and policed by them. Failure to adhere to its principles is not only disapproved of as an anti-social act warranting temporal punishment; but more important, it is a violation of the moral order which may invite a spiritual curse - illness or death according to the gravity of the violation. Conversely, a distinguished adherence to the ideals of *cieng* receives temporal and spiritual rewards.

Cieng is seen by the Dinka as a heritage that has proved its worth over generations and has become sanctified and elevated even though it may have negative aspects. Such negative aspects are hardly ever visible to the Dinka. I once asked a Dinka what he thought was negative in his people's ways. After some silence, a puzzled look, and smile, he said, "How can there be anything bad in the Dinka way? If there were, would it not have been abandoned a long time ago?"

When the Dinka see an airplane flying in the sky, or the power of the gun, they are quick to acknowledge the material superiority of the "pink foreigner" by such expressions as "He is a power" or "He is a creator," but this is not cause for negative self-evaluation. If the issue is raised, the usual explanation of the discrepancy is to see it merely as a difference and say, "But they are *juur* and we are the 'men of men'- they have their ways and we have our ways." The implication is unmistakable: "They may have good things in their way, but our way is best." Indeed, conformity to Dinka ways is seen as mandatory since failure to conform threatens physical and spiritual contamination.

Whether it is a way of life or a set of standards, *cieng* begins at home with the family and follows the fiction of the tribe as a family. In fact, *cieng* implies "people" living together in the family, home, village, tribe, or country. The focus of all its various meanings is their way of "living together."

Human Dignity

Another set of principles governing the life of the Dinka are the esthetics of pride, honor, and dignity. These values are inculcated in a child at an early age, and much of the fighting of childhood is in their defense. We have also seen that the Dinka conceive of immortality in terms of maintaining and venerating a man's name which is a function of respect and an offshoot of dignity. It is in youth and in particular upon initiation that this dignity finds its impetus, as a man nears his marriageable age and prepares to start his family line.

An initiated man is *adheng*, which may very appropriately be translated as "gentleman"; his virtue is *dheeng* (dignity). But *dheeng* like *cieng* is a word of multiple meanings - all positive. As a noun, it means nobility, beauty, handsomeness, elegance, charm, grace, gentleness, hospitality, generosity, good manners, discretion, and kindness. The adjective form of all these is *adheng*. Except in prayer or on certain religious occasions, singing and dancing are *dheeng*. Personal decoration, initiation ceremonies, celebration of marriages, the display of "personalityoxen," indeed, any demonstrations of an esthetic value, is considered *dheeng*. The social background of a man, his physical appearance, the way he walks, talks, eats, or dresses, and the way he behaves towards his fellowmen are all factors in determining his *dheeng*.

The opposite of *dheeng* is *yuur*, with *ayur* as its adjective. But to be *ayur* is not so much a fact of physical looks and bearing as it is of social status and conduct.

Although *dheeng* relates to social relations, it should not be confused with *cieng*: provides standards for evaluating conduct, *dheeng* classifies people according to conduct; *cieng* requires that one should behave in a certain way, *dheeng* labels one virtuous for behaving in that way; *cieng* is a normative concept – a means – *dheeng* is a concept of status – an end.

The determination of status by *dheeng* is not always based on the consideration of the whole person. A person may be *adheng* in certain ways and *ayur* in others. Or he may be *adheng* if the balance of positives and negatives works in his favor.

A remarkable feature of Dinka culture is that it gives everybody some avenue to dignity, honor, and pride. The degree varies, the means are diverse - there are the sensuous means concerned mostly with appearance, bearing, and sex appeal; there are the qualities of virtue in one's relations to others, and there are the ascribed or achieved values, material or spiritual, which help determine one's social standing. Some people distinguish themselves by their sensuous gifts; most people try to win recognition by adherence to the norms of *cieng*. Yet others depend to some extent on the social class into which they are born or which they achieve the former being better than the latter. These ways are interrelated and cannot really be separated, but only by seeing them as alternatives and by realizing that all ways lead to the same ends can we understand why every Dinka has some share in the values of self-respect, inner pride, and human dignity. An elaboration of each of these categories will elucidate the point.

It is impossible to exaggerate the importance the Dinka attach to physical attraction and wholesomeness. To be blind, deaf or dumb, or to be in any way and to any degree, disabled or deformed, reduces a person almost to a subhuman level. This singer expresses what it means to be lame in Dinka society.

> *Young son of Mangok of my father,*
> *If people could be molded from iron,*
> *I would ask to be thrown into fire*
> *So that I might begin a new life.*
> *A misfortune which caught me at the Creator's hands:*
> *It is the heart of testicles which keeps me among men,*
> *But I feel myself low,*
> *With a hip which does not allow me to run*
> *No more speed and no more dance;*
> *Girls, when the drums beat*
> *I go and sit like a child on a seat;*
> *How can that be good?*

Of course, one is shown a great deal of sympathy and concern. Refusing such people in marriage is believed to invite a curse. Some may even become distinguished despite their defect. But the loss is immeasurable. Even when a person who overcomes such a defect and succeeds in life is highly regarded, there is always an element of condescension.

To be handsome or beautiful is a great asset, but "sensuous beauty" is much more than a matter of determinism at birth. A man is not an *ayur* because he is born ugly: He is an *ayur* because he neglects his appearance and makes himself unattractive. The Dinka are quite blunt in pointing out physical defects resulting from natural ugliness or from neglect. Some parents are quite openly, often modestly and sometimes cynically, apologetic about their children's ugliness even in front of the children concerned. I have heard of a man saying to his son, "With such ugliness, whose son would they think you are?" I have heard a father say to his daughter, "So proud and yet so ugly, what if you were beautiful?" In a tone more consoling, I have heard it said of a maturing girl, "What was ugliness has become beauty."

Yet, scarcely any Dinka lacks a feeling of beauty and a show of grandeur: Dinka culture is full of ways of enhancing a natural beauty or making up for lack of it. The starting point is ornamentation: Among the objects of beautification for both men and women are beads and shells worn on the wrist, neck, and forehead, ivory bangles worn on the upper arm or the wrist, and long metallic bracelet coils wound on the arm by both men and women and on the legs by women. Both the bangles and the coils are wound so tight that they make the limbs swell, but are loose enough to permit circulation and prevent gangrene. They are a source of discomfort and pain but are also reasons for a proud display of the arm and the legs as one walks. Bleaching the hair reddish or blond begins in childhood, and it is considered a sign of mourning for an adult youth to leave his hair black. It is desirable that the gums be black and the teeth white, preferably with gaps between them. Dinka teeth are remarkably white, a fact they attribute to their predominant dependence on milk. I have known Dinkas to refuse tea and coffee as introduced to them by Europeans and Arabs on the sole ground that they might stain their teeth. Teeth are constantly brushed with charcoal, ashes, and twigs. Most Dinkas spend the whole day chewing on their twig-brushes, putting them aside only to drink or to eat. Washing one's mouth and gargling before and after drinking or eating are universal.

Dinka men traditionally went naked, but in dances or in public appearances they covered their butttocks with well-trimmed skins of wild, bright-colored cats. In contrast to their men and in line with their sexual exclusiveness, Dinka women have always been clothed. A woman wears a pair of goats' skins or sheepskins with one in front and one in the back. These cross around and hang down from the waist, leaving a gap on either side beginning at the middle of the thighs and widening as the skins reach the knees. Until recently young girls went naked at home, although on formal occasions or in the presence of strangers, they always wore short skirts. Married women on the other hand wore, and still wear, skirts reaching to their feet. When women are in mourning, their skirts are cut short and left untidy. Informally, Dinka women go topless; but on formal occasions, married women wear material wrapped around the body which ends with a knot on one shoulder and is opened on one side.

Skirts are tanned soft and black and are edged with decorative beads or shells. Occasionally some natural fur is left on the lower edges. A look at a lady's skirt gives an idea of her social and economic class, for it is not easy to find and afford all that is needed for the best results. In any case, class is a factor in the taste for quality.

In a society that gives overriding value to marriage, women may be subordinated by patrilineality but they are the focus of male attention. A man sings:

Woman is the God
She anoints your head with her own hands
And you sleep like a monitor and like a python.
Her identity is never mistaken.
For a woman, a man spears an animal
For a woman, a man keeps his cattle.

Relatives spend much wealth on decorating their girls to attract men and, therefore, bridewealth. But the notion of the "gentleman" by far outweighs the notion of the "lady" among the Dinka. Indeed, while there is a word for "gentleman" (*adheng*) there is no precise word for "lady," except to use "gentleman" as an adjective qualifying "girl" or "woman."

The Dinka's slavelike devotion to cattle is also geared toward the objectives of *dheeng*. And oxen are the focus of many esthetic activities. When singing over his "personality ox," a man strolls with grace and revealed inner pride, his body covered and loaded with objects of beautification, a bundle of decorated and polished spears in his left hand, his left arm hanging from the angle formed by the large ivory bangle on his upper arm, his right hand holding a spear in a pointed throwing position, his head poised high and above, and his ox ahead of him waving the bushy tassels, ringing the bell, and echoing with bellows in accompaniment. His relatives delight in his performance, for his attractiveness is their gratification and his name their fame:

When I rise to sing, gossipers disappear.
I rise and make them swallow their words;
My words are never questioned;
I am like my forefathers.
I rise to be seen by my fathers;
I rise to be seen by my ancient fathers
And also by the passersby.

29

I rise to be seen walking with pride
As it was in the distant past
From the time our clan was born.

But singing about, and in the company of, one's ox is only an example of a more elaborate association between dheeng and singing and dancing. Among the Dinka, songs and dance have a functional role in everyday life. They do not deal with constructed situations; they concern known facts, known people, and defined objectives. But above all, they are skills of splendor in which a Dinka finds total gratification and elevation. The vigor and the rhythm with which they stamp the ground, the grace with which they run in war ballets, the height to which they jump, the manner of pride and self-approval with which they bear themselves, and the way in which the high-pitched solo receives the loud unified response of the chorus combine to give the Dinka a euphoria that is hard to describe. As the singing stops, the drums beat even louder, the dance reaches its climax, and every individual, gorged with a feeling of self-fulfillment, begins to chant words of self-exaltation.

I am a gentleman adorned with beads
I dance to the drums and level my feet
The girls of the tribe gather before me
The wealth of the tribe comes for me.

O Kon, O Kon, son of Dau,
I am a gentleman who dances without fearing his bones
A gentleman as delicate as something delicious.

When I dance to the drums
I do not dance with a girl who goes out of step,
The confused girl who disrupts the harmony of the dance,

The inferior (fisherman's) girl who lives on the river.
I dance with a polished rising beauty.
I am not simple at dancing to the drums
I am not simple.
I am never challenged in our tribe.
I cannot be dribbled around at Akot.
I am respected as an officer.

Dinka dance is essentially a group activity in which coordination and unity of action is of utmost importance. The whole dancing group, and not only the partners, should be in full harmony. It is a truly impressive sight to see all the dancers jump up and down or stamp the ground at literally the same time. And as the above lines indicate, to be out of step is to degrade one's self as a dancer. But the significance of the individual is not overshadowed by this group spirit. The fact that there are points in the dancing when every individual chants his own exaltations shows the importance of song and dance to the ego of every dancer. In its collective songs, a group refers to itself not as "we" but as "I," which indicates that group identity is fundamentally conceived as an integration of egos identified as one ego. Since every Dinka dances, except for a few high-ranking individuals and old men (although some old men continue to dance), this balance and mutual support between individual ego and group identity not only gratifies the self-image of the Dinka, but also assures him of his identity as a member of the group.

Dheeng is also determined by personal manners and moral integrity. There are, for instance, eating standards that a Dinka is expected to meet. A man must not milk, and becoming of age at initiation is termed "ceasing to milk." A man must not cook or be near women when they cook. Should it be necessary to milk or cook, for instance when traveling without women or children, men do so for one another and never for themselves. A gentleman should not complain

Agar Dinka imitating the horns of oxen in a high-jumping dance,

about hunger except in songs (which provide outlets for much that the Dinka find otherwise embarrassing to say) and then always after the fact and for a noble cause like herding in far-off cattle-camps or suffering in litigating a case of a cow. Even though Dinka eat thick porridge-like food with gourd spoons, usually fragile from decorative carving, a man must be careful never to break a spoon, for to do so is a shameful indication of greed. This implies taking small portions so that he cannot fill his mouth nor have portions on both sides of his mouth:

> *I saw a gentleman the other day;*
> *He had coils on his lower arm,*
> *And an ivory bangle on his upper arm.*
> *Then he filled his spoon;*
> *Gentleman, do you feel no shame?*
> *What three things the man lifted!*

In sharp contrast with Western manners, the Dinka consider it undignified to eat closing one's mouth as if hiding one's greed or to chew silently as though by stealth. A Dinka chews freely and noisily with his mouth not wide-opened, but not concealing the food either. When a man wipes his mouth while eating, the implica tion is that he has had enough. Children are taught that even if this happens by mistake or because of necessity, one must stop eating. A popular game among children is to try to wipe another person's mouth so that he is forced to stop eating. A man must never empty his dish, however small the portion served. He should not overfill, for the stomach of a gentleman should not show. He should not eat any leftover foods; that is for women and children. A gentleman should not eat corn by digging into the cob with his teeth; that is the privilege of women and children. Instead, he should use his fingers to separate the corn from the cob before eating it. In self-respect, a man must avoid unnecessary visits which may give the impression of inviting invitations. Saying "No" to invitations is commonly practiced to the point of hypocrisy.

> *Of magic, I have never been insulted;*
> *Of theft, I have never been insulted;*
> *Of unnecessary visits in which a man goes*
> *And even sleeps in a strange home*
> *When he has nothing to look for*
> *I have never been insulted;*
> *And of greed*
> *In which a man never says,*
> *"No, please have it yourself,"*
> *I have never been insulted.*

The following singer had shared the camp with a greedy man who used a large spoon likened to a hollow bell.

> *A man who has damned himself [to camp with a greedy man],*
> *He is better who licks his honey alone at home;*
> *A man who has acquired a hollow bell,*
> *He is better who has clubbed a man on the head;*
> *A man who shares the camp with a man who does not know*
> *the word "No,"*
> *He is better who shares the camp with a madman*
> *And knows that he must dodge a spear.*

The above are only examples of restrictions that dignity imposes on a Dinka. Except for those situations in which I made the contrast clear, these rules apply to women, although to a lesser extent. For instance, unless she is a guest, a woman can break a spoon or empty her dish without shame. But it is much worse for a woman to be greedy than it is for a man. However, Dinka women are generally very small eaters. As the Dinka put it, "They eat with their eyes" while they cook.

To those looking for material explanations, some of these rules may appear to have been dictated by insufficiency of food and are geared towards its equitable distribution. While this reasoning is valid, it does not fully explain the situation. There is no marked shortage of food in Dinkaland. Even when what is cultivated does not suffice because of lavish consumption, there is always food in the forests and in the rivers to provide supplements. To the Dinka these are simply rules of dignity.

With respect to human relations, *dheeng* has two strands: a constraining one consisting primarily of respect through avoidance and one that implies and requires a positive duty to confer benefits. Avoidance is mostly associated with in-law relations, especially between men and women. It is less marked between age-mates among whom raillery is recognized. The concept of an in-law relationship is extended to all those who can theoretically enter into such a relationship. Any married woman who is not a relative is a potential mother-in-law and must be given special respect by those who could marry her children. In fact, people in such a relationship sometimes address each other in in-law terms even when no marriage has actually taken place between them.

The relationship of in-laws is extremely courteous and ritualistic. A man must not eat in the home of his girlfriend or of her relatives. Even when married and given to her husband, he and some senior relatives, men and women alike, continue to abstain from eating in the homes of her relatives and from eating any food she might bring from her relatives or be bought with their money. Abstention ends with a ritual of "washing the mouth" which requires a gift of a cow or cows to the abstaining person. The respect behind abstention from food also requires that a person be self-composed and behave with great care and constraint in the presence of his in-laws, especially of the opposite sex. One does not speak face to face with a senior relative-in-law of the opposite sex. It is common to see a man on one side of a tree and a woman on the other side, or one inside a hut while the other remains outside, the two solemnly discussing an issue which may not be all that serious. When a man meets a woman on the road, he snaps his fingers loudly saying, "May we meet?" "May I come?" or "May I pass?" to which she replies, "Yes, with virtue."

When a Dinka woman approaches her sitting males-in-law or any men who might fall into that category, she kneels quite a distance away, announces her appearance, and approaches on her knees, stopping several yards away to talk. In serving food to men, a woman kneels a distance away from them, crawls on her knees, places the food in front of them, crawls backward on her knees until she is some distance from them, and then stands to walk.

Dheeng postulates high moral standards for the Dinka. Major Titherington, whose encounter with the Dinka goes back to the early days of colonialism, wrote of

> *... the higher moral sense of the Dinka. Deliberate murder—as distinct from killing in a fair fight—is extremely rare; pure theft—as opposed to the lifting of cattle by force or stealth after a dispute about their rightful ownership —is unknown; a man's word is his bond, and on the rare occasions when a man is asked to swear, his oath is accepted as a matter of course.*[3]

And after association with various African peoples, Major Court Treatt wrote: "The Dinka ... is a gentleman. He possesses a high sense

---

3   Major G. W. Tirherington, "The Raik Dinka of Bahr-el-Ghazal Province," Khartoum, *Sudan Notes and Records*, 10 (1927), pp. 159-169.

of honour, rarely telling a lie,"[4] and "... I must add a rare dignity of bearing and outlook."[5]

Taking cattle by force or by stealth is frequent, but it is always on the basis of disputed rights and is not considered, nor even called, "theft." Theft as such hardly ever occurs; and when it does, even if such a small item as a piece of tobacco is involved, severe ostracism and punishment is inflicted by the culprit's age-set.

The personality ox of the alleged thief, or of her brother if a female, is skewered to death by his or her age-set. The functional importance of the age-set, the dramatic circumstances in which the killing is done, and the speed with which the news spreads are sufficient indications of how far punitive measures outweigh the crime. Gossiping, which is seen as a form of "lying," is repugnant to the moral character of a gentleman.

In our camp, Mangar of Tong d'Ajing,
I have never gossiped with anyone;
I have never been strangled by my words;
May I die, I hate words that gentleman whisper like the
hissing of snakes.
When the word of a gentleman is peeled like sugar cane
His honor is forever gone.

One is an *adheng* by having an indulgent disposition and to some extent by having material means in abundance; but an ideal *adheng* is one who combines generosity with wealth. A generous but poor man is an *adheng*; it is good enough that he does his best. He is also on the threshold of *yuur* in the material sense. A rich miserly man is an *ayur*; it is not enough that he gives if he does so reluctantly or not

---

4   Major C. Court Trearr, *Out of the Beaten Track*, New York: E. P. Dutton & Co., Inc. (1931), p. 115.

5   *Out of the Beaten Track*, p. 116.

in proportion to what he has. But he is also something of an *adheng* because of his wealth. The ideal *adheng* is one who will open his door and be hospitable to anyone at any time, derive pleasure from doing so, and is able to afford it. Such an *adheng* will readily slaughter a ram or a bull depending on the importance of his guests or on their numbers.

To be truly an *adheng*, it is not enough to fall suddenly into wealth as a result of a stroke of luck. Conversely, to fall suddenly into poverty from a known wealthy background does not entirely diminish the attributes of *dheeng*. Something of an inherited status is always considered. There is therefore a great deal of overlap between beeny (chieftaincy or aristocracy) and *dheeng*. There is also an overlap between being a *kic* (commoner) and being an *ayur*. It should, however, be stressed that being a chief, an aristocrat, or a rich man is only to speak of power or wealth and not of the total status of *adheng*—except insofar as the ideal attributes of dheeng are usually expected to be observed by the Chief and the rich who have better opportunities than the commoners and the poor.

For the same reason of descent, a person may be considered an *ayur* if, even without his fault, he is fatherless or without dependable relations. This may not be so bad as the following song implies, but the poem illustrates the point:

> *When they nearly beat me at Abyei*
> *If it were not Deng, the Patterned One*
> *Who would have rescued me?*
> *Is not the Chief the father of orphans?*
> *What misery!*
>
> *That I should be shouted at, "Man whose father is dead!"*
> *O Dinka, I did not eat my father!*
> *There is no one whose mother cooks for death.*

The Dinka word for an orphan means "the person taken along [by the dead man]" (*abaar*), which indicates the serious impact of a man's death on his dependents. The status of orphanage extends into adulthood. It is then that being fatherless pains the most because of the responsibilities that fall on a person.

In order to appreciate the dignifying value of *dheeng* to all Dinka it is perhaps useful to have a closer view of who follows which avenue from what status to achieve what alternative status. As material and inherited means to *dheeng* are mostly controlled by the male elders of the lineage, young men and women preoccupy themselves with such values as singing and dancing which, though engaged in by youth in any society, are given a special function by the Dinka as substitute values. This way, the desires of the have-nots are satisfied and their latent hostility pacified.

Dheeng is opposed to obstreperousness and aggressiveness, attributes which Dinka childhood stresses as components of courage and the development of physical strength. At the threshold of adulthood these must be controlled and usefully channeled. Young men are encouraged to engage in activities which require courage, adventure, and endurance without causing destruction or unreasonable risks. They travel far to fell trees for drums; they herd in far-off camps for better grass; they hunt wild animals dangerous to livestock and men; they compete in gymnastics and sports; they punish age-mates who disgrace them with moral wrongs; and, of course, they defend the land and the herds from aggression or otherwise sublimate their aggressiveness with war-songs and dances.

The sublimation of aggressive dispositions in youth is remarkably evident in the significance young men and women give to cattle, in particular to bulls and oxen. They sharpen their horns and encourage them to fight. Castrated bulls (that is, oxen) symbolize the qualities of gentleness and submissiveness on the one hand and of aggressiveness and physical courage on the other. In their ox songs, young men and women praise their oxen or the oxen of their husbands or boyfriends for their aggressiveness and valor even as they criticize them for the same. To a young man or woman, an ox symbolizes wealth. The pride in one's family's wealth is usually expressed in ox songs and in relation to one's ox. Thus, by owning an ox or a few oxen, a young man, his wife, or girlfriend feels as rich as his father who controls the herd. The fact that oxen, though castrated and subdued, are pivotal in the esthetics of cattle is symbolic of the fact that young men and women, though subordinated to elders, occupy a high position in the esthetics of Dinka society.

The significance of esthetic values as "compensational" or "alternative" avenues to *dheeng* is evident in Dinka terminology. A man is said to be *alueeth* (a liar) though in a less derogatory sense than the word normally indicates—if he is not particularly good at singing or dancing, not essentially handsome or wealthy, or otherwise not distinguished as *adheng*, but puts on an impressive show of being a good singer or dancer, bears himself with such exaggerated style as though strikingly handsome, shows excessive hospitality as though wealthy, or is otherwise pompous in any situations involving *dheeng*. At the same time, a man who is distinguished in singing, dancing, handsomeness, wealth, or any attribute of dheeng and acts in accordance with his awareness of, and pride in, this distinction is also referred to as a "liar." Every young man and woman is considered essentially vain by virtue of preoccupation with esthetic values, and to the Dinka this is not really a criticism; indeed, it often is a paradoxical compliment.

Singing is seen in a similar way. To compose a song is "to create" a song (*cak dit*); to tell a lie is also "to create'; words (*cak wel*). *Cak* is also applied to God's act of "creation"; and although it might be pushing the analogy too far to consider such creation "telling a lie," there is a common denominator of making something that was formerly nonexistent. In the case of songs, "telling a lie" may indicate the usual exaggeration and distortion of songs, but there is also the analogy that they give young men and women positive values where there might otherwise be none in terms of the standard values used by the elders who determine the acceptable ideals of the system. This is not to deny reality to the function of songs nor to imply its limitation to youth. Songs mean much to all Dinkas of both sexes and of all ages; otherwise, even their significance to youth would be largely meaningless. It is nonetheless significant that it is this group which is preoccupied with them.

Dheeng is thus a concept of status that may be achieved through esthetic means used by youth and through material means controlled by elders. Youth's ways are seen to a lesser or greater extent as winning an "illusory" *dheeng* while the elders' ways provide the "real" *dheeng*. But so ritualized, mythified, and glorified are the values of youth that their forms and their impact on society are more conspicuous and attention drawing than those of the cool-headed, take-it-for-granted status of their elders. The result is a purposeful, proud, psychologically gratified, and socially integrated youth delighting in the pleasures of today yet aspiring to the utilitarian promises of later age. In satisfaction, they conform to the essential norms of the system: the dictates of their elders.

Chapter Three: Birth

Birth Control

T
he rate of population increase among the Dinka is one of the highest in the Sudan, and this is no accident since procreation is an overriding value for them. A couple aspire to have as many children as fortune will grant; but apart from the misfortune that often intervenes to limit the total number of children a couple can raise, the Dinka have practices that tend to control birth and space children even though they are not regarded as birth-control methods.

The Dinka have a high mortality rate-which is particularly striking for infants. According to the 1956 population census, the average life expectancy in the Sudan was only 28 years. The same census indicated that the Sudan, with 52 babies born per 1000 people, had the third highest birth rate in the world, while the death rate, though considerably lower than the birth rate, remained strikingly high at 19 per 1000. According to a pilot population census conducted in 1953, out of every 1000 babies born, 94 die in the first year. Both the fertility and the mortality rates of the Southern Sudan are twice as high as in the North.

It is hard to find a Dinka couple who have not lost at least a child or two. Such names as "The Doomed One," "The One for Whom There Is No Hope," or "The Surviving One" are not infrequently used to indicate past tragedies or helpless expectation of further deaths. For the Dinka to say that a child is too young to be called a person is more an apprehension of death than an indication of age or sexual neutrality—as seems to be the case with the present-day application of the English pronoun "it" to a baby.

Women whose children die regularly fall into a kind of class. The low position they occupy is partly a consequence of the belief that they are in one way or another responsible for the loss. A woman whose children died continually sings in misery:

Jurcol, wail,
Wail O Maleng de Deng!
Each year comes
And with it, I wail!
Each year comes
And with it, I mourn!

In the following song, a man ascribes the continuous death of his grandmother's children not to her guilt, but to God's whim and the curse of the owl.

My grandmother,
My grandmother, Aluel, daughter of Col,
She came with a glory which God denied,
A great lady who bore multitudes of children
But finished the hoes in digging their graves
Leaving my father a lone bull of the buffalo.
We would now be after our herds of cattle.
The owl cries all night in our home

The evil bird of the night has bedeviled us;
The bird cries in the night saying:
"When it dawns, when it dawns
O son of Deng, when it dawns
You will bury another man."
The bird of the night has cast an evil spell on my father.
Our land, our land,
Our land at Biem, my father has covered with dead bodies;
There is no ground left for a foot to step.

Deaths partly check population explosion, but the rate of population increase among the Dinka is lower than death alone can explain; nor is death verbalized as a justification for wanting more children. Experience seems to have taught the Dinka that uncontrolled birth imperils the health of the mother and the children. Among the controls used are setting a minimum age for marriage, abstinence by a nursing mother from sexual intercourse, termination of sexual activity by the mother of a married girl or an initiated boy, and other measures that might be taken by unmarried couples to avoid pregnancy.

Although the Dinka used to marry earlier than they now do, their age of marriage was never as low as is generally assumed of traditional societies. A man may present a young beauty with a wristlet long before she is aware of its betrothal significance, but marriage cannot be concluded and consummated until the girl reaches puberty. Even that is a legal theory for, in practice, girls marry in their late teens and twenties. An only son of a dead man may hasten into marriage to beget children lest his sudden death end the family line, and the eldest son of an important man may marry early to discharge some of the social obligations of his status; but no man can marry before puberty. Most men marry years after initiation which, at least among the Ngok, takes place at age 16 to 18. Those lacking in material means may wait until their thirties or forties. But all Dinka men and women eventually marry. If a girl remains unmarried for too long, her relatives may take the initiative and give her to a man even if for a nominal payment. Likewise, if a man cannot afford to marry, he may be given a girl for nominal pay in the hope that he will make up for the bridewealth in the future, if only through their children.

Long betrothal, lasting at least several years, is characteristic of Dinka marriage. One practical reason for prolonged engagement is the difficulty attached to the payment of bridewealth. Marriage being as expensive as it is, no one is normally expected to pay his bridewealth without the assistance of friends and relatives. Such assistance elevates the status of the marriage as it demonstrates the extensiveness of the man's social circles and, therefore, his security. But to mobilize help is one of the most trying experiences a man must undergo. Each relative and friend must be visited and made to feel important in the venture. Some make the task even more difficult by being so miserly that several visits become necessary before they surrender their cattle. Some men are so disadvantaged that they can neither afford marriage independently nor get assistance from any relatives or friends. These are the ones who may wait until they are in their thirties or older. Long betrothal is caused by more difficulties than those involved in collecting bridewealth: On the bride's side, the cattle have to be distributed within a wide circle. All significant relatives have to be quantitatively and qualitatively satisfied with their share. To meet these demands is a difficult task, often taking much longer than the parties desire. This network of personal interactions and the long period of betrothal it necessitates facilitates a gradual but more reliable coming together of the parties and their respective families—an important factor in the stability of Dinka marriage.

Since betrothal normally takes place after both parties reach marriageable age, a long engagement significantly extends the age of marriage. But such extension is not purely an outcome of practical considerations. It is generally recognized that boys and girls should experience something of independent life and sexual maturity before they face the responsibilities of married life. Free association between the sexes is encouraged, and although it sometimes results in premarital intercourse, the standards of sexual morality and self-restraint are such that this freedom is rarely abused. Experience and maturity are especially required of men. While it is shameful to remain unmarried for too long, some young men in fact resist early marriage and prefer more of the free unmarried life of the cattlecamp. Later marriage means postponed birth and a shorter period of childbearing.

Birth is also controlled by the fact that for the two to three years a mother breast-feeds her child, she must abstain from sexual relations. To do otherwise is to inflict on the child a diarrhea known as *thiang* which is believed to be transmittable to any suckling babies in the neighborhood. Since a suckling mother is not supposed to share her husband's bed, violation is not difficult to detect and, in any case, is very rare. Polygyny, which gives sexual alternatives to the husband, and the overriding value the society places on children (which adds to the mother's gratification in nursing the child) account for the rarity of violation. Only when a child has been weaned and sent to the maternal kin can the mother resume sexual relations. This means that, at least among polygynous families, the minimum age difference between one child and the next is three to four years. Polygyny is a form of population control since the chances of contact with the husband are broadly shared.

The limitation of the total number of children a woman bears is also due to the fact that women stop having children before the age of menopause. It is considered unbecoming of the mother of a "gentleman" or a "lady" to continue bearing children. Consequently, she must stop when a daughter is married or a son is initiated. This may seem paradoxical in a society that places so much value on children. The objection is not so much to middle-aged women's having children as it is to permitting them sex. Sexual activity tends to intensify the jealousies of co-wives which, though strongly curtailed and less serious than might be expected by monogamous standards, are nevertheless real and recognized. Senior wives are expected to reveal much less rivalry than junior wives, and it would be too undignified for them to compete for the husband's bed with junior wives who may be their own children's age. Among some Dinka tribes, a junior wife should address her senior co-wife as "mother." And to place them in sexual rivalry would be almost like making a mother share a man with her daughter.

Furthermore, the Dinka maintain that status should not be confused. When a woman's child marries or reaches marriageable age, she is ready to be a motherin-law and a grandmother. Whether she is really or potentially a mother-in-law or a grandmother, she acquires a new status in which norms of respect are highly recognized, formalized, and applied; otherwise serious consequences follow, entailing secular liability or spiritual condemnation and contamination. A woman having the status of a mother-in-law who risks the "danger" of pregnancy confuses statuses. This not only makes the observance of the norms difficult, it is in itself a violation of the norms.

Birth control is more overtly practiced by unmarried couples. The Dinka do not fuss about virginity, but pregnancy outside marriage is loathed. Except for daughters of important persons (who must be extra careful), badinage, flirtation, and courtship are acceptable quite independently of marital intentions. Occasions like dances and feasts are usually attended by people from different sections of the country who are not related and, since the rules of exogamy prohibit marriage or any sexual associations between relatives, they are particularly useful for matching unrelated couples. It is acceptable for a man to approach any girl and introduce himself. Girls often pretend to be uninterested in making such acquaintances and some females may even be serious, but many friendships grow from these encounters.

A boy is permitted to visit a girlfriend as frequently as the two young people please, provided they meet on the fringes of the girl's village—or farther away—in deference to her relatives. This freedom of association is governed by very rigid, though subtle, principles which may not catch an outsider's eye. Dinka girls are so prudish that any impression of promiscuity would be grossly mistaken, but Dinka boys and girls love mixed companionship. Couples spend whole nights under the moon, or in huts, sitting and talking in the highly artistic and philosophical language of Dinka courtship. It may take years of such friendship before a girl can accept to converse with her boyfriend. It is then that they sleep together. This is not necessarily an acceptance of intercourse and is perfectly acceptable. In some areas, special huts are built for girls to entertain their suitors; otherwise, they use abandoned huts. Sometimes the girl is accompanied by a girlfriend or relative whether the man is with or without a male companion. Such companionship introduces both sides to each other's circles, but it is also geared toward ensuring that the norms of proper conduct are not violated—especially by the man. The Dinka do not scrutinize such relationships to determine precisely what takes place. Nor does it really matter if the girl is not too intimate with too many men. Popularity and courtesy are esteemed; but promiscuity, though accepted in men, is unacceptable in women.

While responsible sexuality is ignored or tolerated, pregnancy outside wedlock is to be avoided. The Dinka do not have illegitimacy in the Western sense, for a child is always integrated into one family or another. An adulterous issue is "The child of the cows" [the bridewealth given for the woman] and therefore of the husband. The child of an unmarried woman goes to the reputed father. However, if two or more men are implicated, which is possible among the Dinka, the claim of the first to have intercourse with the girl prevails. A child unwanted by the reputed father stays with the mother and goes with her to any man who subsequently marries her; otherwise the child is affiliated into his maternal kinship. But the children of illicit relationships occupy a low social position, and there is little or no interest in their birth. The ancestors and the deities may be invoked to induce their stillbirth or cause their death partly because they remind people of the dishonor. The indignation of the family varies according to social status. Whereas an ordinary man may be content with compensation for the wrong, a noble and, in particular, a chief is most likely to curse the child and may disown his daughter, if not in fact, in effect. Most illegitimate children die because of the treatment they receive from society, lacking affection and adequate care as they do. Even the mother, whose love for her baby is rarely shaken, may be so convinced of paternal curse that she despairs and the quality of her care is adversely affected.

To avoid pregnancy the Dinka use such controls as external friction without penetration, the rhythm method, and withdrawal. Although it is said that in some areas of Dinkaland girls use certain herbs to induce miscarriage, abortion is hardly known. However, when the mother's safety requires the loss of her baby—whether the pregnancy is illicit or legitimate—some experts, through physical therapy backed by religious blessings, help to induce miscarriage. In a perilous delivery, a form of Caesarean operation may be performed to deliver the baby, but it is usually born dead. However, grief for such a baby is often overshadowed by joy for the mother's survival; for she will bear more children.

Thus, while family planning is not consciously practiced, the Dinka control the size of their families and space their children. Rarely do women have more than five or six surviving children. Four seems to be the average. Yet, in no way is conception or pregnancy interfered with in a manner denoting disapproval for children. Even when such disapproval is expressed, as in the case of illicit conception, the child is resented only as evidence of a disgraceful union and not as a person. The traditional Dinka are shocked when they hear of birth control as a means of limiting the size of one's family or the population of a country. Envisaging a human being and slamming the door of life on him on the grounds that the available resources are not sufficient would seem inhuman to the Dinka. It is true that they have arable land in abundance and food is also available, but the issue for the Dinka is one of basic moral values. They cannot imagine preventing life to improve it.

Let me illustrate this with a personal story: When my father died, he left over one hundred wives, many of whom were very young and some childless. According to Dinka custom, his younger wives were to be inherited by his brothers, sons, and nephews. We held a family meeting to decide how this was to be affected. All my father's sons are Muslim or Christian converts who had been taught that such a custom is immoral and should not be practiced by converts. However, most of us were living in the Dinka setting and had gone beyond the initial excitement of conversion back to the basic values of Dinka society. Many were, therefore, willing to conform to the custom to preserve the honor of the family in the eyes of the Dinka. I expressed the opinion that we should give the women the choice of remaining or leaving. I argued that, according to the dictates of modern life, even in Dinka society children should not be born in unlimited numbers as we had to consider their education and standard of living. My father had a great many children and this was going to be hard enough, but it was bound to be worse because of the increasing impact of modernization and because distributing the widows would mean many more children than our father alone would have begotten. One brother, a medical doctor who had also been abroad, supported me, giving the example of areas in the world where men and women not only control birth but sometimes practice sterilization. All laughed as though the change we had undergone was not only unbelievable but disgraceful. The oldest uncle in the meeting told us to stop pushing the point, adding "You talk as though you have been too long in the land where they castrate men." That was that. We gave in.

There is a religious angle to all this. A child belongs to the lineage - a long line involving the deities, the dead, and the still-to-be born. It is not for the couple alone to decide whether or not to have a child. Too many interests of too many people who cannot get together and agree are involved and those who count the most (the ancestors) are believed to want the family tree to branch, flourish, and continue.

Conception and Pregnancy

The Dinka recognize basic biological principles of birth, but they also believe that certain factors are involved which are beyond the full cognition of man. Conception is not purely an outcome of sexual relations between a man and a woman; it is also the creation of God and the blessing of ancestral spirits. The cooperation of the father, the mother, and the spirits in the venture is verbally conceptualized. The word *dhieth* means both "to beget" and "to give birth." Dinka view of conception does not distinguish between the roles of man and woman. They copulate to "beget" jointly and "give birth," while God intercedes to "create" and the ancestors assist in protecting the creation from the malevolent powers of destruction. Every individual is therefore the outcome of a human act, God's creation, and ancestral blessing. All these are fathers, grandfathers, mothers, and grand- mothers. Even God is referred to in such personal terms as "Grandfather" or "Father" and his paramountcy implies his transcendent fatherhood over every person and over humanity at large. Conversely, the father is conceived as a kind of God.

The conceptual fusion of the parents' roles is pushed almost to a linguistic absurdity. A man is said to bear his wife a child in the same way she is said to bear him a child. The expression is also applied to sexual relations to have children. Thus, in the institutions of levirate and ghost marriage, asking a kinsman "to enter the hut" of a widow is used interchangeably with asking him to "bear her children."

This close identification of the roles of the sexes is in a sense a justification for the superior claims of the father over his children as compared to the mother. He not only fulfills the normal functions of the father, but is also perceived as sharing those of the mother. Like God, he is the external force acting upon the mother to make conception possible. In copulation, the woman is expected to be a passive receiver and the man the actor who injects the "urine of birth" from which God makes the child. Impregnation is sometimes expressed in terms of a man's putting a child in the woman's womb. Even the child is spoken of as the child of his womb. It is not uncommon to see an aggravated father patting his belly and uttering the words, "How can a child of my own belly do this to me?" This is believed to be very dangerous—and possibly even fatal. Since the father's relatives —particularly brothers and older men—are viewed as "fathers" or "grandfathers," this source of power is vicariously conceived and invoked. An uncle, even a more distant member of the lineage, may similarly pat his belly, utter the "Son of my own belly" formula, and curse with an equal, if not more, effectiveness since the mitigating effect of affection is likely to be less.

Dinka women are not expected to curse their children in this manner. It is said that at birth a mother incapacitates herself by placing a bit of the blood from birth on the tip of her tongue, praying "God of my father, may my tongue be cool against this, my child, even if my heart should be blazing hot." Supernatural powers may take their own initiative against any child guilty of gross violation of maternal rights. Since the relations between a child and its mother are such that mothers hardly ever reach the extreme bitterness possible between a child and his father, the intercession of supernatural powers is rare, but much worse when it occurs as the intensity of feelings would well explain.

While the superior power of man is related to his greater, though fictional, claims in the activities of birth, he is rarely held responsible for childlessness or defects in birth. Since it is in women that the combined activities of God and man take effect, failure is mostly conceived as their barrenness. In most cases, such barrenness is not seen as a result of biological derangement, but in terms of moral wrong on the side of the woman or her relatives. If her fidelity is doubtful, her present and past sexual morality is scrutinized; if her relations, especially with her co-wives are not adequately harmonious, they are examined for any significant violations on her part; and if her family background is morally questionable, it is investigated for inherited or acquired wrongs.

There are, of course, many situations where women or their families are not suspected. Barrenness may result from the spell of an envious eye; from the curse of a bitter man whose kinship rights, especially with respect to sharing in the bridewealth, are not met; from the refusal of ancestors to bless a marriage in which their share of bridewealth is denied or delayed; or rarely, as the Dinka see it, from some biological defect in a woman for which she is not to blame.

Whatever the reason for barrenness, it is detected through the services of a diviner. Once he knows the cause, he may suggest the cure. Usually, it is to undo the wrong that has brought the mishap. If there was a moral wrong on the side of the woman or her kin, she is ritually purified by an appropriate expert according to the nature of the wrong. If it were the result of a spell, a benevolent magician is used to counteract the power of the evil one. In the case of a justified curse by a wronged person, his forgiveness is sought, a payment of appeasement is made, and after a ritual of atonement, he blesses the woman to conceive. God and ancestors may also be propitiated and invoked to help. Such powerful leaders as prophets can also bless barren women to conceive without the need for investigating the rights and wrongs involved. In view of Dinka emphasis on procreation as the foundation of marriage, incurable barrenness is a ground for divorce and return of bridewealth. Most husbands would avail themselves of this ground if they did not have, or could not afford, other wives to bear children. Conversely, it is very hard to divorce a mother of children. Children are the Dinka's best security for the stability of marriage.

Once in a while, childlessness is attributed to impotence or male sterility. Suspicion is aroused if a man has two or more wives and none of them conceives. Of course, an odd pregnancy amidst childlessness can only add to the dishonor of impotence or sterility. Sometimes, a woman who has been subjected to investigations, divinations, and other indignities may commit adultery to test herself or to let the facts speak for themselves. As male sterility or impotence is rarely attributed to moral guilt or evil spell, it is seen as a masculine failure and therefore more shameful than barrenness. So, if a woman proves this point, the indignation on her husband's part may end in a quiet divorce, but in most cases, he is prevailed upon to permit a relative to play the role of a genitor secretly while the impotent or sterile man continues his public image as the husband and the father. The more quietly the situation is resolved, the better for all concerned. Word might spread through rumor, but it is an accepted institution that is unlikely to scandalize the husband's name beyond occasional, indeed rare insults, which call for severe punishment and even appease-ment-compensation for the defamed husband.

Where pregnancy is associated with infidelity, such as concep-tion out of wedlock, either the pregnant woman voluntarily reveals paternity, or a great deal of pressure is exerted upon her to confess. One of the anomalies of the Dinka view of conception is that several men may be held guilty of impregnation (adulterous or otherwise) if they had relations with the woman within a defined period of time, usually a month. Compensation alone or nowadays with imprison-ment, depending on the marital status of the girl, is imposed.

Except with infidelity, the Dinka do not show any excitement over pregnancy. It comes almost unnoticed and while anything leading to a child delights a Dinka, no demonstration of pleasure, far less celebration, is made.

Although lack of faith in the survival of the fetus might be a significant factor, the apparent calm of the Dinka over pregnancy must not be mistaken for lack of interest. There is always the fear that the attention of the evil-eyed might be drawn by overplayed joy so that indifference might be the result of inverse concern. This is evidenced by the intensive care quietly given the pregnant woman from conception to delivery. Her diet is carefully watched. She should avoid sweet things and eat sour food. Since pregnancy is associated with divine will, she must symbolize purity and righteousness. If the woman is a twin or of an otherwise spiritually significant background, she may be required to carry a sacred spear during the period of her pregnancy. Every pregnant woman must avoid going barefoot lest she tramp on a spot polluted by the urine of an adulterer, the footsteps of a murderer, or the infested excrement of a sinner. Unless they have been cleansed by appropriate rites, she should avoid the company of such people. A feeling of discomfort on her side may be sufficient to arouse suspicion, and it is always safer for her to leave the company then.

While sexual immorality endangers a pregnant woman and her baby, and while intercourse with a lactating woman is tabooed, the Dinka believe that the baby should be "hatched" (*gur*) by sexual intercourse. Sex between the couple during pregnancy is believed to be good for the development of the baby and for facilitating delivery. As is evident in the use of the word "hatch," the function of the man is likened to the chicken's with her eggs, and the idea is connected with warmth. It is, therefore, not surprising that the Dinka call a difficult and painful delivery *aril* (meaning "chills"), the same word used to describe what a baby suffers from when it is not given the warm bath that is an essential part of infant care.

Depending on how advanced a woman's pregnancy is, she is

encouraged to lessen her work; but Dinka women are never quite idle until delivery. Whatever her conduct, a pregnant woman must not be beaten, a punishment to which women are sometimes subjected. Apart from the physical and psychological stresses, this exemption may partly account for the grumpy temperament for which pregnant women are generally reputed.

The degree of ill-temper varies considerably. If a woman is especially obstreperous with men, it is believed that she has reason to expect a boy; and if she is so with women, she is believed pregnant with a girl. The positive attributes are also indicative: If a pregnant woman is particularly gentle and graceful with men, she is believed to expect a daughter; and if she is so with women, she is said to expect a son. Although the Dinka, particularly women, enjoy chitchatting over such evaluations, these judgments are merely some of the universal myths often exploded at the time of delivery.

Delivery

As the time for delivery nears, certain preparations are made. For a first delivery, the woman usually goes to her agnatic kin; otherwise, her mother comes prior to delivery to assist with the prenatal preparations and postnatal care of both her daughter and the baby. The crucial signal comes with the "biting" pangs recognizable, especially by senior women. The midwife alerted in advance, is sent for. The Dinka have no professional midwives, nor are any women trained for midwifery. Those who perform this function are experienced elderly women whose expertise acquires a proprietary character and can be inherited by a woman from her mother.

A midwife means much more to the Dinka than a mere expert. She is not paid, but some token payment is made which is considered a gift to the spirits who validate and guide the performance of the skill. Otherwise, the gratification of midwifery is in the relationship it establishes between the child and its family on the one hand and the midwife and her family on the other. If there is a parallel to the Christian institution of a godmother among the Dinka, it is the midwife. The Dinka word for her is *geem*, ("receiver" or "acceptor") who receives or accepts God's gift to man—the child. Although a man may be slightly embarrassed in later years by reference to a woman as his midwife, his relationship with her is a lasting and intimate one involving spiritual matronage by the midwife and filial piety on the child's side.

A hut will already have been set aside for the delivery. The final scene is exclusively for senior women. Children and men are strictly kept out. In case there are complications, and assuming that the fidelity of the woman is in question, she is urged to confess any illicit relations she might have had. The institution of confession among the Dinka is a very important one and is strikingly adhered to. Relations the woman had while unmarried which do not result in pregnancy are neither confessed nor investigated; otherwise, as soon as impressions of pregnancy become evident to the expert eyes of senior women, an intensive interrogation is carried out urging her to confess the names of those with whom she has had sexual intercourse. Even a delay in her menstrual cycle may arouse suspicion and pressure for confession. Such was the fate of the girl who composed this song:

People rose against me
Boys, old women, and girls,
"The girl has conceived."
I heard it and dismissed it
It was because of blood which God had kept away.
Because of one cow, I have met with bewilderment
Afflicted with shame as though I was a monkey
I have met with the loneliness of a speared monitor
In the camp of Dun de Kok.

The daughter of my father said,
"Please tell me the man."
I answered, "Not at all,
O sister, there is no man"
I am holding mine with one heart
And people come and color it with lies.
Mine has no legs to wander alone
And meet with the gentleman it likes.

Of course, for a married woman, the presumption is that her relations are within wedlock and in most cases it is her own guilt and fear of supernatural sanctions which pressure her into confession. Supernatural sanction is conceived in illness and the threat of death. A severe fever or headache may be sufficient to threaten death and induce confession.

Some women harbor lovers to the last minute. Even if she confesses some lovers earlier, a woman may resist revealing the name of a particular man either in fear of scandal or to avoid subjecting him to the punishment that follows. Such are the cases that reach the delivery stage. Since every Dinka believes in the threat of divine punishment under such circumstances, difficulty in delivery may be as much a consequence of harboring lovers as it is the reason for confessing them. The pressure exerted by elderly women is by itself hardly resistible. If a suspected woman dies in childbirth, the reason is easily conceived in her refusal to confess at all, her persistence to withhold some names, or her belated submission to total confession.

If the woman's sexual morality is beyond doubt, as is generally the case with married women, and she nonetheless goes through *ari*—hard labor that is—a diviner is called to reveal the cause of the complications. Contravening the rights of deities and ancestors, concealing a crime or some moral wrong, and leaving wrongs against fellowmen uncorrected are the common causes. Appropriate rites of atonement are recommended to be combined with expert physical assistance.

As soon as the baby is born, the midwife sucks out the mucus from its nostrils to enable it to breathe. Because this necessity is so repulsive, it dramatizes the midwife's intense devotion to the child and justifies her spiritual power over it. The first cry of the baby is taken as the signal of successful delivery. The Dinka greet it with words that recall the ideals of human relations already discussed under *cieng*:

> *Praised by the Lord!*
> *Come, your people are in cieng;*
> *The land is in cieng.*

This declaration has two special aspects. The obvious one is that of ensuring the security of the newborn baby. If there is an order within which the minimum standards of *cieng* are observed, then the child is coming into a secure world in which all will cooperate for the welfare of all, and in particular for the child.

The Dinka have known major disruptions in their history. The more recent ones are the nineteenth-century period of hostilities with Arab slave-raiders and the current civil war with the North. In such situations, the breakdown of order may be such that the minimum requirements of *cieng* cannot be met, and the Dinka then speak of their world as spoiled, the direct opposite of the country's being in *cieng*. But even here, the surrender to anarchy or the view of the world as spoiled may be relative to the complex and multiple view of their social order. The nation, the tribe, and the village may be broken down, but the home and family may still hold. Certain values may be compromised, others may be emphasized—but some continuity is maintained. So, although a child born in times of peace and order may hear the words of reception loud and confident, a child born in times of war or any disaster will still find enough *cieng* for the verse of ritual reception to be recited.

The people really addressed are those present and not the infant who can hardly be considered aware. There is, of course, a projection of awareness, for, if the people addressing the baby symbolically wish it aware, the situation is created in the Dinka mind that the baby is aware of the social security promised and such a wished or projected awareness helps mold the expectations and the demands of all concerned, including those of the baby as it grows. But, while the symbolic focus is on the child, the effective participants in this process are the adults, both present and absent. It is they who will help raise the baby; it is they who will create an atmosphere in which the baby will grow learning about Dinka *cieng*; and it is they who, as they fulfill their obligations to the child and those around them, will also expect from the child those benefits he owes them as members of his family or community.

Since men and children are excluded from the scene of birth, this symbolic meaning applies only to women. But apart from the fact that a symbolic meaning transcends physical phenomena, the Dinka find women's jealousies the greatest threat to unity and harmony. Therefore, when the symbolic presentation of *cieng* is made by women to women, the society addresses itself to what it sees as the source of social ill. Dinka women, and far less Dinka men, do not see that the real cause of disharmony is the inequity of the social system to women, and not women's jealousy.

Although it is the women who utter and hear the verse of reception, word of the successful delivery goes out to the anxiously awaiting men and children. Both the baby and the mother are then washed. Anxiety continues if the placenta has not been expelled. This may take days and may even cause death. When expelled, the placenta is carefully buried near the hut. The umbilical cord is broken by cutting it with a sharp sliver of a cane or by tying it tightly with a thread or a hair from a giraffe—never with a knife or a blade. The Dinka associate blades with spears and spears with war and danger (except for sacred spears which symbolize invocation and protection). The remainder of the umbilical cord is left to dry up and drop off in due course.

If the woman has given birth to twins, the rites of birth become more elaborate. The Dinka attitude to twins is very complex, and it is not at all easy to tell whether they are desired or merely accepted. The birth of twins is laden with religious significance even though it is not clear whether they are seen as a specific gift of God or just as a manifestation of divine power. In any case, so many are the demands of God and the ancestors in relation to twins, so elaborate are the ceremonies and rites connected with their birth and life, and so great is the threat of evil in consequence of any violation of these rites that twins are seen as a liability to the family. Cattle are dedicated to them that should not be disposed of; the milk and the dairy products from such cattle, even the containers in which they are kept, must be avoided by fertile women. Twin's circumcision, the customary removal of their lower teeth, and their initiation can be done only under special circumstances; even their marriage and funeral rites require special formalities. These are but a few examples of the great care and attention they must be given under the continuous threat of evil in the event of default. All this gives them a special status, but it also makes them abnormally demanding. Given a choice, they would be better avoided. But this is a thought no Dinka could consciously hold since it implies questioning the Divine order of things—perhaps the only area in which the Dinka are truly humble and modest.

I have never heard of a Dinka woman giving birth to triplets, far less quadruplets or quintuplets. If there were, it may be assumed that the same treatment would apply to them in intensified form. As a matter of fact, twins rarely survive together, another reason why the birth of twins is more a cause of anxiety and apprehension than of joy. This is perhaps why the dedication of cattle, which is normally done to the dead and the deities only, is also done to twins.

The Dinka associate twins with birds. Indeed, the word for twins in most Dinka dialects is "birds," (*diet*). *Madit* (female form; *adit*) one of the names reserved for twins, literally means "birdman," and *achwil*, another twin name, means "kite." Twins are not said to "die" but to "fly," an expression that is applied only to them. The Dinka explain the association between twins and birds on the grounds that birds symbolize multiple births. But why birds out of all the creatures that give multiple births? An educated Dinka once answered this with reference to birds as symbolizing peace, but that is evidently an adventitious thought.

It is perhaps significant that the Dinka also associate birds with supernatural powers of illness, especially mental disorders. A man suffering from any such disorder is said to "have had a bird done to him," by which it is meant that black magic has been used against him. The treatment for illness, and especially a mental disorder, includes waving a chicken in circles over the patient's head, then sacrificing it and throwing it away—for it must not be eaten by the patient or by any member of his family. A link may thus be found in the physical and mental strains of caring for twins, the spiritual dangers of failing to meet the religious demands of their status, and the constant fear that at least one will probably die. The association of twins with mental abnormalities may be more direct. Having twins has a religious significance and religious or ritual patterns of behavior, such as those of religiously inspired persons, often reveal varying degrees of mental abnormalities. There would thus seem to be a link between the fact that it is abnormal to have twins, that such abnormality implies a religious and ritual status, that mental disorders are normally associated with similar religious and ritual manifestations, and that birds are generally associated with mental disorders.

Chapter Four: Infancy

The Naming System

Personal names are of great importance to the Dinka, for they do not have surnames. Instead, they combine personal names to constitute the lineage. Selecting them is, therefore, very significant though casual and without rituals. There is no precise moment when a child is named, nor is there any designated person who selects the name. Several days after birth, suggestions for names begin. The result becomes more a matter of which name catches the popular ear than it is a matter of formal choice. Priority goes to the common names of the lineage—the names of the ancestors and the totems of the clan.

Some names are predetermined. For instance, according to their order of delivery, the first set of twins are named Ngor and Chan if males, or Anger and Achan if females. The second set by the same woman are Achwil and Madit if males; if females, Achwil remains unchanged and Madit becomes Adit. Singles born after twin births also have special names—beginning with Bol for a male and Nyanbol or Nyibol for a female.

Other names are partially predetermined in that they are associated with certain events or circumstances surrounding conception or birth. For instance, I was named Mading because a bull of that name was sacrificed on my mother's marriage and people prayed that her first-born be a son. Being her firstborn, I was named in honor of the bull. To give other examples: Monyyak, "The Man of the Drought," was given to a child born during a severe drought; Monylam, "Delivered by Prayer," was given to a child born after a difficult labor necessitated sacrifice and prayers; and Nyapath, "Girl for Nothing," is a daughter of a woman whose children had consistently died, leaving little hope for her survival. Since such names tend to be nicknames, they are sometimes supplemented with the names of ancestors, but they tend to overshadow, though, the ancestral names in popular usage—perhaps because they are more intimate and more expressive.

The Dinka vary names a great deal to express affection for children, to praise them, or to tease them. Male children are also given metaphorical ox-names, which are usually based on the colors of their personality oxen. Each son in a household is allocated a color-pattern or color-patterns depending on his mother's order of marriage and his own seniority of birth. Thus, the eldest son of the first wife gets as one of his color-patterns Majok or Mijok, which is a black head and shoulders, with white flanks, and either black or white hindquarters; the first son of the second wife acquires Marial, white body with a long black stripe across the shoulders; and the first son of the third wife gets Mangar, a striping of white and black. When a bull calf is born from a cow belonging to any member of the family or when one comes to the family as part of a bridewealth, it goes to the person whose color pattern it is. When initiated, a man then identifies and is identified with the ox of his color. For both respect and intimacy, he becomes known by the name of the color-pattern of his ox and by the metaphorical names derived from it. Examples of the imagery used in metaphoric ox-names are: "Pollen Grabber" for a man whose ox-color is that of bees; "The Dancing Head" after the color-pattern of the crested crane, which the Dinka believe may dance when sung to; "Swimmer over the Reeds" after the color-pattern of the pelican; "Shining Stars" for a man whose ox-color is a dark body spotted white; "Ambusher of the Animals" after the color-pattern of the lion. There is no limit to such ox-names. When applied to children, ox-names are used in a purely "playful" manner in that they are not always based on oxen actually owned by the children, but on the theoretical ownership of colors allotted to their statuses or on the bulls after which they were named or even on the color-patterns of the oxen of their senior namesakes.

Praise names or nicknames may also be based on physical or behavioral characteristics. Such names as "Big Headed," "Big Bellied," "Flat Faced," and "Narrow Bottomed" are joking insults; an unusually black child may be called "Dinka" as opposed to the name "Arab" for an unusually brown Dinka; if a boy remains uncircumcised beyond the normal age of circumcision, he may be given the name "The Foreskinned" or "The Uncircumcised," which may continue to be used even after he is circumcised; a clever and manipulative child may be called "Fox"; and an unusually tall person may be "The Tall One" or even "The Short One."

While insulting names tend to be applied only to particular persons, ordinary names and praise names of the eldest children are used to signify parenthood as a sign of respect. If, for instance, the child is a daughter by the name of Adau, the father's name becomes "Adau's Father" and the mother's, "Adau's Mother." In a polygynous family, each of the wives gets her name from her eldest child. The father's name is based on the name of the eldest child of his first wife even if a child of a subsequent wife is the oldest of all his children.

The normal system of naming for genealogical purposes is the reverse of this. A man's name is combined with his father's name as, for example, "Kwol, son of Arob, son of Biong, son of Allor"—and on to the degree necessary for identification. To state the relationships involved it may be necessary for a person to introduce the names of his father, grandfather, and maybe the founder of his clan. Among other things, this serves as a guiding chart for the observance of exogamous bars. By knowing each other's ascendants, a couple can more or less tell whether marriage between them is permissible.

The link between a person's name and that of his father is a "d," a "de," or an "e" according to the dialect used and according to whether the father's name begins with a vowel or a consonant. Thus, "Kwol, son of Arob, son of Biong" is Kwol d'Arob de Biong. Sometimes, nothing is used between the names, but the combination nevertheless implies a father-son relationship.

For ordinary purposes, only the normal names are used, but for such pur poses as praise in song, a father or an ancestor may be referred to by his ox-name or by some other praise name. Thus, Deng, son of Kwol whose ox-name is "The Pied One," may simply be called "Deng of the Pied One." A jump is sometimes made so that Deng, son of Kwol, son of Arob, The White One, may simply be designated "Deng of Arob" or "Deng of the White One." This way the lineage is perpetuated through vital names while some are inadvertently dropped and for gotten.

Lineages and clans are known by the names of their founders. The founder's name is preceded with the prefix "*pa*," an abbreviation of *paan* which is the possessive form of *baai* meaning family, home, or people. Pajok is therefore a lineage or clan founded by Jok. A particular experience in the mythology of the clan may be a basis for its name. For instance, *Dhiendior* ("Clan of The Womenfolk") was founded by a woman who begot a son without a man.

Personal names are so significant in social organization that hamlets, cattlecamps, sections, subtribes, and tribes are sometimes referred to by the names of their leaders. Where the leadership has consistently remained in one lineage for successive generations, refer-ence may be made to any one of the leaders, but the frequency with which a name is invoked depends on the degree to which the leader is revered.

Infant Care

While a successful delivery brings an end to the anxieties of pregnancy and birth, it gives rise to new concerns about the health and the general well-being of the mother and the baby. These concerns are shared by a wide circle of relatives, friends, and neighbors; but expertise is necessary for the care of the infant and the mother, who is regarded as a postnatal patient.

If delivery takes place in the woman's agnatic home, her mother takes care of her and the baby. Even if she delivers in her marital home, her mother normally comes for this function. Otherwise, a senior co-wife takes charge.

In contrast to the compassion of females, males generally demonstrate an attitude of esthetic revulsion toward a woman who has newly given birth. Her hut is a nursing home, and since adequate means of disinfection and deodorization are lacking, it is by no means a pleasant place for people who have been kept out since the earliest signs of delivery. Indeed, the atmosphere appears so unhealthy for the baby that a modern observer might be surprised any Dinka children survive. In that small circular hut, a fire burns to give warmth in a cold season and to smoke away the flies and mosquitoes. Leaves of certain herbs are added to the fire to give incense, but this does not entirely eliminate the distinctive odors of the birth-hut.

On a hard but smooth oiled skin lies the baby, a product of the blackest of races, yet so light brown in color that the Dinka word for a newborn baby is "light brown child." Supporting its back as it lies facing the mother are rolled-up leather or nowadays cotton dresses (oiled and odorous). Sitting or lying by the infant's side is the mother, with a broad leather belt tied around her waist to support the disturbed belly, yet wearing only light and loose clothing to relax her strained body. Her inadequate clothes may be a factor in discouraging men from her hut, but even small boys tend to avoid it on esthetic grounds.

Nevertheless, the baby is a focus of attention and affection. Within weeks of its birth, it is adorned with beads and shells for both decoration and spiritual protection. Visiting elders offer their prayers, sprinkle it with blessed water or with the spittle of blessing. Some cut into halves the "holy cucumber," a ritual the Dinka associate with wishes of physical and spiritual well-being. Many people come to see the baby, hold it, smile at it, and chat over it; but not a compliment about its appearance is uttered, nor are the parents congratulated. These are believed to cause an evil spell even if said with good intentions. Much is said about the beautiful child it was, if it should die—but never while it lives. Only when a person is fully grown may such praises be uttered, and even then with restraint and in limited circumstances.

The mother and her baby are believed susceptible to fatal contamination if they associate in any manner with people afflicted with certain impurities. They must avoid adulterers, murderers, and other sinners who have not undergone the appropriate rites of purification. Even unsuspected associations with them must be guarded against. This entails a rigid observance of certain taboos. The mother's utensils must be exclusively hers. She should keep indoors as much as possible; but, if she must go out, she should wear shoes and carry a sacred spear for spiritual protection.

Shortly after delivery, there commences a regular nursing process called "bathing," a hot bath. For the baby, the bath is elaborate. Every morning and evening a huge pot of water is boiled. On the bathing, site are large separate containers of hot and cold water. The mother or the senior woman bathing the baby sits on a wooden stool near the containers. With a small gourd, she mixes cold and hot water until she gets the correct temperature for the baby. On her thighs and legs lies the baby, crying. As the mother pours the water onto the baby with the small gourd, she turns it from side to side, massaging and exercising its arms, buttocks, genitals, thighs, legs, and even its toes. During all this, the baby continues to cry in terror, but that is expected and bothers no one.

For the Dinka cleanliness is not a factor behind these hot baths. Cleanliness can be achieved with cool or milder water. The Dinka say these baths are necessary to avoid the child's "freezing" (*ril wei*), but it is not really the literal effect of cold weather that they fear—nor is the warmth they want the ordinary function of atmospheric temperature. A hot bath is administered even in the hottest of seasons, and births are not timed in Dinkaland. The Dinka conceive birth as affecting the mother's circulation of blood. That she bleeds is, for them, evidence of a concentration of blood, which must be put back into circulation. They believe hot water helps. Furthermore, her body aches all over; and a hot bath is, to the Dinka, a standard treatment for most bodily pains. The same argument applies to the baby. In addition, it is believed that a newly delivered baby requires something of the same temperature as the mother's womb while it gradually adapts to atmospheric temperature. A hot bath is also seen as essential for the proper development of a child. It helps the baby to grow up healthy, well-built, and well-poised. A child who grows up crooked, or clumsy in build or poise, is believed to be—at least in part—the product of improper bathing. This is why there is such an emphasis on the techniques of massaging and exercising during the bath.

Whatever its real aims and worth, so significant is a hot bath for the mother and the baby that the whole period immediately following delivery is termed "The Bathing Period." For the mother, it lasts only a few weeks; for the child, it covers most of infancy, but after a year or so it becomes less essential.

Child Care

When the mother can take charge of most of the activities associated with child care, the grandmother returns to her own home. Bur child care remains essentially communal, and at no time is the child without the close attention of someone, by no means always the mother.

Perhaps the only exclusive function of the mother is suckling the baby. The Dinka believe that there can be no real substitute for breast-feeding. When a woman dies leaving a baby, another woman must be found to suckle it. Such a service amounts to "saving" the baby. So, "a blood tie" is created between the woman and the child. This creates an exogamous bar that is extended to one generation of the wet-nurse's descendants.

The frequency of breast-feeding is not standardized. A mother may suckle the baby whenever she deems it appropriate or when the baby demands. Since the Dinka have no pacifiers, suckling is also used to silence babies. Mothers are, however, discouraged from being too permissive in breast-feeding as too much mother's milk might be hazardous for the baby, and too much permissiveness is obstructive to the development of its capacity to endure.

An important supplement to the mother's milk is cow's milk. The amount a child drinks increases as the mother's milk decreases; but except for the very early postnatal period, cow's milk constitutes an important diet for a Dinka child. Even when a baby is given other foods, milk is usually added. Only once in a while is it given solid food—sometimes said to be necessary for developing the teeth.

Dietary restrictions are aimed at securing the health of the child, which the Dinka see as threatened largely by internal diseases. The Dinka lump together children's diseases as *weeth*. This term is also applied to some chronic adult diseases, but it covers mostly various stomach troubles, usually with diarrhea or constipation—again lumped together as *thiou* (a word which is also used for guinea worm and the swelling it causes its victims). There are, of course, many other children's diseases in the category of *weeth*. Infections of the mouth, the nose, the ear, and the eyes are rather common. So are tonsils, mumps, and similar diseases. Since physical wholeness is highly valued and deformity miserably degrading, hunchback is among the most dreaded diseases of infancy.

The Dinka regard children as "innocent" so that their illness does not imply any moral wrong on their part. In certain cases, especially where an illness falls outside the categories of common children's diseases or where a disease otherwise considered curable becomes fatal or uncontrollable, moral wrong is attributed to adult relatives or to an envious evil-eye.

As soon as a disease is identified and classified, a specialist is asked to appear or the usually anxious mother rushes the child to the home of the specialist with or without the father. These specialists are usually men and women who have once suffered and recovered from a similar disease. Their illness must have been severe, and in most cases must have left some physical evidence. Some payment, if only nominal, must be paid. The specialists generally use multiple and concurrent methods of cure, including medicines from herbs, physical therapy, cutting "the holy cucumber" into halves, blessing with spittle or with sprinkles of holy water, chasing away the evil spell with whistling sounds or other symbolic action, and, of course, praying.

The wide circle of relatives, friends, and neighbors is keenly interested in providing the child with the attention and protection necessary for secure physical and psychological growth. The word *aguen*, a very affectionate term which may be translated as "darling," is used by female relatives and other associates in much the same way it is used by the mother. Among males or females, a child goes from hand to hand, freely kissed by all those in whose hands he finds himself and jounced to the rhythm of lyric praises, beaming as he or she is made to dance. If a mother is away or otherwise occupied, there is always someone to babysit, and, of course, for free. As people sit outside in the evening to converse near a fire, the mother, or another female relative, continuously fans the mosquitoes away from the child as it lies sleeping on her lap or on a skin. The need to smoke mosquitoes away from the sleeping hut is especially great when there is a baby. This is done early in the evening so that by bedtime the smoke would have largely disappeared, leaving incense from the burnt leaves.

Songs of all types are sung as lullabies any time the baby cries. At night, people in the hut—indeed in the village—may wake and be kept awake, but no one objects or complains. The baby may long have slept, but the singer may continue merely for the fun of singing. Dinka find this very entertaining, and, given the stillness of rural nights, one does not need to be in the hut to be entertained.

The normal task of assisting the mother in caring for the child is done by a young girl whose functional title is "baby-keeper." Her function is to take the baby when the mother is occupied with other household work, but she also assists in keeping the house, especially during the early period following birth when the mother is mostly confined. In a sense, she is a servant, but not a paid one; her services form part of the mutual solidarity of kinship.

Since the naturally felt affection of the maternal kin is considered more reliable than the demanded solidarity of the agnatic kin, the baby-keeper is usually a mother's sister, her sister's daughter, or her brother's daughter. Apart from the mother herself, she is the closest to the child. Coming shortly after delivery, she stays until weaning. But her attachment to the child continues and must be especially honored by the child when he matures.

The complex ambivalence of the Dinka about the greater attachment to the mother and her kin on the one hand and the greater loyalty demanded for the father and his kin on the other hand interplay in the rearing of the child. Frictions with the "baby-keeper" are by no means rare. She may even be insulted as an "outsider" by the less scrupulous children of co-wives. But her role is to keep the coals of maternal ties glowing amidst the flames of agnatic ties. This means that, while much of the more meaningful care for the baby is hers, a wide circle of agnatic kin is involved in all the developmental phases of the child.

Lest we fall into the trap of idealization, the negative implications of women's jealousies in the upbringing of Dinka children must be recalled. Since children symbolize the success of a marriage, it is easy to see how female jealousies affect them. Indeed, some of the fears of evil spells are associated with such close relatives as co-wives, stepmothers, and other step or half-kin. As the saying goes, "Evil-eyes know no ties." The handsomeness or beauty of a co-wife's child, its individual qualities, and its popularity, especially with its father, may be reasons for envy and a source of an evil spell. Because these threaten unity and harmony, they necessitate greater emphasis on agnatic solidarity. When a child wanders into the hut of a stepmother, any prejudiced treatment against him is noted. Prejudice is seen in a failure to show extra courtesy and affection. When the children of co-wives quarrel or fight, any alignment with one's own child is detested as favoritism. Failure to take the other side is enough to arouse suspicion. When a child commits a wrong and is caned by a co-wife or the older child of a co-wife, any reaction by the mother in defense of the child is seen as jealousy.

In any of these situations, punishment may be imposed by the head of the family, or some form of public criticism and perhaps ostracism may result. By the time the child reaches the age of cognition, the postulate that solidarity with halfkin must be reinforced and jealousy against them fought becomes imprinted on him. The same external compulsion that mobilizes the kin group to raise him in an atmosphere of solidarity demands of him conduct befitting a member of the agnatic group. Any child who violates such kinship norms is promptly reprimanded and may be physically punished.

Nevertheless, a greater, though subtle, attachment between the mother and the child in preference to wider half-kin associations is understood, tolerated, and expected.

While the father is the principal beneficiary of procreation, he and the male kin, in general, are hardly involved in early child care. This is especially the case in large polygynous households. A father, of course, likes to see the child every now and then. He may visit the female compartment to do so, or the child is brought to the male quarters. It should be recalled that close association between the parents is limited by the taboo against sexual relations during the lactation period. But the negative role of the father in early child care is more than a function of separating the parents. It reflects something of the discrimination on esthetic grounds which I have said men demonstrate against women who have newly given birth and their newborn babies. It is with a sense of sacrifice that a Dinka father holds his baby at this stage. As these lines indicate, for a father to do so for a length of time is an exception:

> *My wife called me,*
> *"Hold my child*
> *Things are getting wet in the rain;*
> *O son of my mother*
> *I am not disdaining you;*
> *Hold my child*
> *Things are wet in the rain*
> *I am not disdaining you."*

The man in the following song requests his uncle to procure him a wife who will bear him a child:

Uncle, uncle, I want a little one who will hug me;
Uncle, uncle, I want a little one to whom lullabies will be sung;
One who will cry ngee ngee while his mother makes his food;
Then I tell my sister-in-law,
"Come and see what the little one is doing."
O our age-set, then I would say to my sister-in-law,
"The son of your sister is crying;

The father, of course, compensates himself for lost companionship when the male child gets older and becomes clean and predictable. His role as the symbol of unity and of lineage continuity becomes the point of emphasis throughout the rest of the child's life.

The father's lack of involvement in the day-to-day care of the baby does not mean more work for the mother. As she has sufficient help with the baby, she can carry on her normal housework without any significant impediment unless the baby is a particularly difficult one who will accept only a few substitutes for its mother. Otherwise, the mother cooks, fetches water and firewood, works in the fields, and even visits friends and relatives. When the baby is still "light-brown," the mother should restrain from unessential traveling; but if she must travel, the baby is carried on her head, lying in a large basket. When it is over a year old, it is carried in a leather sling tied around the mother's shoulders and hanging down her back; the child's legs are spread around the mother's waist and its arms stick out on either side of the sling. From about age 3, a child is carried sitting on the base of the adult's neck with its legs hanging down to both sides of the chest. The child's hands are either on the head of the carrier or held down by the carrier with both hands. While the first two forms of carrying children are exclusively female, the last is done only by men.

When the child is about to be weaned, the mother begins to discourage it from suckling. She may simply avoid giving it her breasts or she may begin to travel freely with less concern about being back in good time or even on the same day. It is then that a child should learn to take the mother's absence without crying. A boy is particularly teased if he cries because his mother is away; and, although a child continues to be largely identified with his mother, this is the stage when obvious identification with his father begins. It is also the stage when the father begins to approach the mother on the issue of weaning. There may be some resistance from the mother's side. This may be because of her attachment to the child, but it is generally the shyness of women on matters of sex, for to speak of weaning is an indirect and discreet way of asking for the resumption of sexual relations. As both are also eager to have another child, any resistance is short-lived. The taboo is ended, the child is weaned, and off to the maternal kin it goes to spend the weaning period.

Chapter Five: Childhood

Weaning Among the Maternal Kin

The dividing line between infancy and childhood is easily determined by the child's change of residence from that of the parents to that of the maternal kin. This introduces him to a new set of relationships and values which, though subordinated to those of the agnatic kin, are highly regarded and, in some respects, are more intimate and more reliable.

The Dinka word for the maternal kin is *naar*, which is based on relations with the maternal uncle—also designated by the same term. This means that the Dinka conceive of the relationships with the maternal kin as focusing on the maternal uncle. In a sense, grandchildren are the substitutes for their grandparents who, in most instances, will have died when the grandchildren reach the age of maturity. It is, therefore, with the maternal uncle that kinship ties are retained over a period of time.

But when a child is sent to the maternal kin, the real intention is to transfer him to the care of the grandparents. They are the best substitutes for the parents because of their long experience as parents themselves. But there is more to it than that. Paradoxically, the babies and the grandparents fall into somewhat parallel points in the cycle of life and in a manner of speaking they are quite suited for companionship. The pleasure of seeing their own line continued even longer, the ability to carry out the functions of parenthood with the skill of long experience, and the ease with which they are able to get along with the children—partly because they are self-assured and can afford to be less bossy—all combine to make the grandparents among the most affectionate relatives a child can have. They even excel the mother because they truly love to the point of spoiling the child. In this sense, the immense deprivation a child feels in being torn away from its parents, and especially the mother, is easily compensated for.

The total commitment of the grandparents to the welfare of their grandchild may be illustrated with an experience I am closely acquainted with. A child was sick and nearly died. Nothing was left undone that was divined and prescribed. In the end, the child's maternal grandfather, a spiritually powerful man, took his sacred spear; got up in the middle of the night; and prayed the rest of the night for his grandchild, begging God, the spirits, and the ancestors to take him, if need be, in redemption of his grandchild. He had married his favorite daughter to the Paramount Chief with great expectations. The daughter had already been betrothed to another man who had paid a substantial betrothal fee when the son of the Chief, later to become the Chief, came along to contest the betrothal in competition. This intervention was seen as improper as the two men were related. There was, therefore, opposition by relatives on both sides—and from the girl herself. The son of the Chief would not be dissuaded. It was even said that he carried a gun and threatened to kill his opponent. The father of the girl himself favored the marriage: First, he did not want a blood feud surrounding his daughter. Second, his favored son from his first and favored wife was the youngest child, a twin, and an only surviving son among daughters. The proposed marriage would provide an important aid for his son's leadership in the lineage. The lineage itself, though integrated into society and a leading one, was only five generations old from immigration into the tribe. The marriage would elevate it to a high political and social level. These objectives could best be achieved if their girl had a son. On celebrating the marriage, therefore, her relatives sacrificed a sacred bull praying that her firstborn be a son who would grow up to be an important link between the respective families. The desired birth had come to pass, and the grandfather had become very fond of the grandson. The child was now dangerously ill. His maternal grandfather deemed his own death not too big a price for his grandson's survival. His prayers were answered: the child survived. Some six years later, the grandfather died. To the Dinka way of thinking, the causation was clear despite the passage of time. That was my grandfather, and I was that grandchild. I grew up ignorant of this. Indeed my mother has never told me about it: When I was about twenty years old, I returned from school where I had just recovered from illness. Word of my illness had reached home. Among the maternal relatives who came to see me was my uncle—the favored son. Commenting on my illness and recovery, he remarked in a typical Dinka fashion: "Mading, son of my sister, there is no disease in your body. My father cursed himself to death so that he might redeem you from death. Nothing will cross your path."

Just as the mother is particularly close and devoted to her child, so is the grandmother. But the mother's father is in many ways much closer than the father and the father's father. The close tie with the mother's parents extends to all the maternal kin. The degree to which it does depends on the proximity of the relationship. The emire maternal circle is generally more affectionate, more secure, and more pleasant to be in than the atmosphere of the paternal home which is strained with competition over the father's affection and attention. Of course, the maternal home, too, has its jealousies; but they hardly ever reflect on the child, particularly at this early age.

Jealousies are even more repressed against the child of a daughter and any breach is more severely punished. A child among the maternal kin has the affectionate care and the attention of the women, especially the mother's mother; the privileged companionship and the wise guidance of senior men, especially the mother's father; the protection of his mother's relatives, especially the maternal uncle, against the aggressive impulses of Dinka children; and the highly unusual exemption from punishment. He learns from his elders by mutual love and not by coercion.

Contrary to the rules of the naming system, maternal relatives call a child by his mother's, not his father's, name. Whatever his father's status, they delight in ignoring him or being indifferent to him. "It is your mother we know" and in the place of "your mother" her personal name is used. While such designation would be very insulting in the paternal house, even to the mother herself, it is loved coming from the maternal kin. In all respects, the child symbolizes the return of their daughter, a compensation more gratifying than the cattle paid for her bridewealth.

The de-emphasis of the father's side must not be exaggerated. The dualism of lineage identification among the Dinka is infinitely more complex than that. Even as a child delights in being identified with the maternal kin, he takes pride in his agnatic lineage and is quick to take sides if the rights of his paternal kin are in question. Such an attitude is expected by the maternal kin as a mark of agnatic loyalty, pride, and dignity, which must not be destroyed in a child, particularly a son. The future of the child, including what he can do for his maternal kin, lies in that lineage. It is, therefore, in the immediate interest of all concerned that the child be prepared to participate effectively in his agnatic lineage. Questions implying great expectations may be put to the child; and the answers he gives may be revoiced in such a way as to highlight his ambition, intelligence, wisdom, and confidence. Some children may have these qualities to a notable degree; but the reputation a child acquires is bound to exaggerate his qualities in order, wittingly or unwittingly, to establish myths around him that will motivate and encourage him. These myths do not end among the maternal kin but are transmitted to the paternal circles. As the child grows up, whatever he does that is seen as an achievement is interpreted as a step up the ladder. Naturally, in the same manner that these myths are positive, they provoke suspicions and perhaps conflicts—with competitors who have also been conditioned in the same way, if not to the same degree.

The exaggerated de-emphasis of the father's side and the stress laid on the mother's side during the period of weaning could be a way of reminding the child of both the overriding status that society gives the former and the close maternal ties that a child is supposed to honor throughout his life. In this ambivalent complex of interests, the mother's side enjoys natural love and affection while the father's side enjoys prescribed loyalty and devotion.

Since paternal interests are primarily the aims of procreation, they are more organized, more structured, and more dominant in the later years of the child's socialization. The maternal relatives make use of the weaning years. Lest the child should become too removed from the demands and expectations of agnatic dominance during these years, visits between the child and his agnatic kin are encouraged. The child's visits are usually brief, and he is treated more like a guest than a member of the family. Those visiting the child are shown great respect and honor: Beasts are slaughtered, beer is brewed, food is made in plenty, and the best of decorated gourds are displayed in serving them.

As the days of weaning near their end, the child, now about the age of six, will have become used to his new home. His maternal grandparents have become his parents and his maternal uncles, aunts, and their children part of his immediate family. Once more, the break is bitter as the child returns to his original home, but his ties with the maternal kin have sufficiently grown their roots and will continue to grow and to be honored. The real "debt" is on the child who will usually discharge it out of love. But should he fail to do so, the consequences are disastrous. It is believed that of all the relatives religiously empowered to curse, the maternal uncle—indeed the maternal relatives—are the deadliest. The Dinka adjective for a person powerful enough to cure is "bitter," and the coincidence of the English translation is apt: For such a power often lies in the indignation of an embittered person and the guilt it arouses in a well-tutored conscience. The greater the justification for a great expectation, the greater the embitterment in case of violation. The immense love and affection that the maternal relatives show their daughter's child deserves great returns. All they expect and claim are modest objects of wealth, most important of which is a share in the bridewealth of their daughter's daughters and perhaps their descendants. Such cattle are not only of material value to the Dinka: They are a means of honoring human relationships. To deny them to people who have been pivotal in the physical and psychological welfare of the child during its crucial years is to expect the kind of indignation and embitterment which can hardly fail to affect the conscience of that person or those closely associated with him. Unless these disappointed relatives are propitiated and appeased to save the afflicted person, death may result. The relatives who are thought to love each other the most are the same who can most easily kill each other. A man sings:

> *Kur Malual never slipped his tongue against the maternal kin,*
> *Ajang Malual never slipped his tongue against the maternal kin;*
> *When the maternal kin begin to disapprove of one,*
> *Things fall apart like the inside of a coward.*

It may seem paradoxical to say that the power of the maternal kin lies in their loving care while the mother, whose love is unquestionable, is ritually incapacitated to curse. A closer examination indicates that the mother's potential power to curse is transferred to her agnatic kin because the child is permitted to demonstrate love and affection for the maternal kin but not for his own mother. It is easy to see why such strong and recognized, but repressed, feelings must find an outlet. And the closest relatives of the mother are the best alternative to her.

Reorientation to Agnatic Values

Modifying the orientation the child has undergone among the maternal kin is the first concern of the agnatic kin when their child returns from weaning. But this is only an intensification of what had long been introduced to the child. As soon as he begins to speak, he is taught to recite the entire agnatic genealogy at a time when a person never goes beyond a few generations of his mother's line.

Countless relatives question a child as to which of his parents he loves, not which of them he loves the most. Rarely is a Dinka child innocent enough to say "Mother." To say so is to expose one's self to ridicule and shame. Even the mother is bound to be embarrassed. In her own interest, she must see to it that this does not happen.

On returning from weaning, a child will have reached the age of cognition, and it becomes even more essential to work on his mind. It must be remembered that agnatic values are more a function of the mind than of the heart, since society dictates that one should show greater solidarity and loyalty than is usually felt. Prudence tells the mind to condition the heart if one is to avail one's self of the advantages of conformity and avoid the deprivations of nonconformity.

A child may be teased or insulted by calling him with reference to the mother's name; otherwise, using the father's name is the norm.

Even the mother gladly foregoes the privilege of having the child identified through her by her kin. Indeed, I have heard mothers get angry simply because their children had been identified by the mother's names. Intimacy with the mother and respect for the father have it that a child addresses her by her personal name, but must address him as "Father." This is also expected and accepted by all including the mother. Only in songs, when the Dinka allow many exceptions to rules, may a child call a father by his personal name and a mother by her status as "mother."

The rules of agnatic integration are more strict in connection with sons than with daughters. Sex roles begin to be differentiated after the child returns home from weaning. Education, which is largely a family affair, begins to prepare the children for assuming and continuing the family skills and profession. Boys learn from men; girls from women. Boys stay with men in the cattle byres or in the open around a fire adjacent to —or amidst—the tethered herds; girls stay with their mothers in the huts or in the female sitting area outside; even trees for shade in the daytime are segregated. It is not easy to prevent little boys from associating with their mothers; this subjects them to teasing and ridicule as their mothers' sons. A girl who associates with boys is also ridiculed, not as her father's daughter, which would be complimentary, but as a "bull-girl" or a "men-seeker." Even at that age, to be accused of acting like a man or of seeking men is embarrassing.

Boys are segregated from women to immunize them against their contagious jealousies, tensions, and conflicts. They are also made to value and develop the sense of solidarity demanded and expected of them as the core of family unity, harmony, and continuity. One of the ways in which this is done is eating together. Each son brings food from his mother to share with his half-brothers. The institution of *agoor*, whereby a woman leaves some special food for her husband, son, or other male relative to eat behind closed doors, is generally recognized as an affectionate gesture and a means to a man's heart. But it is also condemned. Usually, these two attitudes are combined in that a woman expresses her affection and female exclusiveness by providing *agoor*, and the man expresses his male communal sentiments by calling or joining others to share with him or by sending it to them—at the same time appreciating the woman's concern.

Another angle of the solidarity of the sons is fighting in defense of one another or of family honor. Much of the violence of Dinka society, to which I have already alluded, is directed toward this end. But the need to fight for the family is so much a part of the general need to develop an independent courageous character in a boy that it is not possible to separate them. The Dinka believe that grievances must not be nursed. Between adults, they should be voiced and resolved. Since reasoning is more limited among children, controlled violence is permitted and even encouraged between relatives or strangers. Quite apart from the normal fights in the course of life, there are standard ways of provoking fights among children. When herding in a group, boys usually sit in one place under the shade of a tree and go in turn to prevent the cattle from straying. When a boy is away, a plan to provoke a fight is conceived. On his return, he is told that a certain person has insulted him in his absence. The insult is almost invariably against the honor or the dignity of his family or of a particular member of his family. The normal pattern is for him to ask the person who had allegedly insulted him whether he had truly done so. The answer is bound to be "yes," otherwise the alleged offender is accused of cowardice and ridiculed. A fight erupts.

There are many other forms of fabricated provocation. I know one from experience. I was in the cattle-camp one day with several of my half-brothers. As we were playing Dinka field hockey, a senior boy came to tell me that my younger half-brother had been insulted by a boy about my age. According to the story, he came to our section of the camp, seized the ox of my brother, and took it to their section. This was a challenge that could not be resolved by words. The boy might not have taken the ox, but he had to say "yes" when I rushed over and asked him. Insulting him, I challenged him to a duel. Standing by was a group of inciting spectators. As is usually the case in such situations, the fight was regulated. We first wrestled. When neither was thrown, we were asked to hit with bare hands. The Dinka do not punch: they slap their opponent's face or torso with open hands, defending themselves with one arm as they attack with the other. We fought this way for some time and were then asked to switch to prepared branches of trees. After a short while, my adversary threw his branch away and, in breach of the rules, bit me on the jaw. We were then separated. I bled a lot and the wound became so infected that I had to be sent home.

The Dinka like a fair fight and detest undue advantage. In tribal wars, killing by stealth or ambush is considered most dishonorable and gives rise to bitter feuds and heavier legal penalties in the form of increased blood wealth. Among children, fighting a younger child is considered cowardly and vile. When a child is bullied by an older child, the older is said to leave the flank of the dangerously "horned" *ngok* fish to attack the hornless *ayic* fish. A standard practice for small children who have been bullied by older children is to sit some distance away from the people, mumbling with their heads bent down:

> *In misery I sit and moan*
> *Because I have no brother.*

Children say this even if they have a brother. They mean that no one defended them when they thought they were entitled to defense.

Agnatic values and the differentiation of roles are also expressed in labor. The role of the male children is very much tied up with animal husbandry. That cattle are used for marriage indicates their special importance for the sons. Taking care of cattle, sheep, and goats is a full-time occupation for boys. In line with the difficulty of the task, cattle are cared for by older boys while the younger boys care for the sheep and goats. The work is essentially similar in character. During the rainy season, those herds which are not taken to the cattle-camp are put into the cattle byres at night. Boys get up early to release them for "breakfast-grazing" prior to milking or to tether them outside while they clean the byres. Since cattle byres become very messy at night, cleaning is a formidable task. Dung must be removed and spread outside to dry for fuel or must be thrown into the adjacent fields to decompose and fertilize the soil. Urine must be removed and the byre floors dried with the ashes of burnt dung. A smoking fire helps the drying process and deodorizes the byre. If the cattle have spent the night in the courtyard, that area is cleaned. When the cattle are untethered, the ropes are collected and hung. Those ropes that might have been broken or weakened are mended. After a short while, the lactating cows are returned to be milked before they rejoin the herds to graze under the care of older children. Calves, particularly the suckling ones, graze away from their mothers and, like sheep and goats, are herded by the younger children. If the calf should be allowed to graze with its mother, a ring of long thorns is tied around its mouth. This pricks the mother's udder and prevents her from suckling her calf while at the same time the calf is permitted to graze.

Sheep and goats are permitted to suckle their young during the day and only those without sucklings are milked at night. They are, therefore, not segregated when grazing. The objective of the herding boys is to keep the animals from straying and getting lost, or from destroying crops. If the season or the area of grazing is such that the animals may fall victim to lions, hyenas, or leopards, adults instead of children accompany the herds.

Usually children herd after breakfast. As they wander far from home, they collect wild foods according to the season; but generally, they return hungry and thirsty in the late afternoon. This is a noble forbearance which speaks well of a man and about which even adults sing in self-praise. It is one of the early means of testing manhood. The young herdsman must not show a weakening. When he returns, he leaves the animals to graze on the periphery of the village and continues his work in the homestead. It will be recalled from the general description of a Dinka village, that every homestead has a courtyard in front of the cattle byres. This courtyard contains a large area covered with pegs, amidst which are cattle hearths with pyramids of smoldering smudges. In this area, depending on the season and the weather, cattle are tethered outside for the night or for the early part of the evening before they are put into the cattle byres for the night. Sheep and goats are tethered inside the byres unless it is the season when humans and animals sleep outside.

Calves are tethered in the area immediately facing the doorway of the cattle byre and are usually taken home from grazing earlier in the afternoon. As the cattle linger near the villages, the atmosphere is filled with the sounds of calves and cows bellowing and lowing to each other, recognizing and longing for each other, but kept apart until milking-time later in the evening.

Before tethering the cattle, the boys, singing jubilantly and competitively, collect the dung that had been spread out earlier in the day to dry. With it, they make smoky fires to chase away the flies and mosquitoes. Then they tether the cattle, each beast to its own peg and by its own rope. A Dinka child has the extraordinary ability to identify hundreds of pegs and ropes in relation to individual animals. This is taken for granted and it is not even seen as a measure of ability, although failure is considered cognitive weakness. The task is even greater with sheep and goats as they are smaller in size, generally more numerous, and are usually tethered in the darkness of cattle byres.

A girl holding an unruly cow by the nostrils as it is being milked. (Courtesy of the Sudan Government)

When the tethering is completed, a short period of rest follows in which the boys sit around the smoldering fires of the cattle-hearth waiting for milking time. Generally, it is the women and girls who milk, but young boys may be required to milk for initiated men who are not supposed to milk. In milking, the calf is allowed to join its mother and permitted just enough sucking to arouse the mother to release the milk. It is then snatched away and tethered in front of the mother who comforts it by licking as she is milked. When the first flow of milk is dried out, the calf is once more permitted to suck until the cow releases some more milk and the second milking is done. If the calf is small, it is allowed to suck the second flow. If the calf is newly born, the mother is not milked at all; such a calf does not graze and must feed on its mother's milk exclusively. Some cows hold back their milk whenever the calf is withdrawn, and it may be necessary to have three milkings to get the most out of them. Since the suckling of its young is essential for a cow to release her milk, a lactating cow that has lost her calf is made to adopt another one. Otherwise, a dummy calf made from the skin of the dead calf is placed in front of her to lick while she is milked. Where a cow has no calf, or where it has a calf but refuses to release her milk, she may be induced to do so by a person's blowing into her vulva. Some cows resent being milked and react violently if the attempt is made. In such a case, it may be necessary to subdue them by tying and holding them by the legs, the head, and maybe the nose. Milking entails sitting on one's legs under the cow with the container resting on the thighs. The teats are then emptied by the pressure and downward movement of the thumb and forefinger. Sometimes little children are fed with milk straight from a cow: Sitting next to the person milking, a child places his mouth in a convenient position to receive the flowing milk. As milk flowing from the udder forms a foam, a child fed this way is easily satiated, belches loudly, and hungers quickly.

When milking has been completed, the calf is allowed to suck whatever is left. And usually every cow retains some milk for this final feeding of her calf. A calf must not, however, be allowed to suck for too long, since the Dinka believe that it then swallows excessive hairs that mingle with grass to form ball-like objects which are believed to be hazardous to the calf's health and are sometimes found in dead cattle. So hard are they that children use them for playing soccer.

When the calves are taken back to their pegs another rest period follows, after which the cattle are taken into the byres if they are not to spend the night outside. The calves are taken in earlier, just as the children normally go to bed before adults. Inside the cattle byres are pegs surrounding a central hearth lying in a circular arrangement of long poles. These poles support the roof at the point where the first set of rafters is joined by a second set. This combination of rafters gives extra height to Dinka cattle byres and distinguishes them from ordinary huts, which have only one set of rafters. In the hearth is a conical smudge from dried cow dung filling the byre with thick smoke. Partly feeling their way, the boys tether the cattle. Poised between the poles surrounding the hearth is a hard platformbed on which they sleep to guard the cattle at night. With the heat, the smoke, the bites of those mosquitoes that resist the smoke, and the snoring or kicking of animals, this is hardly sleep. On top of that is the need to sleep lightly and shout at restless and aggressive beasts and the even more demanding need to be on the alert to rise and tether an animal that may break its rope, splinter its peg, or pull its peg out of the ground. Dinka boys get used to this. Being on the alert even while sleeping and, therefore, resting with as light a sleep as possible is assumed to be part of the military and defensive character of men. A boy wakes tip to face the new day's challenges without complaint. Similar functions are also performed by children in the cattle-camps; but because of the dangers of herding in distant camps, children are not allowed to accompany cattle to the pastures. That is for the adults.

Although each son generally takes care of the cattle of his own mother or his section of the family, he must not discriminate against the cattle of his step-mothers. For instance, he should not hesitate to do anything that might be required of him either because he is on the spot or because the half-brother normally in charge is unable to carry out his duty. Herding, in particular, is collective work; and whether it is done by turn or together, one is expected to give equal care to the whole herd. Mothers sometimes discourage their own sons from overworking by extending care to the cattle of co-wives, but sons are expected to rebuff such mothers and assert the theory of collective ownership: the cattle of his half-brothers are his father's and, therefore, his own also. When he comes to marry, it is not from his cattle alone, but from the whole herd, that his father will provide the bridewealth. The degree to which children's jobs fall on a boy depends on his age, but the skill of cattle-care is one that every Dinka boy must attempt at an early age and aim at perfecting as he grows.

The task of boys is not only concerned with cattle, sheep, and goats. Since the Dinka do not have domestic servants, it is the children who render the services normally reserved for servants, and this is one of the factors that distinguish them from adults: They must milk for adults and serve the milk. When an adult is thirsty, it is a boy—if not a girl—that he sends to fetch water. A child must be ready and willing to do any errand an adult requires of him. Refusal means a beating from which no father, mother, or any other relative will defend him. Respect for age has few limitations in the eyes of the Dinka, and the performance of such services is one of the central functions of childhood. This singer cites it as a fulfillment of his obligations to his father, implying that it is now for his father to discharge his paternal duties by finding him a wife.

> *I am a man with a confounded mind,*
> *I do not know to whom to give the seat of my father*
> *To go and sit on the discussion-bed.*
> *I do not know to whom to give the bed of my father.*
> *Our words have ended with the times he used to send me*
> *for water*
> *And the times he would say, "Go and bring a mat from the*
> *cattle byre."*
> *I would bring them in front of my father.*
> *Is that not the goodness of a person's son?*
> *But now, people have confused our relationship*
> *So much that I am like the son of a stranger.*
> *My father has tapped his chest in refusal.*
> *O clan of my father, should I be only a tribesman?*

The socialization of a Dinka girl differs markedly from that of a Dinka boy. While she is also expected to identify more with her father than with her mother, it is realized that she is closer to her mother than the son is. It is through her mother that she learns to be a wife and mother. Since she will marry and leave to further the interests of another lineage, her role within her agnatic group is limited. Her main contribution is to attract bridewealth which her brothers and other male relatives will use for their own marriages. Through marriage, she also widens the circle of relatives and thereby enhances the family's sources of kinship values. Yet, the Dinka speak of her as "a slave" to be "sold" and "a stranger" who will "leave" her own kin group for another. These terms are used only metaphorically, but they indicate something of her subordination to her brothers.

Her violation of the rules of preference for the father does not arouse the same degree of resentment as violation by a son. For instance, she may call her mother "Mother" without being ridiculed. The need to foster her agnatic solidarity is also less pressing than is the case with a boy. For instance, it is not necessary for girls to eat collectively with their half-sisters. Usually though, they choose to do so at a much later age. Also, girls are not trained to fight for the family or for one another in the same way boys are, although this is more a matter of violence being less encouraged among them than it is a matter of laxity in the requirements of agnatic solidarity. And a greater measure of jealousy is expected and tolerated from girls than from boys.

The subordinate status of the girl, which leads to the application of such words as "slave"—metaphoric as they are—implies that a girl labors more than a boy. Depending on how ample boy-power is, she may be required to help with much of the care for sheep, goats, and even cattle. She may have to take the sheep and the goats for grazing, although only in nearby pastures.

With respect to household work, while the Dinka segregate and

Women carry burdens on their heads and men on their shoulders. The grass in the foreground of the photo on page 95 has been burned to clear the ground for cultivation. (Courtesy of the Sudan Government)

grade the functions of male children as opposed to male adults, those of females remain identical from childhood to adulthood. When a man is initiated he must abandon much of what are considered children's ways. But a woman may retain these without degrading herself, an indication that women and children in a sense have equal status. This may be a lowering of status for women or a necessity arising from the fact that women constantly associate with children since much of their life goes into bearing and raising children. The functions of a girl are, therefore, not so clear-cut as those of a boy. Although a superficial observation may lead to the conclusion that boys work harder than girls, a closer examination reveals the opposite. Her training is essentially geared toward making her a woman, a wife, and a mother: statuses that involve greater demands than their male equivalents. But the working gap between a boy and a girl is narrower since a Dinka boy works harder than his male seniors.

Girls start learning to cook at a very early age, initially using tiny pots specially made for them, substituting sand for real flour, setting up pot-supporters, and arranging "fire-twigs" under the pots—but without fire. As they grow older the pots get larger, flour substitutes for sand, the fire burns, and real food is prepared. A type of porridge called *por*, made of milk (usually goat's milk) and flour, is their popular dish. Little girls accompany older girls and women with little containers to fetch water from the river or pools. And they take part in the collection of firewood, carrying bundles appropriate to their sizes and ages. While their female tasks remain constant in kind, they increase in degree and intensity as the girls grow older. They pound the grain and prepare the meals; they milk the cows and churn the milk for butter; they make the beds and sweep the huts; they clean the compounds and help in the fields. Indeed, most of the functions of women fall on young girls as the "servants" of older women. But when they reach marriageable age, their load lessens for they must look their best to attract men and should not be overworked. Yet the balance is delicate, for they are also to impress observers as good housekeepers and excellent cooks. So when a guest visits, they are given the opportunity to display their industry, courtesy, and skill.

In serving food to men, and especially in front of strangers, girls, as well as young women, must show exceeding deference. A girl or a woman approaches men well-poised and with her skirts properly held in place. Some yards away she kneels and approaches them on her knees. Sitting on her legs in an almost ritualistic manner, she places the food in front of them, crawls backward on her knees until she is some distance away, and then stands up to go, holding her skirts in place and walking with the self-conscious yet dignified poise with which she had come. This is only a feature of a more elaborate system of respect between men and women, most emphasized between in-laws, whether real, potential, or even fictional.

While the roles of the sexes are thus segregated from childhood, children are not kept entirely apart. There are many things they do together, with or without significance attached to sex. The guiding principle of their socialization is that agnatic values must be promoted; and in this respect greater attention and a more rigorous discipline must be applied to the orientation of boys than is needed for girls. However, the less agnatic values are imprinted on the girls as future wives and mothers, the more difficult it is to secure these values in the society as a whole, and, therefore, the greater and the more oppressive the agnatic demands on boys and men who are responsible for holding the lineage together. Such are the paradoxes that make agnatic ideals more objective than felt and more constraining than loving.

Socialization Through Games

Dinka children, like children all over the world, play a variety of games that are primarily entertaining but are also subtly geared toward developing in a child an awareness and sensitivity for Dinka values and norms. As might be expected, cattle, marriage, the distinctive roles of the sexes, and the values of physical strength and courage for men are among the prominent features of this educational process. Their educational content can be understood only in the total context of their performance, in the emotional disposition they develop in the children, and from the cultural background nourishing such disposition.

One of these games is a bathing game played in the river. Standing deep enough for the water to reach below their armpits, the children form a circle. One child dives into the center while the rest beat the water on top, chanting collectively:

> *The diviner of that day*
> *From where did he come?*
> *The diviner of Nyandeeng's Mother*

Is that why my mother must die?
My little buffalo, rest in peace,
Mankind is passing on.

On the face of it, the song does not say much. It might be accusing the diviner of bringing a curse on the mother, but it might be that the diviner has discovered the source of evil and has concluded that death is inevitable. The diving and the beating on the water seem to symbolize burial. Whatever the interpretation, what counts most is the total effect on a Dinka child of the melody, the rhythm, and the mystery of a child under water. The game confronts a child with the frightening possibility that his mother might die. What I have already said about the love and affection between a child and his mother explains why a Dinka child cannot imagine his world without his mother. To predict or assert that she must die, indeed even the mere association of her health with a diviner, whose notion generally connotes serious illness, is a terrifying confrontation. But despite its shocking effects, the game orientates a child, subtly, but surely, to the tragic and inevitable realities of mortality.

With a somewhat similar though less shocking effect is a game played at home in the evenings. Children sit in a circle and beat their laps with their hands while singing collectively. In the center is a girl—always a girl—sitting on her legs, vigorously hopping and turning while she beats the ground with her hands and joins with the group in singing songs of a mystic nature. As the excitement increases, the girl in the center becomes frantic and may get possessed. The elders then intervene to stop the game, or remove the possessed girl. Again, the words of the songs do not say much, but the whole context develops a sensitivity about such matters as the importance of giving senior members their rightful share in bridewealth or facing the consequences of spiritual danger that is sometimes evidenced by the diabolic possession of female relatives. At the same time, the game trains women psychologically to be capable of inducing possession, or being receptive to it—which is one of the ways in which they exert their otherwise repressed influence on men.

Certain games concern themselves with ordinary life. Small children make cattle-camps, using shells as cattle or making figures of cattle with clay. They even make cattle-hearths and fires of dried cow dung. As they grow older, children begin to act adult roles. Using a slice of sugar cane, boys have their heads scratched with temporary initiation marks. They decorate themselves with the adornments of the initiates, compose initiation songs, and sing and dance to them with all the pride and dignity of adults. They also sing. about fictitious oxen, sometimes decorating billy-goats with tassels and bells to imitate adult personality-oxen and driving them around and singing over them in competition with one another. Wearing small versions of the catskins normally worn by adults for dancing, using the large root balls of the onion-type plant called *agurbiok* on their upper arms to represent the ivory bangles the adults wear, and bearing themselves with the pride and dignity of the initiated, they imitate adults. While adult age-sets travel far to fell special trees for drums and hunt wild beasts for drumskins, children use old mortars and women's skirts. In the late evening when all sit chitchatting outside on moonlit nights, children may be heard throughout the village chanting words that are meant to ridicule those reluctant to join the dance. As these are chanted, the children pour into the open space near the homes and start their evening dance. While babies and very young children are put to bed early, older children are called from their play when it is time for all to sleep—and sometimes they are the last to go to bed.

Usually, people do not go to sleep immediately after going to bed. All, children and adults alike, compete in riddle and storytelling. One of the more elementary examples of Dinka riddles is, "Guess a milk gourd that is upside down without spilling milk." The answer is the udder of a cow. Another one is, "Guess gentlemen challenging one another and not meeting in a duel." They are the sky and the earth.

In storytelling, one person tells a fairy-tale, with the understanding that another one will "pay him a reverse bridewealth" by telling another story. The last to tell a story is usually the last to sleep. Stories act as lullabies and sometimes send people to sleep. They are, however, educational and are meant to be heard. Their importance in symbolizing the heritage of Dinka experience is epitomized by their opening expression "There is an ancient event." As the lion figures prominently in them, fairy-tales are called *koor* ("lion"), by the Ngok. But the fusion of the world of man with that of beasts is commonplace in these stories and extends to inanimate beings. In them, the Dinka do not, of course, mean to tell the real truth. They do not speak of "telling" a story but of paar, a difficult word to translate; it is close to "guessing," but implies an attempt to construct as much of the truth as possible from the scanty information available. The following is an example:

> *This is an ancient event. A small rain fell at the beginning of the rainy season. Angiic, a small brown ant, came out to cool her children after the rain, because the outside world had become cool. When Angiic returned to her hut to do something, the bird called Awec came and ate her children. As he was about to take the last child, Angiic saw him and when she saw such a thing, she poured salty water into his eyes. Awec ran blindly and sat on a tree called Adhot. Adhot fell because Awec was too heavy for him. He injured an animal called Amuk which was under him. Amuk ran wildly and entered the house of the Chief's wife. He knocked down the Chief's wife who was sitting in the doorway and broke her teeth. He was brought to court to be tried.*
>
> *Asked by the Court why he had done such a thing, Amuk said, "How can such a big tree as Adhot fall on a person and*

the person still be expected not to run?" The Court turned to Adhot and asked him why he had fallen on Amuk. He said, "How can a person not fall when a big bird like Awec sits on him?" The Court turned to Awec, saying, "Why did you sit on Adhot when you knew that he too had life?" Awec answered, "How can a person see when such a lot of salty water is poured into his eyes? I did not know where I was sitting." Angiic was then asked why she had poured salty water into Awec's eyes, and she answered, "When it had rained, bringing a cool breeze, how could one be expected not to cool her children in the breeze? And when one's children are then eaten, how can one be expected not to pour salty water on the person eating them?" "Rain, why did you fall?" asked the Court. "When people's crops were drying up," answered the Rain, "How could a person be asked not to water them?" The Court asked the crops, "Why did you go dry?" In answer, the crops said, "When a big animal like Arou [the tortoise] excretes on people, how can they be expected not to dry up?" "Arou," the Court asked, "Are crops your forest where you excrete?" Arou answered, "When such a large animal like Akoon, the elephant, steps on a person unexpectedly, how could he be expected not to excrete?" Then Akoon was asked, "Why did you step on Arou?" He answered, "When drums beat so loud and well, how could a person be expected not to run to the dance? I was overwhelmed by the joy of dancing and knew nothing else." Then the Court addressed the drum, "Why did you sound so loud and well?" In answer the drum said, "When a person is beaten by two drumsticks (theet), how can he help sounding loud and well?" The Court asked the drumsticks, "Why did you beat the drum?" The sticks said, "It was a mistake! What should be done when a person realizes that he has made a mistake?"

And so the sticks were forgiven.

Courage and strength form a recurrent theme. So does the need for affection and for curtailing co-wives' and step-kin jealousies. As the following story indicates, virtue is rewarded and evil punished:

> There were two stepsisters, Acol Aretret [that is, the unruly Acol] and Acol Adheng [the gentle Acol]. Acol Aretret was very disobedient and ill-mannered. Acol Adheng was her opposite. One day, they heard drums beating in the night, and Acol Aretret suggested that they attend the dance. Against the advice of elders and Acol Adheng, she insisted. So they went. The dance was a mixed human-lion dance. They danced with two lions, Lual and Lual, who were half-brothers. One Lual was vicious, and the other gentle. As Dinka girls choose their dance-mates, Acol Aretret chose to dance with the vicious Lual. As they danced, the vicious Lual started to turn wild; and as his tail and fur emerged, his stepbrother warned him in his dancing mioc [a poetic exclamation that accompanies one's rhythm]:

> Lual of my father
> O Lual of my father
> Beware of the Dinka girl.
> The vicious Lual answered:
> O Lual, my brother
> Dheeng has excelled.
> Acol does not know the words;
> Acol who does not know the words,
> Where have you come from?
> I shall eat her
> Between the upper hut and the pillar.
> The gentle Acol noticed what was happening and warned her sister,

Daughter of my father
Where goes the long tail?
Her sister answered,
Isn't the tail the sign of beauty?
For a tail, a girl will choose a man. He came with black hair,
The head heavy with the hair.

After the dance, the two men escorted the girls home, and as they entered the hut, the vicious Lual seized Acol Aretret and ate her.

Akin to fairy-tales are legends explaining certain facts about the animal world. The following song illustrates such legends: The singer whose ox is gray (which is why he later mentions the camel) touches on various legends which are not fully explained, but which have bearing on the color-pattern of his ox. Among these is the myth of God's withdrawal from the world as a result of a wrong committed by a woman. God then sent the finch (which is gray) to cut the rope that still linked Heaven and Earth, thus ending the complete happiness that had prevailed and turning man into a suffering and mortal being. *Guuk*, a species of the dove (also gray), who was then betrothed to God's daughter and had already paid 100 cows, lost both his bride and his wealth. Another legend is that of the grackle, which borrowed the eyes of the moth (also grayish) and never returned them, leaving the moth half-blind. Yet another legend is that of monkeys who are believed to have descended from boys and girls who were gathering *kei* (the roots of water lilies) which stained their hands black. The girls refused to return to the camp with unclean hands and so they, together with the boys, went into the forest to form a separate race. There is also a mention of the fox (also gray) who is presented in many legends as the cleverest animal who outwits all other animals. Apart from these several explanations, there are details I am unable to explain.

Feud, the ancient feud for which hundreds died,
He will find a bird and grab its jaw.
The feud of the storm,
The ancient feud when the finch cut the rope
And turned your mother into a mortal being;
Then the grackle did it again
And the bird disappeared with no vengeance from you.
O Moth, you are a man in vain;
If you had turned into a man,
You would have continued chasing after your eyes
Even if you be defeated by the grackle.
In the past when disaster nearly killed women
If it were not for the wit of man
Things would have burnt into ashes.
It was a fire which could not be extinguished,
A fire which could not be seen,
A fire without smoke.
Monkeys are debased;
The great debased monkeys who cry, "oi oi,"
Monkeys are debased:
Their girls are courted on one side of a tree
While parents sit next to them;
The girls of monkeys have messy hair.
Have you seen, they are like dogs.
The ancient girls who refused the people's camp,
"We cannot return without clean hands."
Monkeys, what great things you have left behind.
There are girls who decorate themselves with red ashes
And dance the dance of your race.
When asked, "How is the dance of your race danced?"
Monkeys say: "We cannot dance
But the fox cannot climb."

The girls who dance with many ornaments,
Your girls are reputed to wear pied and beautiful beads.
Animals say that the land is run by the fox.
My head is stuffed.
The case of my ox seen by the tribe
Clan-heads;
The judges have gathered in the Court;
My Malith like the ancient Malith of the dove above.
The beauty of your original world,
A world in which you all mixed.
How the dove dared to marry the daughter of the Chief;
The finch is the person who hates other people's dheeng.
He cut the rope
And a man who was married was left in vain.
The hundred cows of the dove remained above
And in the evening when the sun goes down
God tethers the herds of the dove
And the dove cries: "Has it dawned
So that I may go to divorce World, bring the morning soon
So that I may go to divorce."
The fox calls, "Gwak,"
My Malinh-Jok,
The curve-horned is like a lion.
People see the buttocks of the Arab.
Here he is;
He is the camel which has spoiled the buttocks of the Arabs,
The great one with disordered teeth.

Children also act such adult roles as getting married. These games do not involve any physical relationships; all they are concerned with is the public image of the husband-wife relationship: the man taking part in public affairs while the woman keeps the home and rears the children, for which logs of wood or dolls of mud are used. I do not know the degree to which the status of a child's family determines the form these games take; but in our village we held public meetings, made public speeches, heard cases, and even appointed individuals to public offices—from Paramount Chief to heads of clans—using the names of the real leaders.

There are also games which are geared toward developing in a boy an independent and courageous personality. I have already had occasion to mention that Dinka children are encouraged to fight out their grievances instead of nursing them. Games of violence, however, have a more extensive purpose than training children to fight one another. Given the violent nature of Dinka society, developing physical courage, strength, and skill is a preparation for the task ahead. Fights are still frequently threatened and not infrequently fought despite the new law and order. In any case, training is still a cultural necessity. Physical training entails a variety of sports including *dheek* (a game of tag), *weer* (racing), *lir* (high-jumping), and *acituek* (a form of field hockey). Being tall, long-legged and slim, the Dinka are remarkably athletic; and their not having yet been heard of in the world scene is merely the result of their traditionalism, isolationism, and the inhibiting national situation.

Violence is more overt in wrestling which, though a game, is also a regulated fight. Usually, the objective is merely to tackle and throw a person down. But when a person is thrown, a certain amount of torture is permitted before he is put back on his feet. The throwing person sits on his victim, controls his victim's hands with his knees, forcefully rubs his face and sometimes opens his eyes wide and blows into them to make them dry up—or exposes them to the glare of the sun. The position might be reversed with the thrown getting on top and doing the same. Otherwise, they are made to stand and give it another go. Being thrown is defeat; crying under torture is disgrace.

At a more serious level is the fighting induced between people who have no real cause to fight. An incident that occurred when I was about eight years old might elucidate the point: Two of my brothers and I went to the cattle-camp after we had just returned on our first vacation from school. Even though we had not been long in school, the cattle-camp was a little different and the boys were more untamed. That same evening, a dance was called exclusively for boys. After some dancing the leader, evidently the toughest, called for silence. He announced that there were newcomers whose affiliation into an age-set had to be determined. Unlike adult age-sets, which are determined by age-groups initiated together, boys' "mock" age-sets are determined by physical strength and courage in fighting. The leader wanted to know which age-set we desired to join. We indicated the senior age-set. Although its members were older than we, the difference was not much. The leader then asked each of us to choose someone from the age-set to fight; our qualification was to be determined by the result. At first, we refused to pick out anyone, arguing that we would fight whoever wanted to, or were chosen, to fight us. This was interpreted as cowardice. I made my choice—a one-eyed boy whom I learned later was one of the toughest and had, in fact, lost his eye in a fight. We wrestled. He threw me down. I managed to tackle him and reverse our positions. After several rounds of wrestling in which I was thrown more than I threw, we were given branches of trees for beating, a part I was much better at. So I made up for lost points. Finally, we were stopped. I and my brothers through me were declared qualified to join the set.

Courage in fighting is more valued than actual strength. Dinka believe that cowards, if compelled to fight, are unusually strong. Crying is the worst sign of defeat. A child who cries is rebuked even by his parents. This is preparation for a later demand that men must never cry whatever the situation. Women are permitted to cry, but, from later childhood, more in emotional distress than in physical pain. Women cry in mourning; men should not. When beaten by her husband, a Dinka woman would more often than not cry after the beating when her pains become more sentimental than physical.

For boys, fighting with spears is learned through the use of shaft-like branches of trees which are sharpened on one end to represent spears. In one game, a large ball-like root of the *amiyok* plant is tied to a long string and swung in a circle by one boy while the rest form a wide circle and spear the object as it passes by. This is one of the popular ways of spending the long day herding. These branches are used in fights between children of different sections. Although such fights are only games, they sometimes result in serious injuries that occasionally cause death.

Thus, although the Dinka do not have institutions for formal education and training, the process of growth is educational. Games are not only played for fun; they are a means of disposing and adjusting children to the norms of society. The forms of these differ with age, but the essence is introduced early.

Children's Operations

I mentioned earlier that Dinka children have their heads scratched with mock initiation marks that usually heal within days. There are also patterns of scars made on children for decoration. The ears of most children, and the lips of some, are pierced for wearing rings. But by far the most significant customary operations are circumcision and extraction of teeth.

Circumcision is not universal in Dinkaland. Some tribes look down upon it and are as contemptuous of the circumcised as the circumcised are of them. Among the Ngok, the Rek, the Tuic, and the Malual, every male child gets circumcised unless he is an idiot, mad, or too chronically sick to be governed by the normal rules of decency. It is sometimes argued that the Dinka adopted circumcision from the Arabs. Even if this were so, the Dinka regard it as indigenous.

Unlike the Arabs who practice it on religious grounds, the reason the Dinka give is esthetic. To be uncircumcised is to be dirty and ugly; not to be circumcised at about the age of six is to invite insults for which there are standard songs.

Unlike the circumcision of Arab boys, which is the equivalent of Dinka initiation and entails elaborate ceremonies and festivities, circumcision among the Dinka is very informal. It is also a private affair done by households rather than in large groups. The operation is performed by an expert. Tying the foreskin tightly with a hair from the tail of a giraffe, he cuts it off with a sharp knife and then trims it along the edges to make it smooth and even. As with all Dinka operations, no anesthesia is used. Circumcision is therefore very painful. Since the manifest purpose is not to test courage, boys may cry, although enduring it without crying speaks well of a boy's courage and is admired. After the initial confinement when the wound is acute, the circumcised are allowed to move about, but must cover their wounds with specially cut leather loincloths to protect them from flies.

Extraction of teeth entails the removal of the six front lower teeth, a custom shared by all Dinka of both sexes. A Dinka sings about the value of extraction of teeth as the cultural trait distinguishing the Dinka from Arabs since the Arabs also circumcise:

Three kinds of people met
And some became confused:
There were uncircumcised men,
There were circumcised men,
And men with unextracted teeth.
Even if the Arab should say,
"It's a lie, I have my doubts,
Why is one Dinka circumcised
And the other is not?"

I will answer, "Yours is the lie;
Don't you see, our heads are marked
And our teeth are removed?
We are the ancient race of the Dinka."

As with circumcision, the Dinka do not give any explanation for the custom other than that it is esthetically pleasant and helps shape the mouth to be handsome. They say that unextracted lower teeth push the lower lip outward and make the lower jaw repulsive. Teeth are removed at about the age of ten in an operation more painful than circumcision. It is done by an expert with a fishing spear. The tip of the spear is placed between the teeth and is pressed back and forth to loosen the roots of the teeth and tear them from the gum. The tip of the spear is then forced to the roots and the whole tooth is plucked.

In most tribes, removal of teeth marks the end of operational pain for girls. For boys and the girls of some tribes, another hurdle lies ahead. The most dramatic, most ritualistic, and most significant operation comes at initiation with the end of childhood and the commencement of adulthood.

Chapter Six: Youth

Initiation

Initiation is a crucial event that determines a man's status in Dinka society. It takes place between the ages of sixteen and eighteen and dramatically brings an end to childhood. Initiation ceremonies give maximum value to courage, aggressiveness, and violence. Yet with this is a new demand: for a high degree of self-restraint, dignity of bearing, and responsible conduct must now be displayed. Seeing a Dinka before and after initiation is enough to convince one of the extraordinary results that can be achieved overnight by the ritualized and socialized drama of psychological conditioning. Nevertheless, because of the intensity of their group spirit and their social prominence, the control of youth and the utilization of their vitality continue to be problems until young men fully make the transition into adulthood and are stabilized by the advantages and responsibilities of family life.

The most obvious attraction of initiation for youth is the dignity it gives a man. Until initiated, a young man is a "boy" and we have seen what that means in Dinka society. Apart from milking, uninitiated men do most of the day-to-day work of cattle husbandry. An

uninitiated man may be sent on an errand at any time by any initiated man even though the latter may be younger (which sometimes
happens since initiates known as *anyat* are ahead of their time).
Uninitiated men are not permitted to sing except in children's activities. They are required to lead oxen for the initiated as the latter
sing. Formal dating, dancing, or flirting with girls is not permitted
before initiation. If it occurs, the girl is shunned and ridiculed, and
the uninitiated man may find himself ganged up against by the initiated age-mates of a competitor. They can act only as agents of the
initiated in the processes of courtship. Because of such subordination,
initiation is one of the greatest ambitions of Dinka youth. This is
revealed in the following lines from initiation songs:

> *I hate being a boy.*
> *I will no longer remain a boy;*
> *Even if initiation burns like gas It is better that I die.*

> *Our age-set will lie for pain in*
> *the home of the Dancing Crane.*
> *Is not initiation the good thing*
> *that redeems a man from slavery?*

Shortly after the age of puberty, the designation of an elder as
the "father" of the age-set is considered. He must be from one of the
preeminent lineages and, although he need not be a chief, he should
be endowed with the divine power to bless and curse. When public
opinion favors a choice, he is formally appointed by the Chief.

The father gives a name to his age-set which will symbolize courage
and physical strength. Examples are "The Lion-Man," "The Buffalo,"
"The Great Vulture," "The Determined Crocodile," and "Honeybee."
The name "Turks" has been used to signify colonial power first introduced by the Turks, whose name the Dinka applied to the British as

well. An age-set may receive its name from a bull sacrificed by the father to bless his age-set. Since females have age-sets corresponding to male age-sets, their name is chosen in conjunction with that of their male counterparts; but is always different from it. "The Tawny Cub of the Lion," and "The Shining Shaft of Spear" are examples of female age-set names.

The chosen name is ritually conferred in a ceremony in which the age-set assembles for the first time and commences its corporate identity. Various social activities and consultations with the father follow before the immediate steps toward initiation are taken. About a year before the desired time, the age-set asks its father, the Chief of the subtribe (for age-setting is on subtribal bases), and the Paramount Chief to permit initiation. Permission may be initially granted but later denied on such grounds as the presence of an epidemic disease, a poor agricultural yield, and the unavailability of fish (a particularly important ingredient of the initiates' diet, since they may not drink milk or eat any dairy food). Permission granted, the young men then invite one of the few experts to perform the operation. Not infrequently, they are invited from other tribes—particularly if a number of subtribes initiate at the same time. A period of festivities and dancing follows. The initiates-to-be must then strip themselves of all ornamentation and must be unarmed except for whips and a bundle of *durra* (sorghum) stalks symbolizing spears. The Dinka consider it unnatural for a man to go bare-handed, but unwise for the unruly youth to be armed with dangerous weapons. As the designated time nears, the festivities increase; plenty of beer is brewed; many animals are slaughtered; much cooking is done. There is no question of shortage, for initiation takes place when the crops have just been reaped. The day before the operation is particularly celebrative. Beasts are sacrificed and other rites of spiritual fortification are performed. No one sleeps that night, for excitement is high and the sounds of drums and songs fill the air. Dancing goes on all night and for days to follow. Early in the morning, the operation begins. In their order of seniority of birth and lineage, the to-be-initiated lie on the ground to receive some seven to ten deep and well-ordered marks across the forehead: the bloodiest and most painful operation in Dinka society. Under each man's head is a hole to hold his blood, but the cutting sometimes releases more blood than the holes can contain:

> *Veins bled like a stormy rain,*
> *The head of the bull has been torn apart.*

> *My holes red like the forest of red trees,*
> *My blood flooding the holes like the waters of spring.*

> *Nyandeeng, daughter of Koor,*
> *Please help chase the dogs away*
> *The dogs are lapping the blood.*
> *In my war with the Pelican [the initiator] there is death.*

As the operation proceeds, people cluster around the youths. Women relatives and members of the corresponding female age-sets, with whom association has been suppressed, run wild screaming with joy; men chant their special verses of valor; both men and women running and jumping in a special ballet known as *goor*; and, since modern influence, gunshots fill the air in a rampant expression of joy. The initiates themselves, still and serene, first attempt to chant their boastful words of courage, but soon pass out from excessive bleeding. The initiator turns wild and sometimes stains his face with blood to invoke greater awe. The whole scene is a madhouse. To a stranger, it is madness itself; but to the Dinka, it is *dheeng*:

My dheeng shocked the Arab to hold his head;
My dheeng shocked the Arab to bite his lip;
My dheeng shocked the Arab to close his eyes.
"The thing is death," he cried,
No, it is our ancient deed.

In the name of joy, a great deal of damage is done; houses of others may be burned with the intention of compensating the owners later; livestock may be killed, with the same intention; clothed, women who are unable to swim fall into deep rivers; and, not least, the celebrants' cries of joy almost deafen the ears. The excitement aroused by the fact that a young man has endured the pain implies his relatives' apprehension that he might possibly shame them by fearing initiation—they are supposed to kill him if he should do so. But so flattering is the whole situation that even a coward acquires enough courage to endure the pain. And except for generalized imputations in songs, I have never heard of a man who showed fear of initiation.

The initiates are in a kind of conflict with the older generations. For their initiation is a step toward equality with their seniors. The extent of their promotion is limited and, although it rises gradually, it reaches a high level only when a man is advanced in age. Yet, every step of the initiate toward that status is a further limitation on the authority of the guardians and of the intermediate age-sets. Combined with the resentment at this is the pleasure of seeing one's child or relative rise in age and status. The initiate, in turn, combines his zest for greater freedom with the gentle submissiveness required of a younger man. Conflict and harmony are symbolized in initiation and articulated in initiation songs. The initiator, who represents the older generations, is seen with both affection and enmity. He is pictured as the one with the upper hand who must be faced with courage; for initiation itself is seen as a kind of war in which both sides win, but the rules are created by the older generations to inflict pain on the rising generations for the purposes of education. Following are examples from the many songs with this theme:

We are provoking a war with Deng and Deng, the Chiefs
And with Agok Mijok, our Father;
The big age-set is held back like a fleeing swarm of bees.
A war we started with the initiator, the Father of Acai,
A war we started with our uncle, The Nile Perch.
And the guns of Deng roared.
The Great Bol, the initiator, is spoiled;
He has rurned wild like the lioness, Awek,
And goes around the flanks in a wild run.

I have subdued the Father of Acai with my forehead.
He is a man initiating a full bull.
Even if the knife is sharpened to be like the slice of a cane;
My friend, Carrier of the Shield, I have blunted its edge.
You let Bol pass and did not say "No."
I have stopped him.
The knife wore out on the brow of my eye.
Is Maguith, the Pied One, not yet done?
The initiator is still on his right forehead.
He has not yet reached the left side.
What is the matter?
Are they skinning the man?
Why has it taken so long?

Most references to the father are those of conflict over whether the son should be initiated. The father's argument is usually "You are still a child"; "You will run away"; or "You will fear."

My father said, "You will not lie down,
You will run away."
O Father, I do not care for my life;
I shall lie down under the shrine of Kwol, the Striped One.

The war is also between them, for initiation is a step toward independence and the beginning of the son's own family line. Yet, the father is pleased to see his son rising to perpetuate their lineage while recognizing that the rite signalizes a loss of parental control.

Those who are unreservedly glad are women: mothers, sisters, and other relatives. Females partly depend on their sons and brothers for influence. The sister does not stay long to pursue this; but the success of the mother as a wife is so dependent on her success as a mother that her status rises in direct correspondence with the number and the ages of her children, particularly sons. Initiation is a promotion for her.

Women stampeded with joy,
My mother chanting, "He has endured it
My son has endured the pain of the knife
I am no longer the mother of a boy."

The recovery period that follows initiation and continues for several months is very colorful. Initiates reside collectively by lineages in restricted villages. Considered somewhat impure, they are not permitted to go near cattle and they must eat only porridge, meat, and fish. On these, they gorge themselves. Although confined, they have few responsibilities and many privileges. Indeed, they are "spoiled." From palm fronds, they make long, beautifully designed and dyed headdresses and decorations with which they cover their otherwise naked bodies. With their remarkable bearing of dignity and pride, their songs of bravery and their initiation dances, they are a great attraction to many a man and woman and especially to girls. In settlements known as "houses," they compete in dances that often lead to fights and destruction of property—all the more reason to keep spears and clubs away from them. They continue to be armed with whips and stalks of *durra*.

The initiation dance in which initiation songs are sung consists of a lifting and dropping of the legs with a jerk of the body to imitate the movement of a horse under tight rein. This is accompanied with individual chantings of self-praise. The singer, representing the horse and the rider, makes sounds as though subduing an unruly horse. Sometimes he whips the horse with the reins held tight so that the struggle becomes more marked. These are symbols of their coercive powers, their pride in their forthcoming status as warriors, and, it would seem, their control by the elders and their desire for emancipation. This symbol of the rider and the ridden is new as Dinka did not traditionally own horses. Southern Dinkas still do not. Because of their long association with the Arabs, the Ngok have horses, but think of them as belonging to people of wealth and authority. Yet it is the theme that counts; and whatever symbols they used prior to the advent of horses, the idea is to represent conflict and harmony in a lyric fashion.

Drums are not used in the initiation dance. Instead, the dancers beat the ground with their bundles of canes. They are usually decorated with all sorts of anklet and bracelet bells that produce a variety of jingling sounds as they dance. Added to this are the joyous cries of women dancers. Generally, men and women dance together—or rather, each person dances as a member of a group without any special partners. The only exception to this is a variant of an initiation dance called *ruaath* danced by men of all ages with women of older age-groups. A man and a woman hop around with one leg held across the leg of the partner while the dancers chant:

My father throws a war club at me,
I shall cut my feet.
My father throws a war club at me;
I shall cut my feet.

This song again calls to mind the ambivalences of father-son relationships in initiation. Cutting feet would seem to suggest a break away from "the boys" in order to go ahead and join the "gentlemen."

Ruaath is the only Ngok Dinka dance in which the bodies, i.e., legs, touch and, in that sense, is their sexiest dance even though it is danced with women whose sex life would have ended—since it is considered indecent for the mother of a "gentleman" or a "lady" to continue bearing children or to be sexually active. The dance is perhaps meant as their last fling.

Termination of their status as initiates (*luny*, meaning "release") is marked by all-night dancing and singing. At dawn, completely unarmed, they are mockingly, but painfully, beaten by the older-age set into a deep river across which they must swim and from which they emerge as adults.

Once released as full-fledged adults, the conduct of young men radically changes from that of a child to that of a highly respectable and largely responsible man who must now appear, behave, and otherwise play his full role as a gentleman and a member of a corporate group with a defined vital role to play in society.

Military Role

Among the symbols a man receives when released from the status of an initiate are gifts of well-designed spears. These are considered objects of beautification, and songs are composed in praise of those who make the gifts. But they are really symbols of the military function of youth. This function is not limited to war even though that is the central point; it covers those aspects of the culture which require youthful vigor and valor. These may be directed against humans or beasts, but may also extend to activities that invest physical strength in construction and production. In fact, the military distinction of youth is largely a matter of show, for every Dinka male is a soldier. Once a war erupts, the ideal fighters are those adults who have the strength to fight and children to survive them should they die: they are not still unmarried youth.

The period following initiation is supposed to be one of training not of serious fighting for the youth. Immediately after their initiation, they are forbidden to drink beer (the only alcoholic beverage of Dinka society), not only to keep them physically fit but also to make them less unruly. They retire into the wilderness with their age-set father who instructs them in the art and ethics of war. They must not provoke, they must defend; and when they fight a just war, they are to rest assured of ancestral support and the blessing of God.

> I remain, I do not vex myself;
> I remain, I do not provoke the tribes.
> The man is calm;
> The Sacred Bull is calm.
> Those who point their spears at me
> Beware of the Flesh of my Father.
> Those who hope to raid my herds
> Beware of the Flesh of my Father.
> I remain, I do not vex myself.

Before going to war, they are ideally to be fortified with religious rites, blessed by their divine leaders, and led by their generals who are specialists in the skills of war and who have the religious prerogative of war leadership. The Paramount Chief, the supreme authority in the tribe, does not go to war; his position is opposed to violence, and he should avoid the sight of blood. Added to this is the fact that he must be protected from all possible dangers and should be kept out of the danger zone. When his tribe fights a just war, he remains at home praying for victory, and, if they are the aggressors, he prays for their salvation. If the war is between them, he attempts to stop it by drawing a symbolic line and willing that the disobedient side suffer casualties and the innocent, none—or minimum loss.

The physical side of youth training is largely done through institutionalized fighting with the immediately older age-set. It is called *biook*. While it is a training, *biook* is also a recognized manifestation of generational competition and conflict. The beating across the river in the "release" from initiation is only the beginning of violence between the newly initiated age-set and those they are about to replace as dominant warriors. But the issue is not only a matter of being the dominant warriors. The immediate point of conflict is girls. Although Dinka women have age-sets corresponding to male age-sets, members of a male age-set usually go below their age-sets for girls because of the earlier maturing of women. In theory, corresponding male and female age-sets are potential husbands and wives. Conversely, any courtables are considered age-mates. Corresponding male and female age-sets are mutually courtable, potentially marriageable, and supposedly exclusive. In addition, the younger age-set often has more influence over the girls, partly because of their esthetic distinction and because the girls are closer to them in age.

Through a singing and dancing institution known as ket, the senior ageset attempts to disparage the younger age-set by singing about shameful incidents involving members of the younger age-set. Usually, individual conduct is the subject matter. The songs are not always about facts; and even when they are, the facts are exaggerated or distorted. A dominant theme portrays the younger age-sets as children still attached to their mothers. Their mothers are often insulted. Even if a brother of the younger man is a member of the insulting older age-set, so institutionalized are the songs that he would not oppose his mother's being defamed.

The following are examples of such songs. The first is against the age-set *Cuor*, "The Great Vulture," initiated in 1943. *Aliab*, the singing group, was the age-set immediately preceding *Cuor*. An age-set is ritually prohibited from drinking beer immediately after initiation; years later, they are ritually permitted to drink again, and this is done with a great beer feast. The song tells how the *Cuor* drank beer so much that one Pieng became drunk.

> *The women of that Noong came running to the pool*
> *And the women of the other Noong came heading for the pool*
> *Pieng has fallen.*
> *Pajok, cover him, I see shame coming.*
> *What I saw will not remain unsaid,*
> *What Aliab saw will not remain unsaid.*
> *He sat with a bulging stomach as though pregnant with beer;*
> *Pieng sat tilted on his hip*
> *And women closed their eyes.*

In the next song, a young man, Nyuong, on whom a disease left a deformed face and crooked teeth, is depicted speaking with a girlfriend.

> *Nyanajith said,*
> *"Nyuong, let us smile."*
> *Nyuong replied,*
> *"Smile!*
> *With what teeth shall we smile?"*

When presenting these songs, the older age-set dances the woman-dance to represent the younger as womanly. Because of the respect the members of the younger ageset must show the older, they cannot retaliate in song or dance; they can only fight. Such fights are not only provoked by songs. They are a general manifestation of the conflict between age-sets. In the eyes of the Dinka, they are mock-fights. Only clubs, no spears, are used; but severe injuries are inflicted and death sometimes occurs. Being young and inexperienced, the junior age-set are usually the victims, but the effect is rather to encourage them toward aggression than to deter them from it.

The implications of this aggression are far-reaching and are focused on the corresponding enemy age-sets with whom fights are provoked in a number of ways. In one case, members of an age-set confronted a man from a corresponding age-set of an enemy subtribe. He was walking with his sister on a public road. They stopped them and in a manner appropriate only for girls asked him and his sister to select from among them the men they were attracted to. The idea was to "cow" him and depict him as womanly. Naturally, he refused and so did his sister. They were beaten and then let go. When word reached the enemy camp, war drums beat, spears rattled, and shields were grabbed as members of his age-set ran to attack. The fight was only narrowly averted by the chiefs and the state police. Those responsible were punished.

A usual cause for conflicts is the alleged violation and protection of territorial integrity. Cattle may stray into the enemy pastures, young men may infiltrate and camp in the grazing grounds of the enemy, or a dispute over the boundaries of the grazing areas may occur. Fights may be triggered by such minor incidents as a fight between individual members of opposed groups.

Although the usual conception of tribal warfare does not seem so disastrous from the viewpoint of modern man, to the tribes it is a calamity—and one that has its rightful place in oral history. Within the Ngok tribe, internecine wars have virtually stopped, although there are frequent attempts to instigate them. In other Dinka tribes, and between the Ngok and their neighbors, they still occur. When a provocation has initiated a war, strategies are planned by the generals who work closely with the young warriors. The eve before the attack, war drums are beaten. The first sounds are followed by a "listen," a few more beats, a dead silence, and then a sudden uproar. Armed with spears and shields, helmets on their heads, all men—except the ailing and the very old-run toward the battlefront booming war-songs or chanting individual verses of self-praise. For a man to fear is to afflict himself with grave and permanent shame. It is at such times that the long-legged Dinka really demonstrate their running skill. Amazing distances are covered in surprisingly short periods of time. Women, screaming their distinctive war cries and loaded with food to serve their men, also keep pace. The children and the feeble remain in apprehension; no one knows who will die and who will return in what condition. Subtribes or tribes fall into alliances, and before long the shadow of war engulfs the whole tribe—and perhaps the nation.

In the battlefield the opposing groups, standing within throwing distance, dart at each other with their slim medium-length spears and forked clubs. The art of throwing and dodging spears is one a Dinka learns from an early age. In war the value of early training is brought to the test. A few cowards may retire never to recover from the loss of face. Renowned warriors become frenzied with valor. They are usually the ones who kill and remain unharmed. Some individuals become excessively brave—almost suicidal. The particularly brave and dangerous are among the most aimed at by the enemy, but they are also the most covered by their men.

Age-mates and relatives stand side by side to help one another in critical situations when a fellow tribesman might retreat to save his own neck. Women keep close behind their fighting men, gathering the fallen spears and handing them back. When men are speared and forced to the ground, women fall on them to protect them from the enemy. Dinka concepts of *dheeng* and war ethics require that a person thus covered by a woman not be harmed. There are extreme situations, however, in which the enemy will beat the women away with spear shafts, and kill the wounded. That a man is helplessly injured means nothing to the Dinka. Indeed, it is considered spiritually dangerous not to join in when a fallen warrior is skewered to death; for otherwise, the ghost of the dead man follows one as the only friend among foes. Even a friendly ghost of the enemy is spiritually fatal. When the enemy group withdraws, leaving the dead and the dying as they run, the fight should stop to prevent more loss of lives. Just as ambushing is cowardly and outrageous to the Dinka conscience, so is killing an individual member of the enemy group outside the battlefield. It makes no difference that the individual has just killed a relative in battle. Those who chance to be on the wrong side during an outbreak of war must be allowed to join their side unharmed.

The fight usually ends with the capture of the enemy herds. Some of the personality oxen are disgracefully skewered for meat; and the rest are kept, pending their distribution. Nowadays they are returned, and those killed compensated for. Warriors return carrying their dead and their wounded. Those who can be helped are treated, and delicate operations are sometimes performed. Those who die in battle are not to be mourned; and women, who never resist crying, are urged to stop. But in this silence lies the threat of future wars. Even though the dead are compensated for with cattle, vengeance in future war with the enemy is the most honorable remedy. In the years following a war and for a long time to come, incidents in the battle are retold, stories of brave men are recited with pride, the disgraceful conduct of cowards is shamefully revealed, and the need for vengeance is stressed. A relative of a man killed in battle may provoke another war to get his chance for vengeance. The cycle of war is thus renewed to give the Dinka their warlike reputation.

It all begins with youth and their militancy. Even their constructive roles have destructive implications. Their activities are usually competitive, and sooner or later this brings conflict. Perhaps the best way of showing the degree to which the activities of youth are institutionally integrated, controlled, and esthetically sublimated-yet manifested in ways that spill into provocation and aggressiveness is through the role of war-songs and war dances. War-songs are usually about the courage and the power of the age-sets. Nowadays they may be concerned with forced labor on the roads, in the fields of the Chief and such tasks, all taken to symbolize the adventurous spirit of the age-set. They may also be about more obvious adventures like fighting ferocious beasts: lions, buffaloes, hippoes, and the like. By and large, they concern fights that have actually occurred. Sometimes this may be indirect. It is usual for an age-set to hunt an animal bearing the name of the corresponding age-set of the enemy, and then compose songs about an actual war with this enemy under the guise of the hunted animal. Power, courage, and ferocity are primarily symbolized with the bull - but also with the lion, the buffalo and similar beasts. The Dinka allege in their songs that they are never the aggressors but defenders of honor and resisters of aggression, although in most cases what they consider aggression is emotive and readily conceived:

> *A man threatened me at the borders,*
> *I thought we were at peace.*
> *Do not provoke me, I am bad.*
> *If I should make it bitter one day,*
> *I will be bad*
> *And I will not be passed by.*
> *All people will avoid me in respect.*

Individual conduct in the battlefield may be the subject of a war-song. In introducing the song, an Atuot informant said, "Kiec killed our people, so our people did their best to insult them in war-songs," illustrating the Dinka conception of war-songs as a form of warring:

Son of a witch, do not cry when you began it.
Things have turned bad.
Manyang has wet himself,
Defecating near our cattle-camp.
The sorcerer with four eyes;
The inside of the man is falling out
Defecating like the young of a locust.
People died without leaving wills.
Riak sent word to the town,
"Send me back the things of my father."
But there was no one left to bring the things
The possessions of the man were left alone.
People who did not know the meaning of feud;
I am told to abandon my land,
The land of my forefathers;
I will never leave my land.
Better dead.

War-songs are sung in a war dance that may provoke a war. For it is usually attended by warring units. The dance is a combination of dances. A theme that runs through them is that the man represents an aggressive bull and the woman a submissive cow. The man faces the woman, forming the horns of a bull with his arms; and the woman raises her arms, joining her hands to form a circle over her head. Thus, the horns of the man symbolize danger while the horns of the woman appear harmless. There is a variation in which the man chases the retreating woman, symbolizing the victory of the bull. On the perimeter of the dance, men circling in single file dance the goor, a war ballet that also figures in other dances and on many

During an interlude in a Ngok Dinka war dance in which some men and women perform a chasing dance on the periphery of the main dance. (Photo by M. G. Tibbs)

other occasions. They jump and dodge as though fighting with spears. Other men, in mimed duels, jump up and down, twisting themselves in the air with amazing skill and using spears to imitate a fight.

Subtribes dance together to one another's songs. During or toward the end of the song of one subtribe, another subtribe withdraws from the dance singing their *dor*, a special type of war-song in which a leader, followed by his chorus, excites peace or war demonstrations. The subtribe that has withdrawn then returns, singing a *dor* and running into the dance: outsinging the previous chorus. People begin to dance to their songs. This is part of the dance, not simply a demonstration of aggressiveness. Sometimes a particularly enjoyable song is interrupted or a particularly provocative song is introduced. Then opposing groups introduce war-songs that are insulting to each other. For security, chiefs must watch the dancers to prevent fights. It may be that modern government has increased the expression of aggressiveness, since it is now known that there can be intervention to stop unrestrained fighting. In the past more self-restraint was necessary.

The provocation of songs does not have to wait for dances. A subtribe may learn of a war-song newly composed to defame them and may take up arms to attack the composing group. The trial that follows, in which the Court may want to hear the songs sung by the respective groups, is well provided with a police force in anticipation of more trouble.

A war dance may be on a smaller scale and directed toward a particular objective. An age-set may have been assigned a job and, after completing it, may seek formal discharge by the Chief. Or an age-set may seek permission from the Chief to move to far-off grazings during the cultivation period—a practice that is nowadays restricted. After such a dance has lasted a while, the Chief, assuming he grants the request, will spray them with blessed water as a token of discharge or of granting the request. The dancers then point their spears up, saying together, "*nguoth*"—a word used when a person has speared an enemy, an animal, or a fish.

War dance in all its variances is the standard dance of the Ngok Dinka. Its name is *loor* "drum." There are at least two drums in a dance, a large one and a small one. The two are beaten simultaneously, and their sounds are coordinated. Beating the drums is a skill that all Dinka share, but not all perform on such dancing occasions, for a high standard is required.

There is a special type of dance that follows the war dance among the Ngok, but which has somewhat different characteristics and might be more appropriately termed "ox-dance" than war dance. The songs in this dance are not generally about war or courage; they are about girls and cattle. They are almost identical with ox-songs except that they are shorter and less concerned with poetry than with music. The dance conforms to the man-bull-woman-cow theme; but although the dancers in striking unity stamp the ground with tremendous vigor, the symbolism is more peaceful than in war-songs and no spears are used. Nor are there symbolic duels between the men. However, the insults in the words may be a cause for retaliation in songs and fights.

Since the activities of female age-sets are coordinated with those of corresponding male age-sets, they too take pride in the military activities of their potential husbands. They too compose their war-songs but only in the form of *dor*, which are used to excite emotions in demonstrations, whether in peace or in war. In these songs, they attribute the role of their male counterparts to themselves in that they speak of "I" and "we" when they mean "he" and "they." This is followed by married women in songs in which a wife, singing about the husband, uses "I" and "he" interchangeably when unchangingly talking of him. Female age-sets of opposing tribes, of course, compete in such songs, but the repercussions are not limited to that. They may provoke the men. But the resultant conflict is not with the singing girls, but between the male youths.

The unconstrained aggressive impulses of Dinka childhood thus continue into youth. So much so that, while society attempts to control them, and use them, in an esthetically sublimated manner— or in military defense of the land—they nevertheless cause a lot of ferment. The petty fights and the serious wars they cause leave many a man dead or bearing the scar of a spear wound on his body or of a club on the head.

Youth and the Economy

To speak of an economic role is to imply productivity, but the distinctive attributes of Dinka youth are largely esthetic and sometimes destructive. Youth work in agriculture, and some even win the reputation of being hard working. As age-sets they cultivate the fields of the chiefs, build their houses, and, as any Dinka may do, work for those who hold feasts of beer, meat, and other food. They also hunt and fish as groups or as individuals, especially in far-off cattlecamps when they need to supplement their diet of milk. The Dinka love meat, but hate to kill their livestock, except for sacrifice or hospitality. All these activities are limited and have a sportlike rather than economic quality. The standard role of youth revolves around cattle. And preoccupation with cattle focuses on oxen. Once released from initiation, a man identifies, and is identified with, his ox and becomes known by the metaphorical name derived from its color-pattern. A man must abstain from eating the meat of his ox and anything—animal or vegetable—which resembles the ox in color or in shape. Dinka generally deplore the sale of cattle, but this is particularly the case with personality oxen. Even for such noble causes as marriage, many refuse to part with their oxen. A young man sings:

> *My Mijok is important to me*
> *Like tobacco and the pipe;*
> *When there is no tobacco*
> *The pipe goes out.*
> *His pace and mine are the same.*

Preoccupation with oxen is expressed in ox-songs with oxen as the central theme. At least among the Ngok, they must be composed by the owner. The ox is usually decorated with tassels on pierced horns and a large bell hanging from a collar tied to the neck. A man may ask a girl to make tassels for his ox or to tan the collar leather of the bell, objects that are delivered in festive celebrations. The girl is praised in subsequent songs. The piercing of the horns is also celebrated, and the events are described in the songs. How the ox sounds the bell and waves the tassels are matters of pride also expressed in the songs. Sometimes, there is a detailed description and appraisal of natural phenomena that bear resemblance to the characteristics of one's ox.

Ox-songs may be used to state a claim or to seek the assistance of the Chief, an elder, or a possible sympathizer. Singing may take the form of "begging," as when the singer's ox has died and he needs a substitute. Family and friendly circles are usually praised. Unlike war-songs in which young warriors present themselves as courageous bulls, buffaloes, lions, and the like, in ox-songs a man combines the courage and vitality of a bull with the gentleness and submissiveness of an ox. In these songs, honor might be given to the chiefs, the fathers, the lineages, and individuals. The following is a typical ox-song. It is about two oxen: a gray ox which the singer likens to the lion, the antelope, the elephant, and the buffalo; and a dark-brownish ox, which he compares to the hippo:

> *Rising Beauty, Rising Beauty,*
> *Born by the king of the wilds,*
> *If you reject men, you will be eaten.*[6]
> *The Great Evil-Eyed coming from the wilds,*
> *His eyes glow as he eats a man.*[7]
> *The Back-clouded One rises like a rain storm,*
> *And brightens like a clearing sky,*
> *He is showing his hump*
> *My ox is showing his narrow-waisted hump.*

---

6   The ox is here conceived as an ox and is warned against lions if he is unruly.

7   Back to the metaphor of the ox seen as a lion.

The hump is twisting like a goitered neck,
Staggering like a man who has gorged himself with liquor;
When he walks, the hump goes on twisting
Like a man traveling on a camel.
Gray One of my grandfather, Arab, son of Ajuong,
Your hump has fallen.
Chief, Deng, son of Kwol d'Arob de Biong,
Is like the Creator at the head of the tribe
While I sing over my antelope, Malith.
The ox roars in the evening with a greedy heart
The curve-horned ox roars while the cattle are tethered.
In the camp of my grandfather, Ajuong, son of Col
I sing over an ox with a dark brown body.
His horns have grown as long as the thorns of the acacia.
Malith has a heart like a buffalo,
When he sees a cow mounted, rattles with a breaking peg.
Malek, son of Yak and I are age-mates;
Egg-White One, Malek of the clan of Jador.
When cattle move to the summer camps
Malith grazes on grass as delicate as a ripening girl
Whose sight attracts people and gives them joy.
When he bellows, his voice falls on the ground
Like the thundering of a morning rain.
My Athieng is as dark as the darkness of the night.
Gingerly he places his feet like a girl wearing metal coils on
her legs,
Malith lifts bulls from the ground.
He hides behind the cows of the camp of the Giant Vulture,
Falls on a bull
And the bulls roar as though a lion has jumped a cow.
The girl named after my grandmother, mother of Deng, son
of Biong,

She resembles those of the distant past;
Her marriage brought me a great Malith with an expanded
body
Like the great beast:
Elephant, beware
You are at war with the brown Arab.
Is it true, have I seen what it is to be an orphan?
Is maturity a bad thing
That I have found the sadness of an orphan?
My father left me with the daughters of my mother
And one of them mistreated me.
For the sake of Malith, I have given up the words of the land:
He will not be lost forever
Like the ancient camp for which spears were fixed
And was sought with fire at night.[8]
The sister who is the oldest of us
Will not go into marriage
Without a brown ox like a brown hippo in the river.[9]
I am keeping animals
I am keeping a buffalo and an animal of the river.
The brown one with a shimmering back
Has cleared the grazing ground,
He cuts the grass and swallows it
As a python swallows its prey,
He munches the crisp regrowth making his mouth stink
Like a man chewing onions,

---

8   So determined were the people to capture or regain the camp that they
     attacked at night carrying fire with which to see. Dinka wars are normally
     fought during the day. The singer is as determined to regain his ox as those
     warriors were to get the camp.

9   In her bridewealth.

A head of a clan with a hopeless head.[10]
Mother of Wor, Mother of Wor, The Pied One,
Never have I found so daring a woman;
How she ventured to sell the ox of a gentleman!
What evils the market has brought into our land
That a man breeds the ox of his pride
Then comes a woman and wants him for sale;
For Malith, I have refused;
I redeemed him from the mother of Dau with a black ox
That year; [11]
Then I redeemed him from a wrong I had done [12]
That year;
And I stopped him from being slaughtered for Nyannuer's wrong [13]
That year;
I clear my ox like separating the shell from the kernel
He will remain in our sacred camp.
Relatives who hate me will say "Lual has become a wild lion."

---

10 A clan-head who is alleged to have nothing in town but onions to eat. Reference is made to some of the deprivations of their now-limited power since the government has turned them into tax-collectors instead of the leaders they used to be.

11 The focus on "That year" here and later is significant. The year was a year of famine in which people against whom wrongs were committed, or people who had legitimate kinship claims, were particularly adamant. The stress on the year is a polite way of insulting them.

12 The tone implies that he had committed a sexual offense for which redress was claimed.

13 When a member of an age-set, male or female, commits a wrong against the set, the set slaughters his favorite personality-ox—or in the case of a girl, the ox of her closest agnate, as a punitive measure.

The formal presentation of ox-songs is done in any one of several ways. They are often sung around the cattle-camp where thousands of cattle are tethered in a large circular area, within which are hearths where men stay and fenced areas on the edges for girls and families. So large are the camps that several people may sing simultaneously, but so far apart that their voices do not clash. One of the greatest pleasures of life in the cattle-camp is that there is always a singing entertainment-sometimes all night. In the morning, when girls wake up early to churn their milk for butter, they sing the favorite songs to the rhythm of their shaking gourds. A singer who is attracted to a particular girl may stop his ox near her camping spot until she releases him by a symbolic gift or by an offer of friendship which may end in marriage. Even if she is not specifically designated, an admiring girl may also take the initiative and make the release. In some tribes, release is made by the girl's anointing the man and the boy who leads the ox for him (and who is expected to assist him in singing if the initiated man should lose his voice).

Ox-songs may be sung in a sitting entertainment. Men gather with or without women to compete as individuals or as representatives of groups. When such competition is in front of women, they determine the result; otherwise the male audience judges. In such sitting performances, a man holds his hands up as the horns and moves his head and body in imitation of the ox. Although ox-songs are not accompanied with drums, the jiggling of the bell and the bellows of the ox are considered accompaniments. When there is no ox present, a singer sometimes rings a bell and a companion may make sounds to represent the bellows of an ox. In addition, the occasional high-pitched chanting of those praised, or of their relatives, adds to the accompaniment.

Youth's preoccupation with cattle is shared by women and is expressed in their songs, usually a form of ox-song centering on the oxen of husbands, dancing partners, or boyfriends. The singing woman shifts between referring to her husband as "I" and as "he." Her identity is thus reflected through him. The following is an example:

Ox with diverging horns,
The horns are reaching the ground;
The horns are overflowing like a boiling pot.
I love the black pattern of the Pied Ox of my father,
I love it as I love our Chief
I love it as I love our Chief who is holding our land.
My Mijok, if no disaster befalls our country
People will point at our camp because of you.
But even if people scorn you
Because of those horns, I love you.

The singer often praises her husband and through him, herself, with surprising snobbery. This praise is usually so exaggerated that it is possible only in songs. The following lines are from a song of the wives of Chief Deng Majok of the Ngok; and although their praise for him is enhanced by his power, a similar exaggeration is a common phenomenon.

Striped Ox,[14] you will mix with the bulls
And your father[15] will mix with the leaders of the Sudan.
He is the expert on the words of the South,
His words are strong.
No one can surpass him in the land of Kwol.
Has not my name[16] traveled far to the land of the Arabs?
And to the land where the sun goes down?

---

14 Her husband's ox.

15 Deng Majok, the Chief.

16 Meaning her husband's.

I have never found anything surpassing The Shining One
I have never found it in the land of Lual.

As the above indicates, women's songs—like men's ox-songs—may concern anything of interest to the singer, but differ from ox-songs in that they are not sung on oxen; they are sung in a women's dance in which the dancers form a circle and the owner of the song, or in her absence a relative, leads. While all sing and clap (the only musical accompaniment), a few in the circle jump to the rhythm. Simultaneously, some people, and particularly those whose relations are mentioned, make such loud cries that it is sometimes impossible to hear the words. These piercing cries are in expression of joy, although to a foreigner's ear they might sound like the cries of a woman in distress.

Perhaps the most striking aspect of youth's preoccupation with cattle is their love for the cattle-camp which, while it provides cattle with good grazing, keeps the men away from day-to-day economic production. The reputation of the Dinka as nomadic is based on the fact that young people move from place to place according to the availability of adequate pastures and sometimes according to youth's desire to keep out of the control of the elders at home. When moving the camp (a decision made by the camp leader known as "The Pied Bull of the Cattle-camp"), people wake up very early, milk the cows, wind the ropes around their necks for the cattle to carry, and in the case of "personality-oxen," tie on the collars and the bells. Children and women carry the gourds of milk and butter, while some adults help in driving the herds and others precede the group to select the sites and cut the pegs. Small calves are carried like children, on men's shoulders, while babies are carried by their mothers on their backs.

It sometimes happens that when going to far-off areas young men leave most of the milk cows at home to provide food during the lean season when most cows go dry. They must, therefore, endure hunger.

The hardships of far off herding often form the subject matter of ox-songs in which named persons are praised for their excellence, anonymous persons condemned for their weakness, and the singer is boastful while lamenting. Whatever its difficulties, being in the cattle-camp is a source of dignity and pride. When visiting a cattle-camp, usually in the evening, a Dinka feels its superior atmosphere from a distance as he sees a beacon of cow-dung fires reaching into the sky and marking the location of the camp. As one draws nearer, the singing of the men, the dancing of the children, the bellows of the herds, the jingling of the bells, the jokes and the laughter all indicate the profound difference between the jubilant air of the cattle-camp and the subdued atmosphere of the home. As the visitors enter the camp, it is not uncommon for the children who first notice their arrival to shout "bringing flies into the camp," and be echoed by children throughout the camp. On the other hand visitors from the camp to the villages are guests with a sense of superiority, often healthy and proud.

Cattle-camping is highlighted by the institution of *toc*, (literally "lying down") according to which young men excuse themselves from cultivation, retreat to summer camps, gorge themselves with milk supplemented with meat, and as the word for the custom suggests, lie down, fatten themselves, and move as little as possible. They compose songs about matters of special interest to them, usually pressing problems. I call these "cathartic songs" because they play a "cleansing" role, and indeed, the Dinka call them *waak*, which means "washing." In these songs, young men sometimes acknowledge their desire to evade work at home and praise those who helped to make their leaving possible. In this song, for instance, a man praises his stepmother and his older brother's wife for having sent him to lie down. The claim that the hoe was hidden or thrown away is an attempt to conceal the half-embarrassing truth that the singer did not want to work.

Nyanyaath of clan Pabong has hidden my hoe,
She has thrown my hoe away.
Nyanyaath has released the cows for me.
The woman takes care of me.
And Agorot, the wife of my father,
Has thrown my hoe away.

Another man, who should have retired from youth activities, but whom his wife sent to rest, sings of her:

Ayan Ajack packed my gourd,
Released the cows,
And put her gourds away,
The woman loves me,
She loves me.
She made me cross the land into the cattle-camp.
Ayan is keeping me in the center,
Caring for me like a newly weaned child.
Listen to what the people say:
"Why is Bar not giving up camping with youth?"
"The Black Bull is feeding himself," I say.
If stomachs were to thank their fathers,
Mine would have thanked me a long time ago;
And that of Kwol would have thanked him too.
I will listen to people's words,
Throw myself on the ground
And lie like a Big Black Bull.

Most cathartic songs are about marriage. A man may praise his intended bride and her relatives, urge his own relatives to support him, or mourn her loss if they fail. Inability to marry because of poverty may prompt a song even if the singer has no specific girl in mind. But anything of interest to a man may be a subject of a cathartic song. During the first few weeks of their return from retreat, these young men exert a great impact. They are thought to be attractive as a result of their being fatter and heavier: For since the Dinka are generally very slender and tall, gaining weight usually improves their figures. They attract a great deal of attention as they move around in a group, presenting their songs with a dance and feast for the occasion. No musical instrument is used. The group forms a large circle, with the owner of a song in the center leading in singing and dancing. In dancing, one leg is raised and dropped with a jerk of the body in a manner similar to the initiation dance—but gently, since the dancers are too heavy to move vigorously. They first dance at the homes of those addressed, but may continue to dance anywhere.

By overindulging in the esthetics of cattle song and dance, Dinka youth compensate themselves for their economic subordination to their elders. Disputes between them and their elders do occur, but only in a limited way. Their esthetic preoccupation with cattle makes them fancy themselves wealthy so that competition with elders over resources is largely averted.

Flirtation and Courtship

Since marriage is everyone's goal and the family is seen as the fulfillment of life, the values of man-woman relationships are pivotal for the Dinka. Nearly everything a Dinka does has sensuous and sexual motives. It is this which gives women an ambivalent position in the eyes of the Dinka; they are subordinate but unquestionably the prime objects of male pursuit. Recalling a song quoted earlier:

> *Woman is the God*
> *She anoints your head with her own hands*
> *And you sleep like a python.*

Her identity is never mistaken.
For a woman, a man spears an animal
For a woman, a man keeps his cattle.

Among the many occasions in which boys and girls meet are dances. In addition to the objects of beautification discussed, the dancers anoint themselves with oil and make designs on their skin with red, pink, or white ashes. Immediately preceding the dance, men and women stand in twos, threes, or more, using all sorts of devices to draw each other's attention. Men stand singing, roaring unnecessarily with laughter, or changing special verses known as *nyal rot* by which intimate friends crown their laughter. The words are usually not important, although they may be relevant and sometimes openly insulting. Such diffuse insults are supposed to give girls the impression that a man is witty and hot-tongued. This is supposed to make him attractive. Girls also fear that to dishonor the admiration of such a man might well result in his spreading of scandalous fabrications. Since girls are expected to be gentle, they stand self-consciously—if not nervously—unwinding and rewinding their skirts around their waists. Sometimes they display themselves with their female dance before the collective dance begins. In the collective dance men, and to a lesser extent women, spare no opportunity to show off, which in the eyes of the Dinka is an essential part of the art of dancing.

Although some people are regular dance-partners, girls choose their partners on the spot, and one man may have several girls while another has none. This is called "remaining on the ground" and, as the expression indicates, is a disgrace. Girls sometimes choose a man just to save his face, but generally, Dinka girls are honest in choosing their partners.

When the dance is over, men and women who, because of the vigor of Dinka dances and because of the climate, have perspired intensely, stroll toward the river for a quick and separate bath. The sexes rejoin so that the men can accompany the girls toward their destination. But the men do not walk all the way home with the girls. A man will cover a long distance before resuming his journey home, usually after fixing a date for the next meeting.

Such celebrated occasions as marriages, the piercing of horns, and the delivery of special gifts, often include dancing and flirtation. Usually, men-women entertainment on these occasions is between members of corresponding age-sets. They eat together and engage in a great deal of joking and badinage. In the evening, seated separately from their elders, men compete with ox-songs and girls determine the outcome and choose the men they admire. Once the choice is made, association, though collective, becomes more intimate. Again, one man may be chosen by two or more girls. Polygyny or no polygyny, things become sticky. The man might end up without deepening his relationship with any of them, but future dates are fixed.

Despite intimate conversations within the crowd, a collective debate usually emerges as to whether the girls should sleep alone or with men. This does not necessarily mean any more than transferring the conversation into the bed with more intimacy. The odds are that the girls would refuse to share their beds and only make arrangements for future visits by their chosen mates.

There is no limit to how a man and woman can meet and, if they react well to each other, arrange future dates. Even the market-day, which has become an accepted institution, is seen by young men and women as a courting occasion for which they dress up to meet. This new practice, combined with the old freedom to approach and talk to any girl at any time and in any place, has significantly extended the meeting opportunities of Dinka youth. Although the initiative is usually taken by a man, a girl can ask for a present; and while the Dinka "beg" their relatives, friends, chiefs, and others for genuine needs, asking for a gift is supposed to be an invitation, a confirmation, or an affirmation of a relationship. When done by a girl who is not related to a man, it leaves no doubt about her real intentions. For some reason, tobacco, whether asked for by a man or a girl, is generally regarded as symbolizing an invitation for courtship. Nearly all Dinka, men and women alike, smoke the pipe; and older people chew or snuff tobacco. But it is not necessary for a person to smoke in order to ask, or be asked for, tobacco.

Whatever the method of initiating a relationship, the effect is the same. A successful encounter ends with fixing future dates. It is always the man who visits. No girl will expressly invite a visit after the first meeting and maybe she will not do so even after the second or third. If she likes the man, the most she says while subtly making her feelings clear is: "Guests are not to be rebuffed. You may come." On the appointed day, a man takes his spears and travels whatever the distance in spite of the weather. The harder the trip, the more convincing his intentions and the better the result. Many a young man travels in the darkness of a rainy night when the narrow lane becomes visible only at the flash of lightning and when the roaring of lions and leopards or the cries of hyenas and wild dogs add to the apprehension of dangers.

On arrival, if the people are not in bed and the weather permits them to remain sitting outside, a man stops some hundred yards away where he is sure to be seen. If he is not seen or people have gone into the huts, he coughs or makes some sounds adding, "There is a man standing here." That standard phrase says that the visitor is after a girl and it is the source of the word for courtship visits, *cot* (literally "calling"). Usually, it is not the girl he is suspected to be after who answers. Depending on the time of the night and how safe it is, a girl or a boy is sent to see him. The expected word comes. Sometimes, if the girl has decided not to see him, for one reason or another, the person is instructed to say that she is ill, away, or otherwise unavailable. Usually, the girl will herself go and give whatever reasons are appropriate in the circumstances.

A courter may be dismissed because of clashing visits, which is possible in view of the courtesy of the girl and her desire for popularity, as well as the lack of precision in fixing dates. When a girl desires to keep a suitor, she may ask him to wait while she dismisses other visitors, often with the vague statement "My body is heavy," which encompasses everything from illness to menstruation.

When a call is accepted, the couple may sit a distance away from home. Normally they sit on the ground, but sometimes the girl may produce a mat for them to sit on. This is more the case when spending the night in a hut, whether by necessity, as in bad weather, or because of intimacy: The former entails conversation in sitting situations, the latter sleeping together without necessarily having intercourse. It is for this latter stage that the Dinka use the word *aleeng* "conversation."

The Dinka language of courtship is a highly philosophic, almost poetic, form of expression, full of proverbs and parables. A young man and a girl can sit or lie awake all night delighting in the mutual display of their skill even though there are little or no physical supplements. A man's physical appeal may be sufficient to win a girl, but verbal skill is a highly desirable asset. Some men are more skilled than others and are very much in demand as courtship comrades. Dinka courtship is almost as much a group affair as it is individual. Friends and relatives visit individually or collectively to speak on a man's behalf in his presence or absence. The mere visit of a friend or a relative means representation of the courter's interest; the conversation need not be about him, even though at one point or another it may.

Group involvement generally connotes seriousness and the desire for marriage. It shows the girl the man's social circle and security. Since Dinka girls are open to competition in marriage, the assistance of one's relatives and friends also shelters one against competitors who may duel or may scandalize one's name through gossip or in songs. The wider the circle of one's relatives and friends, the less the chances of "gossip" or of its effect against one.

Whether a man visits his girlfriend with relatives and friends or they go without him, the girl is informed and asked to invite her friends—including relatives. What follows is a group courtship which may be outside, but is usually inside, a hut. As a result of the extra courtesy involved, girls are not asked to choose; instead, if the man is not present, his closest relative or friend engages the girlfriend and may share her mat with her should the group decide to lie down; the others engage the girls they have developed some relationship with in the course of the conversation. While a lot of touching and teasing goes on, such occasions are not meant to involve physical relationship. Still, intimate ties germinate, and additional marriages may result. The immediate issue is to win the girl for their man. A girl nearly always pretends to refuse a man even one she might truly "love" or "like"- concepts for which the Dinka do not have separate words. In its final stage, the issue is openly discussed by representatives of the parties' age-sets. Even if the girl is known to be in love, this group conference is essential. The men make their formal request for the girl's love and, on the theory that her decision rests on the opinion of her group, the girls formally "accept" after some debate. A girl who is not interested in a man may, out of courtesy, nevertheless invite girls who like the man and who are therefore likely to plead his cause. On the other hand, no interested girl would invite girls who will object to the man she loves. In any case, if a girl truly does not care for a man, such a conference is not begun. Group discussion is, therefore, a matter of formality in cases where there is mutual love—or at least where there is no serious objection on the girl's side. Once her age-mates accept, a girl declares her consent, sometimes reluctantly so that the persuasion of her group is required.

This is all pretension in most cases, for unless a Dinka girl is very resentful of a man or very much in love with another man, she is as likely to accommodate his courtship as she is likely to accept him in marriage.

Because of the pride and the sensitivity of the Dinka, coupled with their extraordinary freedom of expression in song, to reject a man is to invite an excruciating insult.

I do not know what has become of me
Why the girl first deceived me
Then turned and said, "I have disliked you.
If you visit our home
You will not be visiting me,
You will make me call my mother."
Could I possibly pick up my spears to visit your mother?
What about the praise you received as a child,
"Darling girl, wash this dish for me
My sweet one will bring cows."
Has a cow ever come alone
And entered the cattle byre
Without a girl talking to a man?
When a girl utters such heartless words
Courtship comes to a bitter end.
I stood amazed.
What words the girl said!
Even to think of calling your mother!
Your mother never quarreled with my mother
And your father never quarreled with my father
They never met in a drinking house
To be provoked by jokes.
The girl spoke with such vileness;
Her heart filled with hate like our clan Pajok:
Our clan Pajok is filled with jealousies.

Although courtesy for men is a splendor in its own, fear of defamation in song is another factor in the way a Dinka girl accommodates friendships with men. The balance is quite delicate for a girl who reaches intimate stages with more than one man, since she runs the risk of being judged promiscuous and ridiculed in song.

> *Nyankiir, daughter of The Spotted Red,*
> *What promiscuity you have gathered?*
> *Will you not grow old unmarried*
> *With a bottom torn apart by men?*

This reinforces the value of sexual restraint in courtship. The application of the word "conversation" for the stage of courtship when a man and his girlfriend share the same bed indicates that the focus is verbal even though the Dinka usage connotes more than just talking. This is why sleeping together, although normally an accepted part of an intimate friendship, is usually objected to by relatives if the man's intentions are not "honorable" or if he is too poor to pay what they expect as her bridewealth—or is otherwise objectionable as a potential marriage contender. In the following song, a man whose courtship was resented by the girl's relatives was beaten at night as he slept in a hut with the girl.

> *I will not swear never to see your land*
> *I shall attend the dances,*
> *I will not swear never to see your land*
> *I shall continue to herd in the summer camp.*
> *As for the courtship of girls*
> *I no longer know.*
> *I shall meet girls from other tribes*
> *But I will not court them again;*
> *I am a man taught a lesson.*

If a man tries to take advantage of being in bed with a girl by attempting to force intercourse, the girl may cry for help or act in self-defense. The following singer, Ring, engaged to Akuol, went to sleep in a hut with her accompanied by her female relative, Ajok. Ring attempted to force sexual intercourse with Akuol who cried out to Ajok for help. Ajok squeezed Ring's testicles, hurting him seriously.

We were three in the hut
Ajok, Akuol, and myself.
They had accepted me into the hut;
I had my spears
And I had my club.
I went and lay still;
I lay still.
And when the evil heart came,
It said to me: "Why are you sleeping near food?
From ancient times, Dinka men who share huts sleep
But they move.
Ring, move!"
But when I began to move, Ajok Arob,
"O Ajok of my mother, help! Ajok of my mother, help me."
Ajok Arob
She caught me in a way I hate to this day;
She caught my testicles:
Then she pulled me like a coconut
And squeezed me like a fruit juice
As though I was a lactating goat,
O Ajok milked me like a cow.

The girl may herself compose a song about such an incident. The following singer had broken a tooth in a struggle with a man who overstepped his bounds.

In the clan of my father
The clan of my father, Ajak,
I was not unleashed into the camp
To be a person in search of a man.
No, I have not found myself so low.
The hidden one provoked a fight between us;
And when I offered to appease him with a cow
He pushed the cow aside
And wanted the hidden "girl."
Our land has become a land in which we must guard our
thighs
Like a man guarding crops from birds.
Young men attack our thighs;
They attack us and break our teeth.
We are tangled in our little huts.
We are prevented from sleep.

Despite all these restraints, the Dinka voice strong objections only to premarital sex that results in pregnancy, especially when the parties are not engaged. It is because pregnancy and offenses like elopement and abduction harm the marital interests of the girl that they are strongly objected to. By the same token, they are sometimes used by young lovers to make possible a union otherwise opposed or impeded by their elders. It should be mentioned that, while Dinka youth engage in elaborate courtship to win each other's love, only the consent of the elders is a legal requirement. The parties immediately involved are consulted as a matter of practical consideration and not as a legal requirement. There is, therefore, a cleavage between the role of youth and that of their elders. But here we come to a junction in which the two roles are so much intertwined and controlled, or at least conditioned, by the superior role of the elders that further discussion more appropriately falls under adulthood.

Chapter Seven: Adulthood

Marriage

Although initiation is a crucial step in age-stratification, marriage is a necessary condition to becoming an adult of full legal capacity. It is the threshold of independence from the family and the founding of a new line. While it is true that flirtation and court-ship among youth are not always geared toward marriage—and it is even considered shameful for a man too readily to voice marital intentions as a means of winning girls—marriage is the dream of every Dinka.

There are many reasons for the prominence of marriage in Dinka society. One is the desire for an established socially sanctioned man-woman relationship.

People ask, "Do you hate women?"
Oh, I love women!
Why would I hate that noble being
The good thing called "woman?"
Who will feel your front
Then ask you, "Is anything wrong?"
And cunningly I answer:

"Yes my own, I have my doubts."
O, the good times of marriage
When adults chat over small things
And then the woman holds her man
And says, "Father of so and so."
Then I answer, "Yes, yes."
I answer as I put my spears away;
I put my spears away after a journey,
Aker, I do so without words.

Among the motives for marriage are the services of a woman. This is sometimes viewed as a relief to the aging mother:

Father, do not hide the truth from me,
It is not that I am old
It is the misery of Aluel Yak
She struggles with the mortar and the pestle,
Drags herself stooping to fetch water from the river
Then comes to cook when none of her age-mates still cooks.

Marriage implies loss of cattle as bridewealth, but it is also a means of acquiring cattle and an investment in anticipation of female offspring. People assist a bridegroom in the hope that he will beget daughters who will be married and reward them or their children with more cattle than they had paid. Conceiving his marriage as hunting an elephant and his future daughters as the elephant's tusks, a young man metaphorically warns his uncooperative relatives not to expect a share from the bridewealth of his future daughters if they do not assist him now:

A son of man should not be left alone
To struggle with people all alone

Like a black bull of the buffalo ...
If it is because my father is dead
And I am blind to the fact,
Then please let me know at once
Let me know the truth ...
So that I stand and face the elephant
To fight a lonely war with the elephant:
But should he fall one day,
Forget the tusks,
Do not ask for the tusks.

Foremost is the goal of procreation which, being a means to other values, pervades the social system. It creates a web of values and institutions crowned by the overall goal of immortality through children, preferably sons. Just as immortality is a lineage concept and therefore of group interest, marriage and all that it entails is group oriented as well as individually motivated. A sharp dichotomy lies between the respective roles of the marrying youth and their arranging elders: The youth and his age-mates concern themselves with winning the girl's love and affection, while the elders engage in winning her guardian's consent and in celebrating the marriage according to prescribed formalities. The two roles are not entirely separate: They sometimes overlap and are always complementary.

The first step is "seeing" the girl. Usually, this means that after a period of friendship with a girl, a man decides to marry her and consults his relatives. This is often the subject matter of cathartic songs in which young men request their elders to authorize them to look for brides or to consent to proposed marriages. While some fathers urge their sons to marry, many reveal ambivalences that may delay their sons' marriages until they reach an age when marriage can no longer be postponed. The usual reason given is insufficiency of cattle and the need to accumulate more wealth.

When the family agrees that it is time for their son to marry, relatives may take the initiative in seeing the girl. The choice of the first wife of the first wife's son is often left to the father or a senior uncle, but any member of the family may make suggestions about any wife. The influence of one's own mother and sisters must, however, be discouraged as part of the general tendency to control their jealousies.

Whoever takes the initiative, the important members of the family, especially the father, must approve. While the biological father is usually the one responsible, another relative—usually the paternal uncle—may be designated the "father" of the groom and charged with arranging the marriage. The real father may be dead, but usually, the uncle has this responsibility because it is a way of expressing and reinforcing the solidarity of the family.

The dissenting opinion of the son is given more weight if the choice was made by someone other than the father or any other pivotal male member. As the groom's consent is only a convenience and not a legal requirement, his father can proceed to marry the girl whatever his son's view, or may choose to repudiate the son. Since the son has no independent wealth, this is a doom only a reckless man would invite. Rarely will a father change his mind about a girl he would like his son to marry, but sons will nearly always concur in filial piety for the father or in surrender to his will.

During these consultations, relatives investigate whether there is any relationship that might bar the proposed union: Blood relationship is an almost absolute bar; marital affinity prohibits marriage between a wide range of relatives-in-law; breast-feeding creates an exogamous bond between a child, the woman, and her children; and age-mateship and a special friendship pact bar intermarriage between the children or the siblings of the age-mates or the friends unless certain rites are performed. Marriage between feuding groups is also tabooed.

Contravening these rules inflicts a curse on the mother and the children, causing a skin disease known as *akeeth* and maybe even death. The curse results from any sexual relationship, not only from marriage. Once confessed or divined, it may be repudiated by a ritual in which a ram is cut into halves symbolizing the severance of the relationship between the parties at the time of the act, but not justifying future behavior.

On the level of social prejudice as opposed to legal requirement, relatives may oppose marriage on the grounds of black magic, an evil-eye, or such mortal diseases as leprosy and tuberculosis (which the Dinka believe to be inherited). Marriage with non-Dinka is despised and in any case is rare. When it occurs, it is considered of lowly status.

Once the family agrees on the proposal, word of an intended visit is sent to the girl's relatives who will already have heard rumors to that effect. Having set a date, they prepare to receive the "messengers" as these initial visitors are called. On the appointed day, the man's relatives decorate a few oxen with tassels and bells. These, along with a number of cows, are to be driven by young men accompanied by the senior spokesmen. The young men arrive singing ox-songs and war chants. Coming to meet them are women singing either separately or in a duet with the men. All run about and jump up and down in the ballet-type dance called goor. Beer would have been brewed, beasts slaughtered, and plenty of food prepared. The guests may be few, but it is part of the honor for the occasion to be lavish. Whatever the intention of the girl's relatives, the cattle are tethered and carefully attended to as a gesture of respect.

Then comes the meeting in which elders on both sides sit to discuss. This is a solemn occasion and, like all marriage negotiations, calls for high art in oratory and persuasiveness. The spokesman of the visitors starts by saying something like: "I have a lie in my heart." To the Dinka, an undertaking that may prove impossible is a "lie," and so is an error of judgment; but in neither case is a person a liar in the abject sense. By calling their aim a "lie," the relatives of the man mean to leave room for failure. This is a strategy of modesty which is both good manners and a shrewd way of checking the material aspirations of the bride's kin for a high bridewealth. Not much else is said. Unless the relatives of the girl are uncompromisingly opposed to the idea, they are likely to say only something like "We have no word to say now, guests are not rebuffed; you may proceed to do the word of your heart and we shall watch." The idea is to invite them to show their determination by the amount of betrothal wealth they pay and thereby estimate the total number of cows they are likely to pay. Besides, competitors may intervene, and it is always safe to be noncommital until the relationships are more stabilized.

There may be resistance to the whole idea. The girl's relatives may be aware of a marriage bar of which the man's relatives were unaware, nurse an ancient feud that the others might have forgotten or underestimated, or oppose the marriage on the grounds of evil-eye or mortal disease on the man's side—grounds that are so deplored that they are better implied and rarely expressed. Unless opposition is serious, the cattle are accepted by one of the senior members pending a final resolution. Dinkas believe that one should not despair in such matters; persistence is seen as part of courtship whether with girls or with their relatives. Minor objections in particular are not of much concern but must be "washed away" with diplomatic language and gifts of appeasement.

Once the offer to negotiate a marriage is entertained, the next step is to pay the betrothal cattle, the amount of which is usually left for the man's relatives to decide. This completes the betrothal, after which the couple are considered, "married" and are referred to as husband and wife and their respective kin as relatives-in-law. To the Dinka, betrothal is a stage of marriage and not merely an agreement to marry. It gives rise to rights and duties that are not equal to those of marriage, but which anticipate a concluded marriage. It does not license sexual relations between the couple, but it permits free and exclusive courtship which, if exceeded into sexual intercourse or pregnancy, causes no offense. Should a third party court a betrothed girl, at least among the Ngok, he commits an offense; and should he have sexual intercourse with her, he commits "adultery," calling for compensation and nowadays imprisonment. Any children that may result are those of "the cows" —the "husband's."

If there is competition, the cattle of the competitors are kept separately by different relatives. Each time a competitor adds to his cattle, other competitors must be informed and given the opportunity to raise their number. But courtship is opened only to the first bidder. Unless and until defeated, his rights are those of a single fiance; the others fall into the category of third parties.

Except in competition when the total bridewealth is determined by the outcome, the next important formality is "counting the marriage," in which the amount of bridewealth is settled. The public mediates between the parties and partakes in the feasting and the dancing. Counting the marriage is the most celebrated and most festive ceremony of marriage. While relatives-in-law must continue to show great respect for one another, it is also one of the most commercial aspects of Dinka life: The girl's kin aim at getting the most, the man's at paying the least, and "the public" at finding the difficult point of agreement (which is reached more by exhaustion than by conviction). The gracefulness, the charm, and the courtesy with which these business negotiations are conducted contribute to, rather than detract from, the high respect and courtesy which the Dinka demand and expect from relations-in-law.

Sometimes after the "counting of the marriage," a ceremony is carried out by which the consent of the parties, although not legally required, is symbolized. Public singing and dancing is interrupted and the couple sing in turn as though in a duet, but with mutually independent words that have nothing to do with the marriage. The bride then anoints the groom while the "maid-of-honor" and the "best man" sing a duet.

The next stage is payment, in full or in part, of the agreed amount. It is followed by the reverse payment, amounting to about a third of the agreed bridewealth, which the bride's kin must make to the groom's kin from their own cattle.

The final stage, "giving the girl away," may follow soon after the payment of bridewealth, but usually a period of months and even years lapses before the girl is given away. Accompanied by female relatives— the bride then goes to her marital home where sacrifices to ancestral spirits combine with the slaughtering of more beasts for festivities. It is then or sometime after this stage that the ceremony of "washing the bridegroom's mouth" to eat in the home of the bride's relatives is performed.

As these stages show, many of the formalities of marriage are done by senior men while the youth merely engage in courtship. This separation of roles frequently implies that what the elders do might be at variance with the intentions of the young parties. In order to assert their will or otherwise frustrate the arrangements of their elders, young men and women quite often resort to such strategies as elopement and unlawful pregnancy. While these sometimes establish the desired union, they often result in punishment and repudiation of the union. Many are the cases in which people who have long been betrothed are separated; and many are the cases in which a young couple who had eloped and begotten children are separated with one, usually the father, being deprived of his children:

> *O Ajok!*
> *Ajok whom I chose when she was carried in a sling;*
> *Ajok whom I chose when she could not dance;*
> *Ajok whom I chose when she was not yet a tribal beauty;*
> *When she grew, another man took her away from me.*
> *What misery! What a way to treat a man!*
> *God has speared me and Mareng has speared me.*

For the daughter of Kat Atem, I have felt misery.
I cry and cry for the sake of Ajok the Brown.
What carries my children away?
O Bird of the tribe, Awan,
What flies my children across the land?

This extreme patriarchy that gives the children to the mother's husband sometimes defeats its own end for, while daughters who have been "given" to their mothers' lawful husbands usually remain loyal to their stepfathers, most sons seek and join their reputed fathers when they grow up. This is usually allowed. Objection would be greater if a daughter sought to leave her adoptive father since she would then be ripe to attract bridewealth. Oddly enough, the utilitarian value of the sons is minimal despite their pre-eminence. These issues go beyond marriage into the family.

The Family

Once the girl is given in marriage, the sharp contrast between the flattery of courtship and the status of a married woman begins to emerge. As a "guest wife," she is the focus of flirtatious attention by her husband's age-mates, or in the case of a senior man, by his children. She is stripped of her jewelry and other personal belongings acquired from her family, but is soon adorned with new beads, dresses, and other objects of decoration. For the first week or so, she is a guest to be served and not to serve, but she soon takes up most of the housework and gradually integrates herself into the normal status of a wife.

Having a child is the first and biggest step in this process of integration, for children give the spouses a common purpose and are a guarantee, as well as a fulfillment, of the marriage. Dinka children are the focus of family affection:

In the evening
We sat around the fire to talk;
Between my wife and me,
The Little One got up to walk.
My wife cried in fear.
"O son of my father,
Come to my side,
The Little One will fall into the fire."

The longer the marriage, the more and older the children, the deeper the conjugal affection.

In larger families, polygyny is a complicating factor because it is a fertile soil for jealousy and divisiveness. But children remain pivotal in the relations between their parents. Indeed, polygyny is as much an integrating factor as it is divisive. The more reasons there are for disunity, the greater the demand for unity. Depending on the character of the husband, competition over his affection gives him the opportunity to manipulate for family unity around him. The rights and duties of the spouses, although not identical nor equal, are reciprocal. The husband is to take care of his wife, build her a hut, help cultivate her field, provide her with cows for milk, and above all "give" her children. On her part, she is to show devotion to him, love him and respect him, give particular attention to his health and nourishment, love his children, respect his sons, show deference and courtesy to his senior wives, and while she must be exclusively his in sex, she must keep an open house and open heart to all his kinsmen and friends. The Dinka say, "Except in her bed, a wife is the wife of all."

But in this reciprocity, should the husband or the wife fail to meet the standards, the sanctions are far from equal. By and large, the main sanction against him is his image as a man. The complaints of his wife, politely voiced in confidence, are useful guides to his chosen conduct, but do not work as deterrents. She could talk to his elders, but that is taking things too far and the home might never be the same. A prudent wife, short of breaking the union, must either endure the situation or use the art of feminine persuasiveness which makes the man adhere to her wishes while leaving him feeling himself the unquestionable "master"—and perhaps more assured of that by her resort to his justice. Of course, there are "bull-women" who lord it over their husbands, but these are rare exceptions. Such women acquire the fame of bullies as their husbands simultaneously acquire fame as cowed.

In sharp contrast to male failure, a woman who contravenes the norms of wifehood and motherhood faces the threat of punishment ranging from reprimand to beating. By far the gravest punishment is abstention from her food, which implies abstention from her bed. This means depriving her of children and is surpassed only by divorce.

Dinka women are aware of these and many other inequities, but they have come to accept them as part of their status as women. It is not unusual for a woman to assert equality by saying "I have the organs of a woman but the heart of a man." The functions of the heart and the mind are fused in Dinka thought. This formulation indicates an acceptance of the logic of discrimination. Some women do not accept it. While they may not rebel against the system, women have customary ways of making themselves heard which the Dinka do not understand as rebellious, but which are essentially ways of expressing dissent. For instance, women get possessed and, while in a state of trance, voice complaints and demands that are attributed to ancestral spirits. Usually, the demand takes the form of dedication and sacrifice of cattle. But a woman who frequently gets possessed acquires the reputation of being frivolous and risks being ignored. Rarely do first wives, who are often privileged, or an otherwise favored wife become possessed.

Another way adopted by junior, often unfavored, wives is unfaithfulness. Dinka wives are generally very faithful, and this is evident because confessions of adultery are very few even though nearly all are confessed because adultery carries a heavy and religious threat of illness or death in default of confession. Although the following singer is unusually liberal for a Dinka woman because of the "sophistication" she acquired from life in town, she articulates the degree to which a woman may become unfaithful as a means of protest against her subordination.

> *Perish, O people;*
> *Perish, people of our land.*
> *With their eagerness to judge,*
> *They grab a person's case*
> *When they do not know its cause.*
> *Marriage of a woman is bad.*
> *When she is married,*
> *She is most admired,*
> *And when she lives*
> *And gives birth to a child*
> *To be a man among men,*
> *She is pushed aside.*
> *So she steps out of the hut,*
> *She is in search for another man.*
> *For her it is good*
> *But to the Dinka, it is evil:*
> *She is a woman who seeks men.*

When matters go that far, they are no longer dealt with exclusively within the family. Although the husband may sue outsiders for violation of his rights over his wife, rarely can she involve the outside world in their affairs. Adultery as a legally recognized offense can be committed only by a man against the hus band of the unfaithful wife and never by a woman against the wronged wife of the husband. Consequently, it is the male party to adultery who is punished and who must pay adultery compensation. The Dinka explain that it is the men who take initiative in these matters; women are largely the victims of male sexual aggressiveness. But they also recognize that women have their subtle, or sometimes direct, ways of involving men. Some men deeply resent the fact that only they must suffer the legal consequences while a willing, and sometimes inducing, partner is left free and her husband is benefited by the wrong. The sentiment is often expressed, but exaggerated, in songs. In the following, the singer had been accused and convicted of adultery, which, if we believe him, was initiated by the woman as they paddled across the river. The song reports only the events in the canoe and not what happened after they had crossed the river.

> *I saw a woman accompanied by two men*
> *Brown ox of my father, she was accompanied by two.*
> *They accompanied her toward the toc;*
> *And when I caught up with them*
> *She was handed over to me:*
> *"Please take this woman across the river*
> *Since you are paddling across."*
> *I thought I was taking the mother of a girl*
> *So I paddled my canoe.*
> *Then she began to smile;*
> *I wondered why the woman watched my eyes*
> *And her face filled with smiles:*
> *We had said nothing funny*
> *Nothing to make one laugh so much that she lay down,*
> *Exposed herself,*
> *Spread her legs,*

And put her skirt away.
The hornless one remained exposed;
The hornless one which cuts through the heart of man.
But I did not accept,
I fastened my heart very tight;
I went paddling my canoe.
She lay her legs widespread
But I did not accept.
I fastened my heart very tight
And went on paddling my canoe.
Then she dared to hold the curved horn of the moon;
She caught and held my horn—the horn of the buffalo.
When I said, "Don't you see the rain has come?"
She went on holding it,
She caught and held my horn of the buffalo;
She held the buffalo by the horn;

Two young men paddling a canoe.
(Courtesy of the Sudan Government)

Then said, "Please do not refuse
O son of the clan of Alic,
Try, so that I may sleep tonight
And, today,
I will never say a word
Try,
I have had no man for three years
No one sleeps with me
Try,
Thiep, Crested Crane, son of The Snake,
Try."
Then I said, "Are we crocodiles to sleep in the river?
Are we fish to sleep in the river?
Have we become fish and frogs?"
I went on paddling my canoe
Until I crossed the River Lol.
I am a man who paddles the canoe
And covers myself with sweat.

While the law holds the man responsible, Dinka morals hold the woman to be more depraved. That her husband has been compensated or appeased by the adulterer is by no means a guarantee that their relations within the family will be amicable. Because of indignation, the cattle a man receives for adultery are usually disposed of in marriage or otherwise; a man does not drink milk from such cows, eat their meat, or eat whatever food is obtained through their sale.

Throughout a woman's marital life, her agnatic kin maintain an interest in her affairs and come to her aid according to need. If she wrongs her husband, they usually appease him with cattle, a payment known as awec. If she is the complainant, they normally consider it a family affair. But in serious wrongs against her they will intervene and may go to court. In extreme cases, conflicts between a husband and wife may end in divorce, whether initiated by the man, the woman, or her relatives. Divorce among the Dinka is, however, strongly abhorred and rare. Even from the economic point of view, divorce is undesirable since the conditions for the return of bridewealth are complex. If the fault is that of the man, he is not supposed to claim the bridewealth until the wife is remarried and the new husband can afford to compensate the ex-husband—which is very difficult since the cattle will have multiplied. If the fault is that of the wife or her relatives, they are expected to return promptly, when possible, the very cattle paid. If given in other marriages or otherwise disposed of, they must be traced and returned. Sometimes, other marriages may break as cattle are withdrawn and no replacement is made. Only if the cattle have been taken to a foreign land will substitution be accepted. Even within the tribe, the return of the original cattle is easier said than done. Divorce is, therefore, better avoided. Even in cases of adultery, the husband of an adulterous woman will usually be content with compensation varying in value from area to area and also influenced by whether or not pregnancy has resulted. Where there are children from the existing marriage, divorce is not allowed except in such extreme cases as the wife's persistent running away with another man.

I quote from the following song in detail because it gives insight into the various aspects of a Dinka divorce, its linkage with procreation, its emotional repercussions, and the social stigma attached to it. Agorot was divorced on the grounds that she was morally responsible for the death of one of her children. In the song, she denies the accusation, but admits that she must be responsible because she comes from a normal lineage while the lineage of her husband are men who die only of old age.

We are agitated, the man of the house, Rialcol and I
We are a sparrow and a hawk in chase at home.

The evil imputed on me did not occur.
In the family of Col, only old age kills men.
Agorot de Biong, stand bewildered
Stand bewildered, daughter of the son of The White One.
The conduct of the left-handed man of Jok Anguek is confusing to all
Even to the brown Arabs.
The Arab said to me: "Why have you left your home?
What is your fault when you have children?"
The case of the daughter of the left handed is painful
Even to the Arab friends of the clan of Arob de Biong,
Deng de Rahma paces back and forth
The Arab paces up and down.
Alas, there is nothing good that does not spoil;
The word is circulating that the daughter of Biong is divorced.
People ask, "Which one of the girls is that?"
It is the girl for whom sons of nobles covered the plains with cattle.
I never quarreled with the people of the house
I was attacked holding my peace.
People ask, "Daughter of Biong,
What wrong have you done in your house?"
Theft, there is not in me
The daughter of Biong is well composed;
O my people; nor have I been seduced,
No case of adultery was taken to court;
I was dismissed from the house with no fault.
I walked away like a hyena surprised by dawn.
I am accused of hiding a cause of disease:
Disease cannot be imputed to a healthy person.
Daughter of the camp of Milang, leave the house
The marriage has refused to work.
Do not try to soothe me, O Marial of Padek
I feel like a person burning in fire,

The words of the land are burning me,
O Bung de Beek, I am trapped with a trap.
A flame has burnt my face.
My quarrel with Lueth will not make me leave the cooking
place empty.
Awien, daughter of Rial, please kindle the fire
Daughter of the clan of Agueng de Kwol,
We are the blood of Monydhaang de Kwol de Jok,
We are not orphaning ourselves, daughter of Biong d'Acuol.
It is all over between me and the bull of Ajak.
The man jumped on me like a buffalo.
In the clan of Col, The Heavy Haired,
Brave men do not die!
It is I who have brought death to the family of Baar.
But I do not know what wrong I have done
O mother, daughter of Ajing, The Spotted Leopard.
Our great clan of Biong d'Allor has always been mortal
We are the ancient victims of death.
Our clan of Allor de Monydhaang has always been mortal
We are the ancient victims of death.

When divorce occurs, children go with the father as he is considered the primary beneficiary of procreation. But because children are usually closer emotionally to the mother, this separation creates a complex set of interrelationships in which the paramountcy of the father's rights are largely of a proprietary nature. The same factors that give the father a superior claim to children militate against him even to the point of conflict with the children. The Dinka definitely align the child with the mother in the complex setting of polygyny, even as they dispose him against the divisiveness of his mother's actual or potential jealousy. In this alignment and competition, the role of the child is to assert his identity and fight for those rights that are his, and by derivation his mother's or vice versa. He must fight for cattle allocation and eventually for his marriage. To face up to one's father in the assertion of one's rights is expected and encouraged in children, particularly in sons. Indeed, the son's character as a man is appraised according to the degree of both his love and respect for his father and his readiness and willingness to oppose him whenever his filial rights are violated—or whenever he sees his father in the wrong with others. The exception is if the conflict is with his own mother. For here the risks of being negatively labeled as a "woman's son" are too great. The delicate balance of criticism and deference in the father-son relationship is evident in these lines in which a young man whose father is dead complains to an elder whom he calls "great father" against his guardian uncle whom he refers to as "father."

My great father, Majak,
You are our eldest
We the orphans of the clan.
If you see me in the wrong
Lock me in jail.
If my uncle is in the wrong
Tell him gently—gently;
The word of an elder should not be rebuked,
Keep it soft.
My father will think alone at night
And if he rejects the word of a son
I will cry inside myself.

As was the case in this instance, such songs often receive a prompt and favorable response.

But the grounds of potential conflict between a father and a son are many and are so interfused into the system that they are an amalgam of accepted positives and negatives. The most obvious ground is the principle of immortality through procreation. Although the father is a protector, he is also an impediment to the son's status (which depends largely on the father). On his side, the father is threatened by the son who not only takes over his role to perpetuate the lineage but also inherits his younger wives to continue procreation. While this must not challenge the exclusiveness of his sexual rights in his lifetime, it raises doubts, tensions, and maybe open conflicts. Almost every father who has junior wives and senior sons nurses some suspicion and jealousy. As he ages, his fear that his young wives will be attracted to his younger sons increases. Adultery by sons, although a rare and most serious offense, does occur.

Threats of hostility and conflict are behind the rules of avoidance between parents and their children. A mother or a stepmother is not to sit on the bed of a son who has reached the age of puberty. With a young stepmother, the rules are more stringent. While a son may enter the huts of his mother and senior stepmothers and converse with them freely, he is to restrain his visits to the huts of his junior stepmothers, avoid flirtatious smiles or lengthy conversations with them, and, indeed, avoid their companionship as much as possible. The senior mothers and sisters are often the watchdogs of the son's interests in such circumstances and are not slow in giving a warning should things appear risky. And there is always the danger of rumors and fabrications by envious or jealous wives who hope to harm their co-wives or win favors from their husbands—all the more reason for extra care and prudence. With respect to the father, senior sons must avoid his bed as he must avoid theirs. They are not to eat together from the same container as Dinka normally do; they are not to keep company—but if they do, the son is to be exceptionally well composed and should be more of a listener than a talker. To an unfamiliar observer, the solemnness and the formality of their togetherness indicates tension. But to the Dinka it is "respect," and its effect is to minimize, if not to avoid, tensions and conflicts. While they are normally avoided or resolved when they occur, conflicts between father and son, unlike those between mother and child, can but very rarely lead to the ritual severance of ties. A father who wishes that such a son be alienated from his family and wider kin is always in for disappointment. For the ritual of severance does not repudiate kinship ties and certainly does not disaffiliate one from one's clan. This is part of the pervasiveness of the Dinka family.

In addition to the extended family in which a paternal uncle may play the role of the father even when relations with the father are amicable, the circle of maternal kin remains a haven of resort for any disaffiliation from the paternal kin. The extension of the family principles into the kinship and other circle of society is implicit in the generous use of kinship terms to cover a wide range of related and even unrelated people. Such words as "grandfather," "aunt," and "sister" are often used in blood and marriage relationships, not only as expressions of respect in a manner familiar to all peoples but also in definite institutionalized relationships with identifiable rights and responsibilities. This is applied even to nonrelatives and is carried to the point where the tribe, designated by the same term as the family, is conceived as a fictional extension of the family with the Paramount Chief as the Overall Father.

Property and Economy

Control of wealth and the productive exploitation of resources rest with the elders. Adults share something of the adoration for cattle, but they do not share the obsessions of youth even though they sanction them. It is through them that cattle and other forms of livestock are acquired. It is they who sacrifice them, slaughter them, sell them, barter with them, pay them in marriage, and give them away in many other ways. It is they who own the land, cultivate the fields, reap the crops, and regulate consumption.

Except for such outmoded means as raids and novel practices as labor in towns, the standard way to acquire cattle is bridewealth. Bloodwealth and other means of compensation are also sources of wealth, although these are remedial measures whereas bridewealth is not. Cattle are also exchanged through gifts of friendship or through trade. Thus, with few exceptions, the normal means of acquisition is kinship, friendship, and similar institutions. The source of acquisition often corresponds to the source of disposition, especially in connection with obligation to kinsmen and friends. Thus, while a man clings to a few cattle of long-standing descent, other cattle are in constant circulation. A man receives them as bridewealth only to dispose of them in marriage; he gets help from a relative or a friend only to return the favor some day. As the Dinka put it: "What is given circulates, and what is consumed is wasted" and "Cattle belong to all." They should, therefore, be used for the common good. Thus, by law a starving man has the right to seize the nearest goat, sheep, or cow with the tacit understanding that it will be repaid by him or an able relative; a man who needs a beast to sacrifice under the emergency conditions of illness, or even for hospitality, may do the same.

Except in songs, and then mostly by youth and wives, to be proud of wealth and irresponsive to the needs of others is to invite a divine condemnation that might result in the loss of wealth. The ancestress of the following singer, Adut Akol, feeling that she had too much milk because of their great wealth, threw milk into the river, angering God so that he deprived her descendants of cattle. But his grandfather's noble attitude toward cattle brought back the family's wealth. It should perhaps be pointed out that this is an unusual song insofar as it criticizes an ascendant; normally Dinka praise ascendants, whatever their past. The singer's criticism is also balanced by his praise.

Adut enjoyed the riches of my ancestor Kueng Angok—
Then she thought big.

It was a thought disliked by God.
The word of a fool is disliked by God.
She poured the milk into the river,
And goat's milk remained smelling;
That is why we had no goat's dung.
My father Ring was convened by his father,
He seated him down by his side,
And then rubbed his head,
And left him these words:
"Son, Ring, there are the cattle,
Cattle are the prosperity of man."

While cattle should serve a common interest, their normal control is less widely shared and is vested in a few. The right to such control is determined by one's position in the kinship values. Since adult males are charged with the payment of bridewealth, they are pivotal in the control of cattle. But it is a chicken-and-egg riddle as to which one comes first: responsibility for payment or male dominance. The head of the family allocates cattle according to houses and their seniority. Each house then redivides among its members, providing that the needs of individuals are satisfied by whomever can afford to do so. A man always leaves a herd in his name as the collective property of the family. Neither the wives nor the children can dispose of cattle without the consent of the family; and in the normal course of events the father, too, should consult with them before disposing of cattle allotted to them. A man cannot dispose of cattle dedicated to God and ancestral spirits except for certain noble purposes like special marriages. To do otherwise is believed to be a religious offense that might cause death.

While the Dinka are mainly reputed as devoted to cattle, they are also cultivators. Cattle, however, have the additional dignity of being acquired by virtue of one's status, while cultivation can be done by anyone and is therefore of less prestige. This singer prays for the combination.

> *O Creator,*
> *O Creator who created me in my mother's womb,*
> *Do not confront me with a bad thing.*
> *Show me the place of cattle*
> *So that I reap my crops*
> *And keep my herds.*

The usual assertion that the Dinka lead a semi-nomadic life is true only in the sense that youth accompany the cattle in temporary camps in search of better grazing areas; otherwise, the villages are permanent. They are always inhabited by the older men and women and also by the younger people when they are not away with the bulk of the cattle for distant grazings.

Theoretically, control of the land is vested in the Chief by virtue of original occupation. In their migrations, the Dinka were led by members of dominant clans whose lineages founded, and still hold, chieftainships. Myth, if not fact, has it that the leader of the tribe distributed land among his original followers and thereby formed the subtribes or sections. The heads of these sections redivided their land among internal groups, and so on, according to the present segmentation of their society. Various rights in land are therefore held by the descendants of these original occupiers. Latecomers acquire rights only by association with those lineages. But this is not of much practical significance today. Every Dinka now has the right, within his subtribe, to settle and cultivate a piece of land, provided that such land has not been cleared by any other person and is not so close to any residential or arable area as to form a part of that area.

Where various rights to land are vested in a hierarchy of social and political institutions, as among the Dinka, the nature of rights and claims becomes confused. The individual member of the community is relatively free to acquire land subject to territorial division, but it is the Chief who allocates land to new comers. Except in war, it is he who protects the land against outside claims; it is he who has the overall power by virtue of his divine prerogative to control such destructive elements as rain, birds, and locusts. Although no Dinka adult can eat of any new harvest unless he has propitiated God and the ancestral spirits through a "Thanksgiving" ceremony called "offering to the land," the festivities of this occasion are most elaborate in the house of the Chief.

The control of the Chief over land is largely minimal insofar as members of his tribe are concerned. Since there is land for everyone to occupy without friction, land allocation among tribesmen is unnecessary. Disputes about boundaries do arise, but they are often solved by local headmen. Those concerning sections' grazing areas are more serious and reach the Chief.

While in Dinka law nobody can sell land, the individual can make a gift of his land, residential or arable, to a member of the tribe. Any change of residence, from one section to another requires the permission of the chiefs of the sections concerned and of the Paramount Chief.

An elementary family usually works its own land and builds its huts and cattle byres, but it can hire other people to help in cutting the grass for thatching or the poles for rafters, and even to carry out the actual work of building. Such hire may be settled by payment or by inviting friends to a feast of beer and food. The exception in this respect is work for the Chief, whose huts are built by the age-sets of the different subtribes. Even then, he gives them beasts to slaughter for meat.

Dinkaland, and particularly Ngokland, falls into the central clay plains that are the most fertile in the country. Among the crops produced are *durra* (sorghum), maize, groundnuts (peanuts), sesame, beans, okra, and tobacco. The main food crop is *durra*, and among the

Ngok it is cultivated twice a year. The first crop is sown in the early rains and cut in September, while the second crop arises from the stubs cut in the first harvest and is harvested in November or shortly afterward. Agricultural work comprises clearing the fields during the dry season, sowing the seeds at the beginning of the rainy season, weeding at least twice a year, guarding the crops against birds and animals, and harvesting and threshing them. These activities require very hard labor. Men and women wake up early to go to the fields—often a distance away—returning only in the evening or sometimes sleeping in nearby homes. During the working hours, the air is filled with sounds of people singing to the rhythm of the hoe, each man in his own field. Except for the often absent youth, most of the work is shared by all, with some division of labor on the grounds of sex and age. In sowing, men dig the holes while women and children follow to bury the seeds. Weeding is shared by both but is the primary function of men. Women do most of the harvesting and the whole of the threshing. Allowance is made for the homekeeping function of women, who usually return earlier to nurse the babies, prepare the food, or otherwise keep the home. In a polygynous family the head of the household has fields which he cultivates separately from those of his wives, although he usually assists them as well. Sons are also expected to assist and, in the interest of family solidarity, usually help their stepmothers rather than their own mothers. Anyone can get help by giving a feast to which he invites friends and neighbors. To this may be added gratuitous help by blood relations or relations-in-law. Beside having available the services of any age-set, which he may ask to work his field, the Chief is also assisted by some of the men attending his Court during the cultivation period.

Land is also used for fishing and hunting, which are done individually and collectively. Fishing in particular is an occupation of all age-groups. The Dinka are not keen fishermen, but they crave fish as a supplement to their diet. Fishing takes place at most times of the year, but collective fishing is more regulated. Rivers and lagoons are officially opened in November when the fish follow the flood-water into the main rivers and in February and March when the level of the water begins to drop and expose the fish. In addition to hooks, nets, and traps, spears are used in all manner of situations. Hunting connotes vigilance and is largely a youth occupation, but adults sometimes hunt. Hunting is done with the help of dogs and is especially prevalent during the very dry season when the animals leave the forests and the dry plains to drink at the rivers near the villages, or in the very wet season when they also come out into the open drier areas near the homes. Meat from hunting, like the meat of sacrifice or feast, is always subject to rules of distribution according to descent and age. The first person to spear an elephant is usually entitled to the right tusk, and the second person to the left tusk even if the wounds they inflicted did not lead to the death of the animal.

Paddling and fish-spearing around a herd of hippos.
(Photo by T. R. H. Owen)

Other activities connected with land are the collection of wild fruits and honey. A person may make a beehive or mark any trees where bees are likely to swarm to ensure that the honey produced there is his private property.

The economic activities of the Dinka are very much conditioned by the four seasons which the Dinka recognize, but which do not correspond exactly to the Western seasons. They allow for some overlap of the months. *Ker*, the season beginning from May to early July, and *Ruel* (from July to October) form the wet season. *Rut*, extending from November to February, and *Mai* (from February to May) form the dry season. During *Ker* the early rains fall, the fields which had been cleared earlier are planted, and the cattle gradually return to camp near the villages while some cows are kept in the villages to provide milk. In July, mosquitoes increase and it becomes necessary to bring the cattle home to be protected in the cattle byres at night. *Ruel* is the period of heavy rains and permanent residence in the villages. Agricultural work, including harvest, falls into this season. The end of the rains is referred to as *anyoic*, the period when crops are ripe and the cattle begin to graze farther away from the villages but are brought back during the harvest of the second crop. This is a period when the fields have to be properly protected from the cattle as they crave the flavor of this second crop. Conflicts often occur between the owners of cattle and fields because of crop destruction by herds. *Ruel* is also the season for select young men to go to their rest period, leaving cultivation to be done by the women and older men.

Rut is the coldest season, marked by the north wind's blowing in November. While younger men start to gather wood and wattle for the repair of homes and cut thatching materials before the grass is burnt, older people remain in the villages to complete the harvest. Road construction by younger age-sets has been introduced by the Government and is also done during this season. As the pasture soon gets exhausted, the cattle are driven out in small herds to graze farther away along the upper reaches of the watercourses. As the Ngok move northward to the higher land where even less flooding occurs than in the mainland, the Tuic and the Malual Dinka, whose land gets severely flooded, move into Ngokland. And afterward, as the Tuic and the Malual return southward, followed by the Ngok, the Baggara Arabs (whose land becomes too dry) move into Ngok land. Ngok territory is therefore of special value to both the Southern Dinka and the Arabs and is often a ground for tribal conflicts which make the task of administration, particularly trying for the Ngok Paramount Chief.

During *Mai* the main cattle camps in the *toc*, which had been started during the *Rut*, begin to be used as there is little grass left near the permanent villages. This is the hottest time of the year: Water supplies are scanty and wells are dug near the permanent settlements. This is the season of disease, and the Dinka eagerly await its end and the blessings of the early rains of *Ker*.

Power and Law

Adulthood gives a person the right to participate in the public affairs of the tribe, both as an individual and as a member of an age-set. Age-sets are permanent and, throughout life, widen the circles of associates by providing additions or alternatives to kinship ties. But the corporate spirit of the age-set begins to wane as people get married and settle as family men. Women's age-set activities end then. Although those of men continue for quite a while, they almost disappear when these men become elders. But men continue to take part in public life, attending the Chief's Court as plaintiffs or as defendants, taking part in the trials of their peers, or otherwise sharing in the decisions of the Assembly of Elders.

Dinka conceptions, institutions, and practices of power and their legal expression have changed a great deal, first as a result of the nineteenth-century upheavals of the Turko-Egyptian and the Mahdist regimes when, to the Dinka, "the world was spoiled"; and later as a result of the Anglo-Egyptian colonial administration. No easy dichotomy can be drawn between what is normal change and what resulted from the breakdown of order under the chaotic conditions of the nineteenth century—or between what was indigenous and what has been implanted by alien powers. The trends have not been uniform throughout Dinkaland: Some chiefs emerged as a result of the upheavals; others disappeared under the purge of the colonialists; while some families held their religious and secular leadership, through war and peace, in tradition and in modernity. This is particularly true of the Ngok, among whom traditional leadership has not only been confirmed by successive administrations but has also been enhanced by Arab influence with its emphasis on stratification.

Traditionally, the Dinka political system functioned through lineages, with each descent group being an autonomous unit. But the system centered around the Paramount Chief, his subordinate chiefs, and elders. Political leadership is considered divine and is traced through religious legends that are continually retold to reinforce contemporary structure. The emphasis placed on such legends, especially in songs, is often exaggerated and the religious beliefs embodied in them may appear archaic. But to the Dinka, they explain why things are the way they are and give stability to the social system.

One example of such myths concerns Jok, the founder of the Pajok lineage, and tells of how on the Ngok migration westward, the tribe was confronted with a river that could not be crossed. Jok sacrificed his daughter Acai to the river. She was carried off by the Spirit of the Water who in return caused the waters to part so that the people could cross on dry land.

A more recent myth among the Ngok tells how another Pajok leader, Arob, saved his tribe by sacrificing his son. The facts of Arab's sacrifice are rather unclear. It is said that a governor during the

Mahdist rule wanted to test Arob's commitment to his tribe in order to decide whether he should be recognized by the Central Government. The governor challenged Arob to give up his son, which he did in the face of strong tribal objection. Some say the child was killed; others maintain he was taken away. It is known that Khalifa Abdullah, who succeeded the Mahdi, kept relatives of chiefs from all over the country as hostages to secure their support. These lines are about the sacrifice:

> *The old are asked about the distant past,*
> *Ask your father about the distant past.*
> *The land was spoiled and did not hold,*
> *And when it did not hold*
> *Arob said: "Sacrifice the child."*
> *But the death of the child dismayed the tribe*
> *All raised their hands aloft and cried,*
> *"Killing the child will spoil the tribe."*
> *My Great Father called the word all right.*

In another song the following dialogue between the grandsons of Arob is presented:

> *Leader:*
> *You, Deng Majok and Deng Makuei,*
> *You are the elders with the words of the tribe*
> *Why was the son killed?*

> *Chorus:*
> *It was a sacrifice.*

> *Leader:*
> *Is a human life simple enough to be given in sacrifice?*

I beseech you give me a better reason.
Why was the man killed?
Chorus:
It was a sacrifice.

Even to my grandfather, Chief Kwol, a young man attributes a miracle:

Of the distant past
I hear that horses used to fly,
In the world of today
Horses no longer fly;
The Land is full of sin
Yes, Miyom, ox of my father, sin is grave.
Of the distant past
I hear that Chief Kwol d'Arob de Biong
Charmed the crested cranes until he caught them;
In the world of today
No one can charm the crested cranes until he catches them;
The land is full of sin
Yes, Miyom, my father's ox, sin is grave.
Even if people pray night and day
No one has that power of spirit
Unless we wake our ancestors from their graves.

The Chief is conceived as the father uniting the living members of his community among themselves and with their dead. In the ceremonies of his installation, he is lifted by representatives of the community so that the will of the tribe and divine acceptance are symbolized. But there is, of course, a struggle for power within the ruling families which corresponds to the familiar frictions within polygynous families. However, these political struggles are more intensified by the importance of the disputed positions. Conflicts may be between father and son, between brothers, or between other members of the lineage. Although primogeniture favors the eldest son of the most senior wife, circumstances can be complicated enough to permit deviation and choice. In the genealogies of leading families, there are cases dating far back in which sons other than the most senior or of the most senior wives, have prevailed over otherwise entitled senior sons. Leadership may even get out of the immediate family: For instance, a chief may die, leaving children too young to succeed. Then his brother, cousin, or uncle succeeds, establishes himself too firmly to give room to the deceased's children when they grow up and begins to pave the way for the succession of his own son. After his death, competition ensues between his children and those of his predecessor. These complications and changes in circumstances give the people a choice so that primogeniture neither creates too much security for good leadership nor imposes leadership on the people. The institution of primogeniture simply limits the circle of choice—a circle duly disposed to leadership, trained for it, and believed worthy of it.

This brings us to Dinka conceptions of what makes a worthy leader. A Dinka Chief is not a ruler in the Western sense, but a spiritual leader whose words express divine enlightenment and wisdom and form the point of con sensus and reconciliation. In order to reconcile between men, the Chief himself must be a model of purity, righteousness, and, in Dinka terms, " a man with a cool heart"—as opposed to a hot-tempered and impatient man. Owing to the family orientation of the society, most problems of social relations are either familial or interfamilial. Within the family these concern individuals; outside the family, they often concern groups, usually represented by individuals. When there is a disaster such as crop failure or an epidemic, the Chief's task is one of mediating between the empirical and the spiritual worlds to correct the loss of harmony and unity believed to have caused the mishap. To achieve this he must invoke the help of his ancestors and the divinities as they are the protectors of the whole tribe. But the role of the Chief goes further than that. As the spiritual father of the tribe, he is the keeper of the people, as a group and as individuals. The continuous theme of self-sacrifice in the stories of chiefly families is a testimony to the responsibility his position bestows upon him. A needy person looks to the Chief for personal remedy. In order to meet these responsibilities, the Chief must be endowed with all the material and spiritual values essential for his duty and hence he should be the tribe's wealthiest and most generous person, without favoritism.

In carrying out his duties, and in accordance with the overriding goals of the Dinka, the Chief is supposed to emphasize persuasion rather than coercion. *Luk*, ("to persuade") also means "court" or "trial." Litigation among the Dinka is designed more to reconcile the adversaries than it is to find a right and wrong side. Unless people succeed in this, the conflict is not adequately resolved. Every detail is examined, every chief and elder who wishes to be heard is heard, and a general dialogue of persuasion continues until the alleged wrong is revealed to the party at fault and the parties concur. Weather permitting, the court or the assembly meets under a tree; attendance is open. Many people who are not interested in a particular case are spectators or participants. Quite often, people are forced to sit in the sun when all the places in the shade are occupied. Order of speech is maintained through the institution of *agamlong* (literally, "The acceptor of speeches"). This man, appointed by the court for this specific purpose, sits in the center of the meeting, repeating in a high-pitched voice the last word or part of the last sentence—or even the whole sentence—said by a speaker. No one can speak without the attention and the repetition of the *agamlong*; and while only a few of them repeat whole sentences, the agamlong sometimes rephrases the idea in a better, more persuasive, way and may even refuse to repeat a sentence because it might detract from the common goal.

In many cases, when a final settlement is reached, a ceremony of reconciliation follows either in front of the Chief or privately. Only then is the case fully resolved and harmony restored.

Women do not take part in trials except as litigants and witnesses. Normally, it is the man who sues. In sex matters, the woman on whom the offense was committed may attend more as an interested witness than a litigant. Some women, however, play a prominent role as litigants either because they have no men in the house or are of a particularly strong character and verbal skill.

The authority of a Dinka Chief is sanctioned by his spiritual powers of life and death through blessing and cursing. Such divine and secular powers, although concentrated in the chiefs, are shared by members of chiefly lineages. Because commoners do not have equal powers they are sometimes, somewhat comically, referred to as *Micar ageer*, meaning "the black bulls with widespread horns"; (A bull with such horns has a hard time fighting with bulls having upward and pointed horns.)

The spiritual power of the Chief can be awesome, but the Dinka know that the Chief should not err and invoke divine power unjustifiably. Abused power is ineffective. The fear of the Chief's religious sanction is therefore not so awesome as it may seem. Persuasion is his primary tool.

The Chief's office is particularly opposed to physical coercion. Ideally, he should not even see blood. In the case of aggression against his tribe, when force is deemed necessary to stop force, the Chief should bless the warriors and pray for victory far away from the battlefield. In a war between his own subtribes, he may draw a symbolic line, place his sacred spear on it, and pray that heavy casualties be inflicted on any group crossing the symbolic line in disobedience to his orders against fighting.

In view of the emphasis on his persuasiveness, it would seem paradoxical that the symbols of the Chief's authority are spears. Since the spears are invoked to inflict a curse, the symbol is that of necessary but reserved coercion. The power of the spear is linked with the power of the divinity Ring which literally means Flesh. It is from Ring that the Ngok Paramount Chief derives his title and all Dinka chiefs derive their authority. At night, when everyone is asleep, masters of the fishing spear are said to "call the word," praying for divine en lightenment. And it is believed that Ring sometimes reveals Himself to them in the form of light. The symbolic spears of the Ngok Paramount Chief are believed to shine brightly at night if they want to draw the Chief's attention to something. The information may accompany the illumination, or the truth may be subsequently divined. Yet, while a source of divine endightenment and therefore of persuasive wisdom, Ring is also a source of divine curse and death. Its revelation through the spears thus symbolizes righteousness that embodies persuasion and the power to destroy evil and its human agents.

It was to stress the importance of persuasion in Dinka society, and its divine and secular bases, that some scholars concluded that it lacked the ingredient of coercion necessary for the Western conception of law. Law, a normative cocept generally desired by every society for the sake of internal order, should be seen contextually. For despite fundamental similarities among all legal systems, each system has its own social policies that it is supposed to serve. In doing so it adopts ways and means that distinguish it from other systems, although it retains the basic principles that are universally common to law.

A conspicuous factor in Dinka law was the minimum effectiveness of the Chief prior to the advent of modern government and the prevalence of selfhelp through violence. It is hard to say whether these were normal features of the Dinka legal system or implications of youth resorting to violence. Besides, the disruptive conditions of the nineteenth century could not have left the legal system unaffected.

While it is common in Dinka literature to speak of the days "when the people lived by the force of the arm," it seems more consistent with the idealism of their legal theory to view this as an attendant evil of a "spoiled world" rather than as a natural aspect of the legal system.

Chapter Eight: Aging

The Paradox of Age

The Dinka respect age and love youth. One brings knowledge and wisdom, the other has vitality and vigilance. Both are complementary, but one supports future expectations while the other involves recollections about the past. To compensate for their economic deprivations, youth are overindulged in esthetics; to make up for their lack of vitality, elders are highly respected and made to feel pivotal even when effective control passes to younger generations. The Dinka ambivalences in this forward-and-backward combination are apparent in these songs:

They say Mangar is too good for a young man,
He is better suited for an older man,
But I will not leave him.
Am I not the older man?
Did I not breed him myself?
Was not an older man a younger man?
And will not a younger man be an older man?

Next Winter, people will gossip and make wishes:
"These oxen are better suited for a younger man."
Where was the younger man during the summer days?
When I bought them in the marketplace
No one was absent, girls and young men,
They were all in the marketplace.

Although the ideals of the system are geared toward them, Dinka elders live on memories of their youth and enjoy telling of their experiences, glorifying the past to the point of distortion to justify a positive image of themselves. This is in part an attempt to project an idealized image of the self, but it also acts as a distraction from the apprehensions of the approaching end. This downward journey is a gradual one. The period of adulthood when a man enjoys the panoramic view of life is expansive. The peak is a spacious plain. But going over the hill is an anti-climax:

Coming of age is a beautiful thing,
Yes, my Ox, Agaany,
Coming of age is a beautiful thing;
Old age is a bad thing,
Yes, my Ox–Maker,
Old age is a bad thing;
It drags a man into indignities.

As usual in songs, the point is overstated; indignity is too strong a word for the status of a Dinka elder.

The threats of a take-over are mitigated for an elder by the fact that his older children would already have founded their own families and moved. In most cases, too, the older children's mothers would long have reached the age of abstinence in sexual life. This means that the influence of their children over them, which may have worked against him (or at least caused a degree of disharmony), has diminished or else found little or no channel. In any case, the women would themselves be quite remote from their married children-especially sons, with whom rules of avoidance between relatives-in-law discourage close contacts. But an elder who is thus removed from his older wife or wives usually marries a young wife. Even if he is emotionally close to his older wife, she herself may advocate his remarriage. She derives advantage from the services of a junior wife and is moreover interested in having small children around the house. She takes care of her grandchildren, but they come and go, while a junior co-wife's children return after weaning.

The family atmosphere of an elderly couple or an elder man with a young wife is a cordial one. Unless the man has a public status or otherwise is socially prominent so that he has a lot of company, such a couple usually retire from public involvement and lead a quiet life. If they are both elderly, the fact that they have lived together for so long is itself a reason and a proof of their mutual affection. Besides, they have a mutual interest in having raised children to be men and women. If the wife is young, the marriage is a commitment of devotion to a man in need. Meeting this need is a challenge for her and a ground of gratitude from him. But he is not just the receiver: Men have a more public life than women, and for a man to be confined and devoted to his wife's limited circle is a rare privilege which accounts for some of her own devotion. These circular and mutually interdependent considerations make for a happy union where the casual eye might see only imbalances. Quite often, such a couple reside some distance away from the cattle byre, which is often associated with men. This would tend to support the observation that the older one grows, the more one returns to the status of children and women. But a more immediate reason is that elderly men are more associated with land and cultivation than they are with cattle. This is an extension of the adult occupation as opposed to that of youth. This does not mean that they are altogether divorced from cattle. They not only continue to supervise the care of cattle, they still control their ownership and the rights of alienation. But tensions with the sons become critical, and some sons take advantage of their elderly fathers by running off with the cattle to faraway cattle-camps and residences. These are the prodigal sons against whom fathers need the help of the chiefs. But in the Dinka way of thinking, the father's control can be exer cised on his bed, for eventually such sons meet with disaster. And if they manage to survive the curse, they eventually return.

Advise but Consent

To say that a son must always continue to show filial piety to his father is not to say that an aged father must continue to be the pivotal decision-maker in the affairs of the family. The take-over from the father by his son is supposed to begin long before it is fully effected by the father's death or senility. Most Dinka fathers prudently start training their sons for this responsibility from the time they ate initi- ated. Others resist to the bitter end. After a certain age, the Dinka recognize that an elder gets out of touch with the facts of changing life, but the whole system is geared toward his remaining in focus. The formula used for solving this riddle is what I have tried to express by the title: Advise but consent.

The essence of "Advise but consent" is that an elder must be consulted and heard even if not obeyed and sometimes openly opposed. An old man may not like being opposed, but he may be convinced—and he will always appreciate being heard. The wisdom of his accumulated knowledge often strikes a happy note if not always the truth. Whatever degree of truth he says bears the additional weight of his age and the deference due to him.

Correlative to being heard at home is the significance of his voice as a litigant or as a member of the Chiefs Court. Many a time a small boy or woman brings an old man, sometimes blind or near senility, into the Chiefs Court to pursue the case of a cow. The idea is not that he will plead the case best, but rather that he will be heard. Even when there is a backlog of important cases, his case will come first. Oftentimes, amidst cases of competitive importance, a Court member may be heard saying "O people! Listen to the word of the elder." And few Dinka, if any, would challenge such a plea and proceed to make their own claims or advocate the claim of a younger man. There is also a degree of bias in settling a case in favor of an elder. But should his claims be unreasonable, the Dinka do not hesitate to say so in the elder's face. Elders take this in good spirit, provided it is done with respect. Disrespect closes Dinka eyes to the truth just as respect opens them.

The Dinka, elders included, know the privileged position of an elder and do not want to abuse it. When an old man is dragged into Court, it is usually because the culprit has been too abusive, the Chief too indifferent, the Court too crowded, or the case too urgent. The status of an elder invokes the sense of protection in the Dinka. Should his need for the cow in dispute (to give one area of conflict) be so great that it touches on his security, a relative must provide for his need. If he has no kin able to do this, then the Chief must. Rather than induce an injustice, these considerations facilitate justice in the elder's favor.

Just as an elder has the priority of being heard as a litigant, he is heard as a member of the Court or Assembly. I recall how in the case of the succession of Chief Deng Majok, an old member of the Pajok lineage was arguing in favor of the rule that a Chief must be succeeded by his son if the boy is old enough. This elder traced the entire Pajok genealogy naming each Chief and the son who succeeded him. Since there was hardly any disagreement on the point and as his enumeration was unnecessarily lengthy, some voices were raised in protest. But an overwhelming chorus responded with

"Let the elder speak." He said, "I will not leave a single one out; I will mention them all; and let no one cut my mouth." Not a voice argued against him.

The attitude of the Dinka toward their elders is not altogether voluntary, for they believe that elders are next to the ancestors in their power to curse. This is believed deadly. So, even from the purely selfish point of view, deference for the aged is a must. The solution is to benefit from their wisdom, or at least make them feel important even if their ideas are not. This principle increases in its validity but decreases in its effectiveness the older a man becomes—until at last it is a matter of dutiful affection and tolerance to hear the elder. That is about at the point of senility. But this point is rarely reached, for few people live that long. If they do, they enjoy immense care without imposing anachronistic views. The principle of interdependence between the sexes and ages, as well as dedication to the interests of the elder and his reciprocal appreciation, interact to produce reasonable unity and harmony even when there is a certain degree of apathy—or perhaps (rarely) antipathy—for the elder.

Need and Reward

The special effort the Dinka make for their elders is part of the expectation expressed by the proverb: "It is what you have born that redeems you." Procreation implies gratitude on the child's part sanctioned by the father's cursing power. But filial obligation is not so much a matter of reciprocity and discharge of a debt as it is an implication of the parent-child relationship. Good care for one's aged parents is part of the ideals of the Dinka system. Thus it enhances the status of a child in society and is self-motivated, if not willed without strings.

The demands of the aged are not that cumbersome. Since the father is supposed to remain the head and in control of family resources until he dies, his needs are more emotional than material. They are reflected in the demand for continued control more than they are a demand for material benefits. We have already seen that adult sons acquire power piecemeal in the family and wield effective control by the time the father reaches old age. This is a delicate matter requiring utmost prudence. Except for fathers in public office who usually monopolize and remain in power, most fathers willingly involve their sons and even confer pivotal positions on them, provided the father's authority as the overall head with the veto vote is not undermined or threatened. This is only an aspect of the wider need to make him feel not only in control, but deservedly so. He must be consulted on every matter, listened to carefully, given his due praise if right, not in a cheap manner but in a discreet and dignified way. If wrong, he is to be opposed, but with respect and subordination. Filial care for the aged is therefore more a restraint on the son's self-assertiveness than it is a demand for positive aid.

From the viewpoint of interaction with the wider kin, the needs and the demands of the aged male call for special attention to the kinship obligations, usually in terms of honoring his share in bridewealth or blood wealth. Obligations that might normally be obstructed are honored with pleasure if owed to an elder. Otherwise, his indignation is dishonorable to his opponents and may even be spiritually fatal. But the Chief also provides a worldly sanction in reprimand, increased payment of appeasement, and nowadays criminal sanctions: remedies that are often executed without the delays of normal procedures.

There are, of course, old men whose material needs are more basic. A man may be poor and his son reasonably wealthy. One reason for this possibility is the reverse payment a husband receives from his relatives-in-law, the objective of which is to establish the young couple. A man may be left without enough cattle to marry sons off, his cattle may die, the son's cattle may multiply, and the son may continue to receive from the bridewealths of his sisters-in-law while the source of the father's income narrows. Such a material need by an elder in the eyes of the Dinka is most serious; the father of able men must not be in need. It is a disgrace that must be promptly remedied, if necessary by the Chief. If the sons themselves are unable to assist because of poverty, the Chief may call upon any other relative— even a distant one—to help. Otherwise, the Chief himself assumes responsibility for the security of the aged.

The more immediate need of an old man in terms of day-to-day care is provided by his wife who, even when senior, is usually younger than he is, sometimes young enough to be his daughter. There is also a tendency for very old men to be left to the care of children who provide them with such small needs as drinking water, fire, wattle, and sitting equipment. Blind people are nearly always led by children.

The material and emotional dependence of an aged mother on her children is greater than an aged father. The further away from her husband a woman gets, the more removed she is from her source of support and the greater is her dependence on her children. The logic of Dinka social relationships works in her favor in that the greater emotional ties with her children ensure their unfailing concern about her security. Of course, contact with the parents is impeded by the rules of avoidance with relatives-in-law, but the mother's care for the grandchildren permits closer ties with her children than are open to the father. The issue is much simpler: The mother is more in need than the father and children never let their mother down.

In compound families, the militant guard against jealousies restricts any partial demonstration of affection, including material aid. Some mothers may encourage gifts to their co-wives rather than to themselves. If the system functions well, the crisscrossing of gifts to stepmothers leaves all mothers provided for. But this is not always the case. Some children are sensitive to these ideals and abide, while others take care of their own mothers. A more intricate combination is sometimes resorted to, whereby sons provide for their mothers' needs in some discreet ways. Nor is discretion used only with mothers and stepmothers. Even if the father's needs are not pressing, the logic of his dominance—material and affectional—indicates that the child gives his earnings to him rather than to the mother; and, as usual, mothers may be the first to tell their sons to abide by custom.

Just as the Dinka family is a complex system that fosters the ideals of human relationships but recognizes factionalism, so meeting the needs of parents is a complex fusion of duty and will. And the relative positions of the father and mother in this are part of the father-mother complexes pulling and neutralizing each other by ascribing objective dominance to the one and affectional dominance to the other. With both usually meeting their due, tension and conflict are pacified, leaving no tearing effects on the children.

The Lonely Years

The central position of elders in Dinka society minimizes their alienation. The life expectancy is such that a man normally dies before the embarrassing age of senility. But some live to be very old and from rough estimates even pass 100 years. Those who live to be old are members of a diminishing age-group who have seen most of their age-mates go and many age-sets appear. With this demographic change is a more pervasive social change. Despite the backward-lookingness of the system, living individuals become obsolete even as they remain the pillars of social values and esteem.

It is characteristic of Dinka elders to appraise the present in terms of the good old days. They frequently express the view that contemporary generations have lost sight of their ancestral ideals; that the ancestors would be indignant if they returned; that even as they remain in their graves, ancestors keep a watch and must not be underestimated as out of sight. Then, as if the absence of the ancestors reduces their insight, elders not infrequently threaten to brief them about the horrors of change. So feared is the ancestors' reaction that the threat is nearly always directed against the group, and not the individual, and is aimed at correction.

The pain of change is gravest when it touches an individual elder. It is not uncommon to hear an old man mumbling to himself in aggravation because his authority is questioned by an insolent son, his kinship rights violated by a disconcerting relative, or for one reason or another, his sense of integrity, honor, and dignity hurt. Grumpy old men talk aloud to themselves, addressing their ancestors and God and complaining about the departure of their age-mates, leaving them alone and lonely among "children." They pray audibly to be taken to join their dead age-mates. But the zest for life and the dread of death never quite leave them. Some old men are known to shift their prayers quickly and, in the next breath, beg to live as guides to the young. Most of the loud prayers for death are really attempts to influence the conduct of the living.

Such old persons, if they are from modest backgrounds with no extra requirements of respect, run the risk of being viewed as idiots in whom people, especially children, find amusement. Although many other reasons account for the custom, it was perhaps in part to avoid the degrading consequences of senility in old age that Dinka Chiefs were not allowed to die naturally, but were buried alive when too old to function or when they thought themselves near death.

Chapter Nine: Death

Religion and the Agents of Life and Death

D inka notions of life, death, and immortality have already been introduced. Here, I elaborate on agents responsible for life and death, what is done to impede death, and what follows death—questions that are bound up with Dinka religion. The Dinka are intensely religious. In the view of some observers, they are by far the most religious people in the Sudan. Dinka religion is not an affair of the soul in a world yet to come; it is rooted in Dinka demands for a secure life in this world and continued participation after death.

In the mythical hierarchy, God is furthest removed; other supernatural spirits are nearer to man and are symbolized by emblems that are more commonly en countered. Nearest to man are the dead whose spiritual existence, proximity, and physkal presence are evidenced by their progeny. Their belief in this complex system of supra-natural divinities tends to blur the monotheistic picture of Dinka religion. Nevertheless, the Dinka believe that God is One and cannot conceive of Him as a plurality.

In their practical life, the Dinka are more concerned with their ancestors, clan spirits (*yieth*: singular, *yath*), and independent spirits (*jak*: singular, *jok*) than with God. There is an important ethical and functional dichotomy between these sets of spirits. The ancestors and clan spirits are partial and protective, while independent spirits are "free" and largely destructive. But the destructiveness of *jak* is not always negative: It may be a resort to a necessary evil to enforce, reinforce, or sanction a virtue. When an ancestor or a clan spirit is provoked, it is *jak* that they call upon to punish the wrongdoer. Thus fortune is the gift of *yieth*, and misfortune the function of *jak*, acting alone or in concert with yieth. Should a man recover from such affliction, it is because *yieth* have been reconciled and have instructed *jak* to withdraw the punishment. Or if the initiative was taken by *jak* themselves, it is *yieth* who have persuaded them to withdraw the harm.

Jak also act as the police of any person who successfully invokes the help of the spirits. An evil person takes the direct route and elicits the support of *jak* by propitiating them, a form of bribery which *jak* readily accept, being fundamentally corrupt. The proper procedure begins with the wronged person invoking his ancestors, *yieth*, or more directly, God who, after considering the rights and wrongs involved, passes judgment and calls upon a *jok* to execute the prescribed sentence. But *jak* do not act only when called upon. All the unexplained suffering is attributed to their malice, although the fatalistic and guilty disposition of man often traces the chain of causation to some human fault, if only error.

The fact that even the virtuous spirits may unjustifiably use the evil spirits means that there is much crisscrossing in which spirits protect or injure people with justification, or as their whims may dictate. A spirit may also be called upon to mediate between man and another good or evil spirit. Spirits usually have particular characteristics that manifest themselves through human experience. Some of them are known to inflict specific types of pain or illness. Some are known to have certain likes and dislikes. When they "fall upon" a man and possess him, they can be identified by the aberrational behavior they induce in him. The relationship between a clan and a particular spirit may be traced to a mythicized incident in the history of the clan. In these legends, the Dinka try to create a protective relationship out of a destructive experience. The evil and the good aspects of the experience are merged into a positive image, and the object and the subject of the experience are reconciled as relatives who must no longer antagonize one another, but must indeed assist each other.

Thus, in the story I told earlier of how Jok sacrificed his daughter Acai, we have a situation in which the river and its powers confronted the Dinka with a potential disaster. The Dinka resorted to the lesser, but also shocking, alternative of human sacrifice. The outcome was a veneration of Acai, who although a female, is now a greater power than individual ancestors. The river where she now resides became a holy place which must be revered. Every year offerings are made to her in the river. In respect for the river the women of the Pajok clan, agnates or wives, must not cross at night.

To mention other examples of how conflicting factors in a bad experience are reconciled by ritual and symbolism, a man who has suffered a serious, often disabling or deforming, disease may become recognized after the disease has passed as possessing an inheritable spiritual power to cure similar diseases; a man whose herds have been wiped out by a disease, rendering him poor, may similarly acquire a power of purifying cattle of like diseases. Not everyone of similar experience achieves the same results; it depends on the impact made upon the person and his community by the memory of his experience. In all cases the memory must be honored by appropriate rites, sacrifices, or dedication of animals or objects. Failure to do so may result in harm inflicted by the neglected power.

Even when the victim is not human, it may be honored. This is especially the case when man is responsible and the victim venerable.

The following song is about a strange bird which was believed to have spiritual powers and yet was killed by members of Bol Wiel's clan. The memory of the bird was eventually consecrated by the clan as their protective spirit.

> *People of Bol, people of Bol,*
> *I am not a bird of your world*
> *I am a bird of the world above.*
> *It was my father who sent me,*
> *"Go and visit the people of Great Bol*
> *Visit the people and return home."*

A personal story will demonstrate even more lucidly the significance of experience in Dinka religion and the attempt to win over destructive forces and reconcile virtue with evil. One day when I was very small, my mother went to see our distant agricultural fields. She was to stay overnight, and I was left under the care of my maternal cousin and a stepmother. Other women also shared the hut. That night a lion came. It managed to strip the door open and peep into the hut, waking all. I was too young to be afraid, and the women were too prudent to cry. There were men in the cattle byre some hundred yards away, but the women knew that it was dangerous to cry or show fear. Lions attack cowards or in self-defense.

So the women rattled the spears to indicate that they were armed and called themselves male names to fool the lion that they were men. This went on for a very long time with the lion wandering about and returning. Eventually, an Arab came traveling along the road singing loudly. When he was near, the lion jumped into the tall corn and *durra* stalks behind the hut. The women took advantage of this and shouted to the Arab to come to the door. When he was told the story, he looked around, saw nothing, and concluded that it must have been a flirtatious man. As he went away, the lion returned.

The episode continued until close to dawn when a crowd of hyenas, including their puppies, came making noises. Lions are known to fear hyenas when they are in a group. As their crowd advanced, the lion went away and the hyenas took over the village for the rest of the night. When my mother returned the next day and was told, she said without excitement: "No lion would enter my hut, and, even if he did, he would not harm anyone; our lineage and the lions have a pact not to harm each other." She then proceeded to tell the story of how her grandfather was eaten by a lion while sleeping alone in his cattle byre and how the people came the following morning to find a dreadful sight, bones, flesh, and fat scattered all over. Members of his immediate family ran into a nearby forest looking for the lion without crying for help. They found and killed the lion. Sometime later, as though settling a human feud, they underwent the rituals of atonement with the lionworld and agreed to be relatives who would never hurt one another. The pact has so far been observed.

It is because the Dinka desire to turn evil into virtue through symbolism that snakes, which among the Ngok bear the expression "bad things" (ka rac), often symbolize clan spirits to be respected and protected as relatives. I recall how my maternal grandfather used to pat dangerous snakes like puff adders with his bare hands, give them butter to lick, persuade them to get into containers, and then take them away from home, saying that he did so not to dismiss them but in fear of cattle treading on them or human beings inadvertently hurting them. One of my brothers, a Christian, once killed a puff adder near my mother's hut. The puff adder is an emblem of my maternal clan. That day, all my sisters became acutely ill with the same symptoms. It was suspected that the curse of the "murdered" snake had caused it; but to be sure, a diviner was employed. He recommended sacrifice and dedication of beasts to appease and reconcile the spirit of the snake. That done, the girls suddenly recovered.

In the story with which the following song is concerned, a sacred tree in the house of the Chief had begun to die and epidemics were attributed to this. The singers, mournful at the death of warriors, pray that the tree goes alone as there are no more men to spare:

Chief on whose branches the tribe hangs,
Do not vex yourself;
I remain, I have not displaced my heart
Even though I know the tree has destroyed us.
Branching tree, did you not go with earlier groups?
There are no other generations to spare.
I wish you would travel alone.
In your nature as a tree
Go, and a new forest will grow.

The significance of experience in Dinka religion has been the subject of study by Dr. Godfrey Lienhardt, who explains that among the Dinka the memory of an experience is projected from the mind of the remembering person to form an image that acts upon him from outside himself. What the Westerners call "memories" of experience and consider intrinsic and interior to the person remembering—and therefore modified as part of the remembering person—are seen by the Dinka as apart from the remembering person and a part of the external sources from which they originate. They continue to act upon him as did the sources themselves. Divine essence is attributed to this externalized image which is understood by the remembering person to be capable of making demands or of conferring benefits. The distinction between interiority and exteriority should not be exaggerated. Although the image takes an exterior appearance, the fact that it originates within the experiencing person and exerts influence on him shows a unity between him as the object and the image as the subject. Indeed, the identities of subject and object become so interfused that at a certain point it is no longer possible to distinguish, and to that extent, it becomes only a matter of labels. The West may speak of "conscience," the Dinka of spirit, but both are essentially the same. This brings Dinka religion and concepts of God to man, and makes them part of his essence even when they are seen apart.

Indeed, the unification of experience goes beyond the self to embrace the whole of man and his environment. Rocks, trees, snakes, animals, the wind, the weather, waves, foam, drums, everything man encounters in life has a spiritual significance. This is why spirits are symbolized by any of the natural phenomena familiar to the Dinka. Men become relatives to those objects and must not hurt them. Their suffering is that of men; and if wrongfully brought about, may result in human suffering and death. A relationship to an emblem may require that certain trees not be burnt, certain animals not be killed, certain bones not be broken, certain sacrificial beasts not be roasted on fire, certain fish not be killed, certain grass not be burnt—indeed, that an object not be treated in a way inconsistent with the respect due to spiritually inspired leaders. Otherwise evil follows.

Individual experiences reflect the power of lesser spirits; God is not limited to any particular feature of human experience, but embraces all aspects of life. He is therefore a unification of infinite diversities. Within his manifold and yet unified mythical system, the Dinka sometimes appear to equate individual divinities with God, an anomaly which recalls the Christian concept of the Trinity.

The Dinka believe that mankind as a totality is subject to the one supreme power of God, for it is God who creates and destroys all men. But at the same time they recognize that different peoples have different gods and, consequently, sometimes different religions. It is thus said that the Arab has his God, and the European his God; and in fact, each individual human being may have his God, although nearly always as a member of a family. The relationship between God as a totality and any individual man is sometimes expressed in such personal terms as "God of my father," or "God of my forefathers," or simply "my Grandfather" or "my Ancestor." I do not recall instances of God's being referred to as "God, my Father"; the relationship seems always to be qualified by "of my ...," which implies the pivotal role of ancestry and the need for at least one ascendant above the father. As a corollary to this segmentation of lesser spirits, it is understood that the exclusive Dinka divinities do not have much power over Arabs, Europeans, or to a lesser extent, educated Dinkas. Likewise, exclusive European and Arab gods do not have much power over the Dinka. The overall God, however, has the power over all.

Since in the order of the proximity to human experience this overall God is farther removed from man than are the smaller divinities and ancestors (also visualized as smaller creators), He is less conceivable to man, less possible to symbolize by natural phenomena, and less understood by man.

Spiritual Cause of Illness and Its Cure

The Dinka explain the ultimate source of illness and death through a myth mentioned earlier in which God is conceived as having once been physically connected with this world. Life was then perfect. According to various versions, the connection with God was severed owing to the fault of a woman: Offended, God withdrew from man and willed that the world be immersed in suffering and misery. A recurrent theme in Dinka religion is the imploring of God to restore the world's erstwhile unity and goodness, the need for which becomes manifest when man suffers the misfortunes of sickness and death:

> *Leave Your home in the sky and come to work in our homes,*
> *Make our country to become clean like the original home of*
> *Deng.*

Deng, bring the rope of the finch
That we may meet on one boundary,
We and the moon and divinity.
Give the rope of the finch
That we may meet on one boundary with the moon.

In the face of all the crushing hardships of life, the Dinka express their helpless bewilderment in God's failure to restore unity:

Great Deng is near, and some say "far."
O Divinity!
The Creator is near, and some say, "He has not reached us."
Do you not hear, O Divinity?
The black bull of the rain has been released from the moon's byre.
Do you not hear, O Divinity?

Superficially, there seems to be a contradiction between the unity of experience as discussed earlier and this myth of division. An explanation lies in the Dinka attempt to come to terms with their ignorance of the unknown, which is as much a reality in their world as the known. Man struggles to explore the whole truth, but when by reason or by experience he perceives the limitation of his understanding, he must ease his mind by finding some logic even when there is none. The Dinka achieve this by attributing full knowledge and control to a superior order and being they call *Nhialic* (God).

Dinka doubts are not altogether resolved, but the question "Does God exist?" is never posed among traditional Dinka. Those with Western thoughts now occasionally ask. The immediate answer is usually a counterquestion: "Who created you?" One might further argue that it is not enough to call the Creator "God," for Who and where is He? The Dinka solve this riddle by the myth of the disrupted world. God was with man but is forever gone. It is because of their awareness of the riddle and their need for an answer that the question of the riddle game: "Guess the gentlemen challenging but not confronting one another" (sky and earth), is combined with the myth of the divided universe. Through this awareness and blocking, the (traditional) Dinka do not ever specu late on the unknown, seemingly implying that it is unknowable.

Although separate from man, God is not entirely removed from his cognizance. Man sees evidence of Him in all the unexplained facts of nature. Among the unexplained phenomena that the Dinka associate with God are thunder and lightning and the rain, all of which are associated with divinity Deng, the closest divinity to God. Thunder is the angry voice of God, and lightning the glittering club with which He strikes the evils of this world. The solar system is known to them only to the extent that it guides them in telling time and following seasonal changes. The sun is understood to travel from the east to the west, returning to the east in the darkness of night. Man must not see it return; the vision of its return, which some occasionally claim to see, is an ominous revelation that would probably lead to death unless Divinity is propitiated. Since God supplements the parents with the creation of every child, the begetting of children is considered a gift of God; he may choose to have a woman barren, but might change his mind when appeased through appropriate rites.

On the human level, there are evil practices against life which may be individually acquired or inherited. Typical of these are the evil-eye *(peeth)* and evil-medicine *(wal)*, the power of which is contained in fetish bundles, distinguished from the curative herbs used by spiritually authorized people. *Wiel* is a more inclusive practice designed to bring death or some misfortune to whomever it is directed against. These various practices may be utilized by a genuine victim to punish a wrongdoer, but they are loathed and deplored because they are believed to victimize innocent people and to counteract righteousness. Many of these evil practices, especially the use of fetishes, are considered originally non-Dinka.

Legitimate power to bless or curse a deserving person is believed to be in every man by virtue of his being a human being. But this innate power varies according to the individual's status and the nature of the relationship it involves, particularly in terms of descent and age. A Dinka must therefore strive to maintain unity and harmony between himself and the world outside, reading cosmological discord into the mishaps of life. Harmony is best achieved by attuning one's demands and desires to the spirits and other fellowmen; it often fails. And when it does, the cause is immediately or eventually divined and harmony restored through such rites and ceremonies as may be recommended by the diviner.

The Dinka who is visited by illness or disaster explores the depths of his inner self or that of a close relative in the hope of finding the sin that has brought on the discord. Whenever a man suffers illness or injury he is likely to attribute it to the divinities. A woman who has committed adultery feels her guilt as physical pain that can be alleviated only if she confesses. A man who swears falsely sees his illness or that of a close relative as punishment for his unlawful deed, and the threat of death can be removed only by his confession followed by rites of purification. Ill-treatment of an elder or a kinsman may be understood as the immediate cause of bodily suffering. A man who has committed a secret murder bears the heavy responsibility for whatever deaths occur in his family. He also fears for his own life unless he confesses and the evil is removed by compensation of the deceased's kinsmen followed by ritual purification.

Even when the physical "cause" of an injury is clear as when a man falls from a tree and breaks his arm, the Dinka often look beyond the evasive notion of "accident" and attribute the mishap to a supernatural force. In searching for a sin that might have caused divine retaliation, the chances are that he will find some fault on his conscience or that of a relative.

It is postulated that spirits have the transcendent right to expect man to yield to their will. When their legitimate expectations are satisfied, they are supposed to rid man of evil; but spirits are not always predictable. It is not always possible to explain their harshness; nor is it always possible to appease them. Since the notion of an anthropomorphic God is revealed through the realities of Dinka experience, He may display a nature which is both harsh and gentle, both cruel and kind. The Dinka are occasionally forced to say "God has no heart," or "God's eyes have no tears," meaning that he lacks sympathy and understanding. Such extreme judgments are passed only when a disaster occurs for which man cannot find justification or when the divinities capriciously refuse to be reconciled by propitiation or to help in any situation where they are implored to do so. The Dinka are thus a submissive people, living in a world they cannot control and subject to the will of a God they do not fully understand.

A man's well-being is the concern of the whole family and the kinship group. "Illness, catch me that I may see my people" is a popular saying. When a person is sick, relatives and friends all cluster around him in prayer or in silent watch. When an animal is to be sacrificed, a group of people form a circle invoking spirits with one person speaking at a time and the rest repeating after him in chorus. Except for hymns, the Dinka have no standard prayers. Each person speaks in much the same way he would to persuade a human being, only more solemnly and ritualistically. The concern of the community for the patient is symbolized by the division of the sacrificial beast among a wide range of relatives and in accordance with strict rules descended from perpetuity. In Dinka metaphor, people are thus put together as the different parts of the bull are put together.

To punish a person, wrongly or justifiably, or to remove the effect of a wrong or curse, the Dinka use a great deal of symbolism which seems to be based on the premise that what is willed in fact occurs. A magician may make out of clay a human figure to symbolize the person he wants to punish and pierce his heart, his eyes, or whatever organ he wants to afflict. To cure, a chicken may be circled about the head, killed in sacrifice, and thrown away, symbolizing the disease that has gone with it. A cucumber may be invoked, cut into halves, and thrown into the air. The half that turns upside down is believed to contain the evil spell and is thrown away; the other half or both, if they fall the right way, are rubbed on the head and chest of the ill person and kept near him.

Symbolism can be even more dramatic. For instance, when I was in elementary school, the Governor General of the Sudan was visiting our area for an inter-tribal meeting of chiefs and administrators from the South and North. There were to be tribal dances, sports, and other displays. Prior to the celebrations, I was walking along the river when the Governor General, other British officials, my father, the headmaster of the school, and a crowd of followers came by. They called me. We had a brief conversation in which I answered such questions as "How are you?" and "What is your name?" English being novel among us, the group was impressed and word went around that the son of Chief Deng had spoken with the Governor General in English. In the school show that followed, I was the first in line for the march. I was given the role of stepping in front of the children to greet the Governor General with some English, Arabic, and Dinka verses. A few days after the celebrations, I came down with acute stomach trouble which the local medical assistant could not cure. My father had gone away. My uncle and mother employed a well-known diviner who was also a magician capable of bewitching and curing. I was reluctant as I had been introduced to Christianity, but I was desperate. The magician came. He was a bulky, short, and crooked-looking man who must have been born defective and was deformed in almost every way: Head, trunk, legs, and even his skin and eyes were bulging and red. He divined that my performance at the show had invited the envy of a magician who had cast into my stomach a black cobra. He asked for a black ram into which he would transfer the snake. The ram was brought, and the operation began. He anointed my lower belly with oil; the ram was held across my upper belly while the magician pressed his eyes on my lower belly and massaged it as though to squeeze the snake into the ram. The ram was in the meantime struggling but was kept in place by several people. After some time, the ram, without any obvious cause, bled from the nostrils and died. The magician said the snake had been transferred, that I might continue to ache over night, but that I would be fine the next day. He was right. I recovered the next day.

I do not know whether the practitioners realize that their technique will work on the patient even though they do not really do what they claim to do. I do believe that some realize their claims are deceptive, but hope that they might be lucky and the patient recover. There are, of course, those who cheat; but they are rare because in most cases a practitioner is paid on success and in any case, repeated failure leads' to loss of customers.

I had an experience with a man who must have been a borderline case. He claimed to remove tonsils and similar growths from children. He went about Dinkaland from Tuic to Ngok claiming great success. One day, he was called by the women to perform in our family. I chanced to be on vacation, and the combination of curiosity and the eagerness of a first-year law student to invoke the law against cheating made me interested in his operation. After he performed on the first child, producing from his mouth a bloodless piece of flesh which he claimed to have sucked out of the child's neck, I acted impressed, told him of my curiosity, and asked him whether it would be acceptable to him if I washed my hands and searched his mouth before his performing the next operation. He became furious, said he had never been so insulted, decided he would never perform in our family, and went and told my father of my insolence. My father laughed and let the matter go. I threatened the man with a criminal charge. My father told me to forget it.

Diviners do not always just cure; they compel a correction of a wrong without which there can be no cure. When a diviner discovers that a wrong committed by the sick person or his kinsman is the cause of the malady, he advises confession as a step toward readjustment. A diviner is called to diagnose the grounds for sickness or diabolical possession only when the patient has not been able to do so. Sometimes the power behind the illness may make itself manifest through the patient's mouth. The diviner may discover the grounds either by going into a trance-like condition or by inducing such a condition in the sufferer or his kin, or both. The Dinka display amazing psychological skills in such circumstances. Diviners induce almost multiple personalities in themselves to act the roles of the unseen powers and be the medium with human beings. They project their voices to appear as though coming from the walls in which some spirits are believed to reside. I have seen a diviner walk into a large flaming fire in a state of trance, singing hymns as she did and emerging completely unburned. Such demonstrations have great impact on a patient, as they enhance faith in the miraculous and healing powers of diviners.

Although I have presented the Dinka as dependent on supernatural forces for physical and mental well-being, this should not imply that their approach to well-being has no secular aspects. In addition to the use of herbs for medication, some experts are skilled in surgery and are capable of performing very delicate operations. Even where the approach is clearly religious, the interconnections of the psychic and the physical well-being are significant. Diseases or other evils are not always corrected successfully. In such a case, the Dinka find an easy answer in the refusal of divinities to be appeased, or perhaps in the failure of the diviner to have discovered the cause. It would seem that where the organic disease is one that psychological cure cannot affect, or where the patient's condition is too serious, the diviner's psychological cure is likely to be ineffective. In these cases, some diviners are honest enough to tell the relatives that they can do nothing and that the man must die.

Death and Eternity

Dinka religion does not promise a heaven to come and does not prepare the Dinka for death. Inevitable as death is, bravely as men will face it, and immortal as they will be made, death is an end beyond which Dinka vision is dim and the fear of the unknown is manifest.

The atmosphere of death in Dinka society is solemn and is seen as spiritually polluted. It invokes sorrow and awe in relatives and strangers alike. The Dinka do not seem to distinguish between a state of coma and actual death. People have been thought dead who regained consciousness later, some after being placed in the grave. But senior men and women are considered experts at death signals. Once the early symptoms of death are visible, children are sent away, women start to cry, men tie their bellies as they "cry inside" and get ready to dig the grave, and strangers withdraw or half-heartedly assist in the digging (usually left to relatives), for the very idea of death is so frightening and so demoralizing that it is feared as contagious.

Before the body stiffens, it is made to lie on the right side, the limbs are bent and the hands are placed under the head as in a sleeping position. If a dead person is not discovered until the body rigidifies, the muscles must be cut and the limbs bent into their appropriate positions. The body is then washed, anointed with oil, and placed on a skin awaiting burial. A male head of the family is buried in the cattle-hearth in front of the cattle byre. Otherwise, a male is buried near the hut on the right side and a female on the left. The grave itself is a round hole about 3 feet in diameter and about 5 feet deep. A special space is prepared at the bottom. When it is time to place the body in the grave, women wail their loudest and become frantic. The body is laid facing east where the sun rises and life begins. The grave is then filled in; the gourds which the dead person had used during his illness are broken on the grave; and the skin on which his body had lain before burial is thrown away.

Dinka attitude to death is astonishingly divergent from their ideals of human relations. People who have lost a person are seen as impure and spiritually dangerous; they should therefore avoid others and be avoided. There is a taboo against their drinking or eating in the home of outsiders or mixing with others on social occasions. For the relatives of a dead person to violate this norm is to invite disaster. I witnessed one such alleged violation. We were fishing with a crowd of people. The river was so low and so full of fish that some fish were visible on the surface. I had a barbed spear. At one point, one of my sisters snatched it from me to spear a large fish that was on the surface. A woman who was using a special women's trap jumped on the fish and met with the spear. It fell on her breast and penetrated through her ribs, just missing the heart. She tried to pull it out, but although a barbed spear penetrates easily, it is impossible to pull out because the barbs point to the opposite direction and catch the flesh. Groaning in pain and despair, she fell. She was carried ashore with the spear in her chest. It was then removed through a delicate operation. We ran in fear of retaliation. I was particularly frightened as the wound had been inflicted with my spear. Our father's absence from the tribe also aggravated our fears. We were later informed that the victim was a woman whose bridewealth was paid by our father for a distant relative. She was therefore our "wife," and there was no possibility of a feud. Rights of atonement were performed on the spot. Later that evening, I heard her fate explained in terms of her violation of the taboo against social intercourse between relatives of a dead person and the outside world. A member of her family had just died, and she should not have appeared in public-far less should she have been fishing, which for the Dinka is a sport.

Appearance tells if a person is in mourning. Women cut their leather skirts, leave them unoiled, dry, and untrimmed with beads. They cover their bodies with dirt and ashes. Both men and women must not wear any ornaments or bleach their hair reddish or blond as is generally done by young men and women. Mourning lasts for months and sometimes a year, at the end of which people are ceremonially cleansed and then resume normal life.

Despite the continued association between the dead and the living, they are paradoxically separated by a ritual known as *cuol* performed three or four days after death, depending on the sex of the dead person. Given the subordination of women, it is interesting that the period is longer in their favor. By this ritual, a ram and a chicken are sacrificed in the middle of the night some distance away from the homesteads. The chicken and the ram are not eaten by the relatives although they may be picked up and eaten by nonrelatives. The idea is symbolically to combat the disease that killed the man and send it away from the living.

The principles and practices applicable to the death of a Chief are different from those applicable to an ordinary person. I have already pointed out the importance of the Chief to the spiritual and physical welfare of his society and how traditionally he was not supposed to wait until he was actually dead before burial, but would request that he be buried alive at the brink of death. This is a debated point among anthropologists. Some believe it was merely mythological and not real. Real or mythological, the Dinka believe that the custom pertained until it was prohibited by the British. My great-grandfather was allegedly buried this way. According to the story he remarked: "Watch my eyes" as the grave was being filled in. Since the grave of a Chief is constructed in such a way as to leave a dirt-free space for his underground shelter, the possibility is not so absurd as it might sound. It is said that my grandfather, too, would have been buried alive had not government agents seen to it that this did not happen.

The rationale of the custom is not clear. The Dinka argue that in the Chief's life lies his spiritual might and protection of the tribe. For him to die is to diminish this power. There would be nothing to pass on and disaster would ensue. The idea then is to lay him in the grave where he lives in his people's memory and his successor takes over what is still vital and unweakened by death. As I have already indicated, a possible consideration might have been that the Chief should not be too ill and senile to rule. Given their privileged position and the protection they receive from the tribe, chiefs usually live much longer than the average person. The dangers of old age were therefore apropos. Whatever the justification of burial alive, whether it in fact occurred or is only believed, it gives a different dimension to death.

The funeral rites of a Dinka Chief are complex and confusing. They weld grief for the disaster of the Chief's death with hope in the inauguration of a new Chief together with the myth that the Chief, although dead, continues to live. The Dinka do not speak of burying their Chief but of "elevating his throne" (*thooc*), an expression supported by the manner in which his grave is prepared. People should not decry a Chief's death. Many, especially members of his family, do cry; but they are reprimanded, and quietness soon returns before the ceremonies of burial are completed. Only on the death of a Chief do the Dinka have singing, drumming, and dancing as part of funeral rites. The songs then sung are the ordinary songs of war and dance, although there are hymns specialized to death and inauguration. The following is used in funerals and inaugurations. It was first sung on the installation of Kwoldit of Pajok about thirteen generations ago in circumstances that did not include burial: When the younger generation was leading the migration of the Ngok to the area they now occupy, Kiec, the ageset of Kwoldit, asked the Chief (Dongbek) to give them his son Kwoldit to lead them as their Chief after they had lost their leader, Kwoldit's brother. Dongbek first refused, arguing that Kwoldit was too hot-tempered.

He suggested another of his sons. When the age-set persistently begged for Kwoldit, Dongbek, after counseling his son, gave him his sacred spears and allowed him to lead the tribe. Kiec carried Kwoldit on a bed all the way to their new settlement singing:

"Kiec, this is a flash of light to light your way."
Dongbek thus honored us with Kwol.
"May Kwol give you the life of my father, Bulabek."
In the land of Bulabek
We had no Chief to guide our way;
No Chief to arrange our words.
Kiec, this is a flash of light to brighten your way.

Some of the inauguration hymns are so ancient that their meaning is hardly obvious. While I was able to make some sense out of the following lines, there were many others I could not understand and unfortunately could not verify at the time of writing:

Some people say, "Our Chief is no longer Chief."
The man who has no Chief may leave the country,
I am taking my Chief into the sun;
He is taking himself to the spirits above,
He remains our Chief.
Father, son of our Chief,
You are going to the spirits in the sky;
You will sit in the center of the spirits above.

As these hymns are sung, the grave is dug after the heir-apparent marks the ground. Digging is shared by the tribe, singing and working in subtribal groupings. Although there are special subtribes who are ritually qualified to inaugurate, all take part. The actual gravedigging, however, is avoided by those who install. All participate in the rites of installation, but the pivotal subtribes, especially representatives of the commoners among them, must be involved or else the installation is incomplete.

The grave of a Chief is arranged differently from that of an ordinary man. After digging in the normal way, the hole is narrowed and dug farther. A bed is made for the body to lie on, and a shelter built on top of it to prevent dirt from touching the body, which rests on a skin and is covered with another skin.

When the preparation of the grave is completed, all cluster around the grave waiting for the body to be lowered. As this is done, they raise their hands to the sky and utter the word nguooth. This is the word a person uses when he strikes in war or in a hunt; it is also used by warriors or any male-gathering when the Chief is sprinkling its members with blessed water. Its use implies success in overcoming, or a wish to overcome, an adversary. In the context of burial, it is a prayer for the blessing of God, a wishful demonstration of success in having obtained it, and an assertion that, despite the tragedy, the country will hold its front against its foes. Looking away from the grave, everyone helps shovel in the dirt, except those who are ritually prohibited. As soon as the body is placed in the grave, even before it is filled in, people rush over to the heir, grab him, and raise him toward the sky. When the burial and the installation are completed, a fast is observed throughout the tribe. No one cooks or eats: Mothers must not feed their babies; cows must not suckle their young; cattle must not graze; and fires must be extinguished. The next day, the slaughtering of beasts begins and days of mourning-feasts follow. The burial of a Chief is a very expensive ritual. Many bulls and oxen are slaughtered throughout the tribe. Some are primarily for propritiating the dead Chief and appeasing the gods; others are for meat in the festivities of installing the new Chief.

As the successor to the Chief is usually known in advance, he is supposed to learn from his father a secret hymn that only the Chief should know to sing in times of his greatest need for divine help. I tape-recorded the hymn from one of the younger sons of Chief Kwol who had heard his father sing it and had memorized it. The death of our father, Deng Majok, brought into chieftainship a generation that had not been adequately instructed in traditions. His successor did not know the hymn. This was a major disqualification that had to be remedied secretly. So I taped the song for the successor to memorize at night, using earphones. The hymn is in such ancient Dinka that it is hardly intelligible. After listening over and over again and asking for explanations, sometimes in vain, I was able to come out with some sense for translation. Some of the names mentioned here are of spirits or possibly of ancestors dating beyond the traceable genealogy of the ruling family which goes back at least 15 known generations. The Dinka do not worry about the coherence of the hymn. Its antiquity gives it a deep logic that does not require understanding. The uncle who discussed it with us said that it is as important as the Chief's sacred spears. Being a secret hymn, I translate it with hesitation; but I do so to save it, as oral literature is now threatened with extinction.

Arumjok, you are the maternal uncle of all peoples;
Jok, I have sent you to the bottom of the sun;
From ancient times, I am stroked into peace, saved from
* dangers I do not see.*
What about the word of Kwol, son of Bulabek?
Do not dodge me; our country will collapse,
Let another word right the wrongs of the past;
Hold the eel by the eyes and hand it to Kwol.
Even if it should destroy the Chief
There is an embracing light:
There is the sun,
There is the moon,
There is the rock,

There is Deng.
Garang, original father
Bring peace,
And you Duper,
And you Ajwol,
And you Kur,
And you Ayiik,
I do not know a cyclone Chief
Like the son of God and mother.
I come to appease my Lord,
He is spoken.
Father, do not cry,
Ours is a country maintained by the Nile
And by Ayiik.
A chief is sent,
The Great Chief Ayueldit,
The children of Garang will always mourn.

The period of mourning a Chief is not one year as is normally the case; it is only one month, after which people shave and return to normal life. Then the inheritance of property and wives takes place.

In the death of a commoner, problems of inheritance do not generally arise because a man distributes much of what he has acquired in his lifetime to his wives and children. On his deathbed a senior man is expected to express his last will about how the family is to be run and what basic reorganizations or changes need be made. This is called *cien*. This is so revered that relatives will cluster around a dying man to catch every word. Sometimes a man is told that he is dying and pressured into speaking. Some people die without making their wills either because of the nature and circumstances of their death, or because they simply refuse to talk. Usually, confusion follows; and the more important the person, the greater the confusion. Even when a person makes his declaration, confusion arises over how his words are to be construed. Interpretations and inferences are made by interested persons to suit their own ends. Those present at death are examined and re-examined in the hope of finding favorable information or objective truth.

Whatever the inheritance and the complications, the youngest son of the mother and the oldest son of the father receive special privileges. The youngest child of the mother, when she dies, inherits the property that has accrued to her. Thus, the special cattle allotted to her from her own daughters' bridewealths go from her to him and continue to accrue in further marriages. The eldest son of the father, if of age, is the executor of his father. He must see to it that his last instructions are carried out and his affairs settled and must also help remedy whatever injustice his father's lifetime distribution has caused some sons. It is the eldest son who inherits the fields of his father and the homestead where the shrines of their clan spirits and ancestors are built and major sacrifices are made. He also inherits objects of ritual significance, the heirlooms of the family. And, as we have seen, the eldest son, through primogeniture, succeeds to any administrative or ritual position his father might have held. All in all, the eldest son "steps into the shoes" of his father. This is no mere linguistic coincidence, for among the Dinka he in fact inherits his father's shoes.

Thus, the Dinka and their religion view death as a dreadful end mitigated only by the immortality of procreation. When a person dies, it is often said that "God brought him and God has taken him" and the incident of death is sometimes described as "outrunning away." But in no way is it felt that a dead man may be gone to a better life. It is life in this world that really matters to the Dinka; it is for it that they pray to God and other spirits and it is in it that the dead continue even as they exist somewhere else. People mourn a dead man, but turn to his children and say, "Your father is not dead since he has borne you" and "Now that you have remained, strengthen your hearts to maintain your father's name." Similarities that might not have been vocal before begin to appear and be voiced: "Exactly like his father"; "That is what his father would have done"; "Spoken like his father"; "In him lives his father." Such opinions not only keep his memory alive but moreover encourage the sons to live up to that memory. Criticisms of dissimilarities may be, and are, voiced but only to correct and direct the child in the path of ideal immortality through procreation, the Dinka's only saving grace from the doom of death.

Chapter Ten: Change

History

T he Dinka were in contact with the Arabs long before colonialism, but the hatred caused by slave raids prevented profitable acculturation and disposed the Dinka to reject Arab ways. However, the leading families of the Ngok Dinka and the Baggara Arabs were always in diplomatic contact as friendly neighbors and a certain amount of cross-cultural influence, especially in the political field, took place. Later, the Turko-Egyptian administration collected taxes, permitted slavery and other forms of exploitation, but otherwise left the "natives" alone. It was never a model for change nor was it interested in change, yet it activated the assimilation of Arab political ideas and practices. But while each culture assimilated what it adopted, each remained distinct and separate. Although the Dinka fought against the Turko-Egyptian rule, the Mahdist regime which succeeded it brought more terror to the Dinka.

With the advent of British rule, these peoples were lumped together into the loose unity of the modern state, but were otherwise kept separate and independent. The Dinka, having just emerged from a world "spoiled" by the ravaging raids of Arab slavers, had memories to keep and grievances to nurse. As children, we were still frightened into silence by such exclamations as "There come the camels." The expectation was that Arabs would capture and put the captives in their large skins on the sides of their camels. The foreign ruler did not hesitate to use this for his policies of divide and rule. But he saw to it that conflicts did not occur, and contact without conflict began to erode away the fears and memories of slave raids, facilitating cross-cultural adoption. For various reasons, which the British considered protection for the South but which did not exclude divisive ness to help them rule, the Southern Policy was enunciated and brought a halt to cross-cultural influence. The South was to develop along its indigenous lines at a very slow pace. With their pride and ethnocentrism, the Dinka were a potential threat to the ruler; and the more they stayed in the abyss of backwardness the better. The notion of the "Noble Savage" added to the policy of preservation. Although some Southern tribes were judged harmless and were receiving more modern benefits than others, the whole of the South remained a museum of nature. Speculations on its long-term political future ranged from affiliation with Uganda to total independence. Initially, unity with the North was not contemplated.

Then events outpaced the British planning. Their foresight had not included the fact that Egypt and the North might favor the Sudan's unity with Egypt or total independence. British control and interest in the Sudan was going rapidly downhill, and the British administrators in the Sudan began to see it. They feared that they would soon be compelled to leave the South culturally different, numerically subordinate, and economically backward. So, they decided that only by accelerated development along Arab lines would the Southerner be able to hold his ground should he find himself united with the Arab in an independent Sudan. As this became imminent, it became clearer to the British that if past injustice against the South was to be corrected, it had to be done then or never. The policy of separate development was abandoned in 1947 and replaced by an integrative policy. This new policy, it would seem, was not aimed at unification; it was based on predicted unity. Under the policy, contact with the North was intensified while the British supervised and saw to it that no one was, or felt, dominated by the other. The Southerner came closer to the Northerner in their common struggle to rid their country of colonial domination. The average Dinka could go into the city and become more exposed to Arab influence; prior to that, going into Arabland brought great shame on a Dinka and invited insult songs. Although migration to the North is still considered not noble, it has become more accepted and is sometimes honored in songs as an economic venture by the traditionally disadvantaged factions of the society.

What followed happened so fast that it is impossible to know who made what decision. The prediction came true: The British left, and on January 1, 1956 the Sudan became independent under a unitary system. Southerners believe they are the price Britain paid for its interests with the Arabs, especially over the Suez Canal; but it is also possible that nationalism swept the British off their ground so that they were unable to protect the South. Still, Southerners welcomed independence on the Northern promise that the Southerners' call for federation would be given due consideration. That consideration has not yet produced much.

The results of Sudanization in 1955 made some Southern soldiers skeptical of the Northern promise. They mutinied that year, igniting the civil war that has continued to this day. At first the Dinka were not involved, and the cry in the North was that the Dinka were "the good guys." They missed the point. The Dinka considered the revolt premature and ill planned. For years many Southerners worked within the system, calling for a federal status within the unified Sudan, but to no avail. Quite the contrary, postcolonial trends witnessed the policy of cultural integration through the Arabization and Islamization of the South. Cross-cultural contacts, which the British had impeded, were not only permitted but were encouraged. Governments changed. Democracy came and went. It was no longer possible for the Southerner even to be heard. Many more joined the language of violence; the Dinka joined the civil war; and the *Anyanya*, the army of the Southern revolt, was formed.

Hundreds of thousands of refugees fled into the neighboring countries of the Congo, Uganda, Kenya, Ethiopia, and the Central African Republic. For a people who had grown up thinking of themselves and their country as second to none, the indignities of refugee life brought lamentation and a feeling of isolation. The fol lowing song was composed by a young Dinka in exile.

> *Gentlemen grind their grain in the land of the Congo;[17]*
> *The Dongolawi, [18] the Arab has remained at home*
> *He has remained in our land.*
> *We left our herds tethered in the cattle-camps*
> *And followed Deng Nhial.*
> *Gentlemen beg in the land of the Congo;*
> *The Dongolawi, the Arab has remained at home*
> *We left our herds tethered in the cattle-camps*
> *And followed Deng Nhial.*
> *When we reached the land of the Congo,*
> *The Congo said, "Dinkas are matata."*
> *I turned and asked Ngor Maker,*
> *"What does 'matata' mean?"*
> *Ngor Maker answered,*
> *"He says we are bad."*
> *My heart became spoiled*

---

17 Normally, women grind the grain.

18 A tribe in the Northern Sudan, here used to refer to all Northerners.

In the land of the Congo, my heart was spoiled
And I thought of Anger, the daughter of Wol Ayalbyor,
I wish I could find her to see her.

In the following song, they express determination to fight for their cause, however long it may take.

William, [19] feud is the task of man;
O Deng Nhial, The feud, the feud,
The feud of the Southerners with the Northerners;
Our feud will never end.
The army of Deng Nhial and Morwell
Are called the Anyanya.
In Bahr-el-Ghazal; we shall shoot
With the Northerners—The Arabs;
We shall cut through Bahr-el-Ghazal,
We shall revenge the evils of the past;
And if we succeed in our vengeance
We shall be praised by God;
Bless us
We are the Dinka.
O, feud, O, feud.

Ironically, as the South becomes an insecure battlefield, Southerners run to the North for refuge from death. The conditions of these "refugees" are just as awful as those of refugees elsewhere. Indeed, they are often worse because they do not have the status, and therefore the sympathy, given refugees in a foreign land. A form of integration *has* to result from this unhappy interaction. But to a Southerner, a cycle has been completed: The civil war recalls the days of the

---

19 Deng Nhial, a Dinka leader who was later assassinated.

slave raids. Although the outcome is unknown, the attitude of the Southerner against forced Northern assimilation is one of rejection. Many Southerners have learned, or are learning Arabic, and many have become, or are becoming Muslims; yet, many have abandoned or are abandoning Islam, more in political protest than because of loss of faith in Islam. Many who had acquired Arab-Muslim names now prefer their once abandoned Dinka names. From the inception of the Southern political movement against the North, Muslims have been among the prominent leaders of the South; and there are Muslims among the extremists in the military wing of the Southern

The response of the Southerners to the Government's declaration of autonomy. In the forefront waving at the crowd is Sayed Joseph Garang, himself a Southerner and Minister of the newly formed Ministry of Southern Affairs. (Courtesy of the Sudan Government)

movement, the *Anyanya*. After all, pioneering enemies of Western domination in Africa were the more Westernized Africans, educated mostly in the West. And although the analogy may not be entirely accurate or acceptable, it should give some warning and guidance.

Northerners have begun to sense this. The most recent step in the direction of compromise was taken nearly two years ago when the present military regime announced autonomy for the South. A Ministry for Southern Affairs has been set up under a Southern minister which may initiate, but mostly coordinates, programs and activities relating to the South. A number of senior appointments and transfers to the South have also been made. Some refugees have returned to the promised autonomy. But the implementation of autonomy has by and large not occurred, partly because most officials do not know precisely what it means: So far, its details have not been spelled out. The Government called for the involvement of the Southerners and offered amnesty to those in exile who would join hands with the Government, help shape the theory of autonomy, and participate in its implementation. The Government has also postulated Socialism for the whole country and the Minister for Southern Affairs has stated that development along Socialist lines is a necessary condition to autonomy in the South. Although it has expressed the intention to construct even if the rebels destroy, the developmental plans are frustrated by the Government's demand for peace before development and the rebels' demand for a political settlement before they will halt the insurrection. While Southerners first welcomed the declaration of autonomy with enthusiasm and voiced their support of the Government, the passage of time without any significant change has brought back skepticism and suspicion. Voices have begun to murmur criticism inside the country, and the Southern militants abroad are ambivalently rejoicing at the seeming failure of the North to implement its promise of autonomy within unity which was beginning to divide the South. All these factors interacted on both sides and threw the country back into polarization and extremism. Violence between the rebels and the Government has returned and intensified. The Southern problem continues to be the greatest problem facing the Sudan, frustrating its economy and claiming the lives of what some say now exceeds a million.

Authority

The historical perspective of Dinka acculturation indicates that the development and the survival of Dinka culture has largely depended on the prevailing political conditions in their country. Consequently, the aspects of the culture selected for planned change and the degree of the change depended on the government interests to be served. The first modern impact was that of the British. Their primary interest was to establish order after the years of disruption, corruption, and disintegration under the Turko-Egyptian and the Mahdist regimes. This had to be done at minimum cost, with minimum personnel, and along traditional lines. Where chiefs did not cooperate with the system or where a cooperative chief was not competent enough, a Government chief was appointed independently of the traditional leadership. Among the Ngok, this was not the case; however, segmental authority was replaced by a concentration of power in the Chief. Sectional chiefs were left with administrative functions, but were stripped of their judicial and executive functions. The clan-heads, once elders in charge of their clans, were appointed by the Chief to collect taxes: a change that reduced their status and necessitated the selection of people most able to discharge the new function. Clan-heads are now the target of many unrestrained insult songs. Traditional authorities, including junior chiefs at all levels, continue to exercise a semblance of powers, and most matters that reach the higher authorities will have passed through them. This is only time-consuming because in most cases the opinion of the Paramount Chief is sought in the end.

The initial importance of chieftainship among the Ngok, the precolonial reception of Arab political practices with their emphasis on social stratification, and the emphasis on the Chief by various colonial and national regimes all combine to make the Ngok power structure even more hierarchical than that of other Dinka tribes and, indeed, of other Southern Chiefs. The effect of a traditional and yet innovating leadership has made the Ngok political system adaptable to, and effective under, the new conditions. The Ngok have abandoned "living by the arm" and have become responsible to the authority of their Chief even more than the other Dinka tribes. However, chieftainship is losing its religious sanctity, and reverence for the Chief as a secular-spiritual leader is now being replaced by fear of secular punishment. Secular punishment is as much open to criticism as it is feared. The Chief and elders continue to practice persuasion, but to a comparatively lesser degree than they did in traditional society.

Where a chief is appointed whose ancestry has no traditional leadership, which has happened in many Dinka tribes, the secular conception of modern authority and therefore the lack of traditional reverence due to a spiritual leader become even more conspicuous. A degree of divine authority usually evolves in consequence of such an appointment. And relatives of the appointee may even claim some ancestral distinction through songs to give traditional validity to their newly acquired authority. The alienation of the people from modern-day secular authority may be illustrated with the fact that the Dinka refer to the government, even that represented by the Chief, as *jur* ("foreigner").

In Court, the Chief and elders are often tempted to consider themselves umpires applying the law and may quickly resort to coercion. The Dinka reaction towards police, flogging, and imprisonment is one of indignation; and to have undergone these indignities is considered a cause for complaint. Until recently a policeman sent to seize a man's cow was likely to get hit on the head with a club. Today, governmental punishment has become accepted as leaving no recourse: something to be feared and yet to be faced with courage and without the usual shame of a convict in Western society—unless the offense is shameful by traditional criteria. The following song is quoted at length because it covers the various aspects of power transformation in Dinka society. Deng, the singer, had not responded to a court summons. A policeman was sent to summon him or seize his personality-ox to compel his appearance. On appearance, he was committed to jail, awaiting trial. Later, the case was settled in his favor.

I went and sat under the Court tree
Of all the people gathered
Not a single man said, "Good morning."
So I sat with a twisted heart.
A court order was written without words
Even my name was not asked.
Why do all people get angry when I state my case?
Do they mean to put me in jail?
"Yes, the wrong is grave
You will go to jail."
Is that why people threaten me with anger?
Only jail?
And what now that I will go myself
Without being driven by the police?
Even if there is a crocodile which catches people in jail,
I will go inside.
I am locked in jail, I am locked in jail
And sweat pains our eyes;
Sweat pains our eyes, while bats stink.

Son of Pakir clan, Mayon de Dan de Kir, [20]
The government is not like your ancient times:
Do not get angry when the police send you,
You will be beaten, and the face of shame will be big,
Shame for the beating of an elder
While young men [21] *watch him beaten;*
A victim of law cannot be replaced.
Let's tie our hearts, father of Nyannuer,
And go to grow cotton.
When we were driven to the field
I walked, tilting my head like a canoe;
I almost refused to work.
The pain of initiation came back to my heart; [22]
I almost did what I almost did.
Mijang de Dak, [23] *do not walk behind us;*
Do not follow us with the whip;
People do not enslave one another
When they are both initiated.
The vileness of the Arab police
A Dinka must not join
To kill his own people.
The Arab ordered me about a dead donkey;
He ordered me to sit in the sun
And said, "Guard the donkey from the birds."
All the birds that fly in the sky
Can I guard against?
I cannot, Micar Aroljok,

---

20 A prisoner who is an elder.

21 Including the singer.

22 He supposedly won respect by initiation.

23 A Dinka policeman.

All the birds that fly
A man cannot guard against.
Because of an animal which will not be eaten or skinned
I sat all day in a burning sun.
Then my case goes to court.
I do not vex myself when a case goes to court
But for this case
If the Creator was near,
I would call my father
I would call my father, the son of Deng
To come and attend my case;
Each man comes with his father
And I venture the courts alone,
I am lonely in my pleading
Lonely as though I never had a father.

Because judicial functions concentrate on the Paramount Chief, his Court becomes so overburdened that the police sometimes attempt to prevent litigation in his house, contrary to the traditional practice whereby a chief hears cases anywhere, any place, any time. People are sometimes beaten away from the Chief's house in pursuance of this policy. In some cases the Chief orders the police to permit the people to enter. In any case, police restraint may reduce the crowd, but hardly ever stops the litigation. One sees people spread over the area outside the Chief's enclosure waiting in twos and threes for the Chief's appearance. When he appears, it is often time for the police to prevent too much encroachment on him, especially as the Chief should be left to walk some distance ahead of his followers, a courtesy normally observed, but sometimes enforced.

Despite the effectiveness of the new judicial system there are still remnants of self-help which are sometimes justifiable by the circumstances and are so much a part of Dinka practice as to be considered customary. For instance, in order to coerce a person into settlement, the plaintiff seizes the offender's cow. Again, to hasten compensation in sexual violation of male rights over women, the relatives of the woman seize many of the best of the wrongdoer's cattle. After the settlement, they are given their due and the rest of the cattle are returned.

One by-product of the secularization of authority and control and the waning of divine authority has been the intensification of power conflicts and the rise of modern political opposition. Ambitious members of the Chiefly lineages, and even commoners who come into conflict with the Chief, in one way or another begin to agitate. Complaints have been raised to national authorities which were calculated to discredit the Chief in one way or another but have invariably failed to do so.

The traditional importance of chieftainship among the Dinka, the degree to which the power of the Chief has been enhanced by foreign influence, the increasing secularization of power, and the tendency toward autocracy have in large measure been affected by the personalities of the Chiefs involved. Ngok leadership has been increasingly reinforced by a long line of great men whose selective adaptability at the crossroad of cultures has augmented their status, won them great influence and saved their people from alien destruction or from negative repercussions of imprudent resistance. Records speak of all modern Ngok Chiefs, Arob de Biong, Kwol d'Arob, and Deng Majok de Kwol as "Arabized Chiefs," an erroneous assessment of their complex process of adoption, adaptation, and assimilation of what they thought best in the ways of the Arabs without foregoing what was best in their own Dinka ways; compromising the egalitarianism of the Dinka only in degree. They inherited a position going back 15 known generations and probably longer, each one building on the legacy of his father and sometimes bequeathing an even greater legacy of office to his successor. Upon succeeding his father in 1905 Kwol rode to El Obeid to secure the protection of the newly established Anglo-Egyptian Condominium against Arab slave-raiders for whom the South was still a hunting ground. It was not until the 1930s that many Dinka tribes in the South were fully brought under the protection of the new regime. Deng Majok, who succeeded his father successfully maintained his own autonomy and that of his tribe against the ambitions of Arab Chiefs with whom he shared the Council. The Paramount Chief of the Arabs, Baba Nimr, whose jurisdiction was extended by this unity over other tribes of the Arabs and the Nuba, could not understand why the Ngok were not included in his jurisdiction; Deng Majok was indignant that the issue was even raised. He argued that the Ngok as a Dinka tribe should not be assimilated into the authority of an Arab Chief. Both the colonial

Chief Kwol Arob with some policemen near the first car to come into Ngok territory in the early thirties. Chief Kwol succeeded his father, Chief Arob, in 1905 and ruled until his death in 1945. (Photo by K. D. D. Henderson)

and the post-colonial administrations consistently endorsed his position, and he remained responsible only to the Central Government
authorities in judicial and administrative matters.

The crisis worsened when in 1965 some Arab Chiefs entered into
an alliance with the Ngok and elected Deng Majok as the President
of the Missiriya Council. These developments strained the relations
of the Ngok and Arab ruling families, with corresponding strains in
the relations of their respective peoples. These strains contributed to
the Baggara-Dinka hostilities of 1965 in which thousands of people
on both sides lost their lives and in which Deng Majok played a
unique role to reestablish and maintain order. Although he called
in security forces, he saw to it that they did not usurp tribal power
and turn their presence into a military occupation and a means to
subordinate the chiefs as has been the case in the South since the
rebellion began. These difficulties left him politically anxious but
unscathed; indeed, they enhanced his already monumental image and
made him a heroic leader even to his opponents within the Ngok
people and to the tribes farther South. As a Southern leader put it,
"Deng Majok achieved absolute equality with Arab Chiefs and was
accepted by the Central Government as such. For a Southerner, this
is a miracle." That he was equal but a Southerner made him an even
more prominent leader than his neighboring Northern counterparts.

The death of Deng Majok in August, 1969, was an unparalleled
calamity for the Ngok and other Dinkas farther South. Ngokland
suddenly ceased to be a secure bridge between the South and the
North. The fear, despair and surrender to the concept of a spoiled
world that came with Deng Majok's death left no doubt in anybody's
mind that a great leader and protector was dead.

We eyewitnessed this crucial phase in the history of the Ngok
when we took his body from Cairo where he had died. Although
it was a rainy season, it had not rained for some days so that with
some leveling, the airstrip at Abyei could be used. The Government

arranged for our flight from Khartoum in a Sudan Air Force plane. On landing at Abyei, we found a reign of terror. Deng Majok's absence had created a vacuum which the security forces were filling with arrests, torture, and murder. Just two nights before our arrival, they had shot and killed a brother of the Chief—a highly regarded and well-established person whom they had suspected of cooperation with the rebels. Among the many who had been tortured was the Chief's own sister because one of her sons was a rebel. Her arms had been rendered paralyzed. The Dinka, including their Chiefs and especially their educated, were under careful scrutiny and in constant apprehension. Abdalla Monyyak de Deng, the son whom Chief Deng had left in charge and who was to succeed him, had tried to fill his father's position; but he had neither the legal authority nor as yet the personal influence to be effective. He was even suspected of

Chief Deng Majok Kwol (fourth from left) with Arab chiefs in 1954 in an intertribal celebration in honor of Michael Tibbs, the last British District Commissioner in the area. In 1945 Chief Deng succeeded his father, Kwol Arob, as Paramount Chief. (Photo by Michael Tibbs)

Chief Deng Majok Kwol eight days before he died in August 1969,
following a prolonged illness.

cooperation with the rebels by the security forces. He succeeded his father without delusions about the size of the shoes he was inheriting. As though his father were to blame, he remarked with tears in his eyes, "We were all praying for him to return and bring an end to all this. Instead, he returns a corpse at the moment of our greatest need."

We were quickly told that we would have to be guarded by tribal warriors throughout our stay. But we accepted the officer's invitation to stay with him as our house was crowded with mourners. The first night we did not sleep. The officer's house was full of whispering people coming in and going out. Something ghastly was in the making. The next morning, we decided to be open with the officer. We told him of our apprehensions throughout the night; that we had been informed of our uncle's death; that he had been very dear to us, but that we were shouldering our father's burden as Chief and must keep the interest of the whole society in mind whatever our personal loss or grief. We, therefore, wanted to know his version of our uncle's death, the security situation as a whole, and how we could help reestablish some understanding to promote the return of order and save Dinka lives. He told us how he had killed our uncle in the conviction that he was a rebel, how the night before he had had our house and the whole of Abyei patrolled because he had had information that local rebel leaders (our cousins) might come to the funeral, and how he had given orders that they be shot on the spot even if on the mourning-mat. He also told us of the authorities' suspicions against Abdalla and expressed doubts as to whether he would be confirmed by the central authorities as Chief. His confidence in us —precarious as it remained—and the abominable situation were perhaps best symbolized by a small gesture. As he was stepping out of the house to play volleyball with his troops, he threw a pistol at me, saying, "In this area, you need it!" It must be remembered that our own people wanted to guard us against them.

We found the suspicions against Abdalla to be utterly unfounded.

We tried to dispel them and labored day and night for a month to restore some workable relationship among the security forces, the Chiefs, and the people. We even tried to pacify the local rebels. But the task was incredible. Complex factors interplayed. Since most educated Ngok are from the leading families, some of the local rebels were relatives of the Chiefs and this gave the Arabs notions of a grand alliance be tween peaceful and rebellious authorities. Those interested in dismantling the established leadership of the tribe made use of this coincidence. The foundation of tribal order was being undermined in many ways, both subtle and overt. The commanding officer rewarded his informants with cattle seized from suspected people. Distortion, and even fabrication of evidence became a means of wealth and vindication. I cite only one example: We agreed with the officer that we should meet with the tribe to discuss the security situation. He decided not to attend in order to allow for maximum freedom. In the meeting, one of our younger brothers advised against encouraging such freedom, arguing that the lives of those who might criticize the officer could not be guaranteed. He said he spoke because he did not care what happened to him. He also said that he was determined to raise the case of his murdered uncle with central authorities and expressed the hope that we would help by talking to the authorities about that and the whole security situation. The next morning we were having breakfast with the officer just before we were scheduled to go to the final meeting, which he was to attend and in which we were to unite all factions to work together for the security of the area. The officer was called into his office next to the breakfast room. He emerged later and sat as though nothing had happened. But while he was still in his office, an anxious boy had come running to tell us that our brother had been arrested and was now with the officer. Dinka feared that being taken to military quarters instead of the police station is tantamount to death—or at least to severe torture. We sat, anxiously considering whether to wait for the officer's return or to intrude. Our brother was very temperamental and was quite likely to do something foolish. We were relieved still not to have heard a shot when the officer returned. We asked him what the matter was. He tried to dismiss the question and would say nothing except that our brother was under arrest at the police station. He would not tell us what our brother had done. We told him we would not go to the meeting without at least knowing the grounds for our brother's arrest. After a heated discussion, the officer told us: He had had our previous meeting infiltrated, and according to his intelligence reports, our brother had publicly threatened rebellion and had requested us to send arms from the United States of America. He was a threat not only to the security of Abyei but to the whole Sudan. According to the officer, the allegation had been made by four of his secret police and must be assumed accurate. To prove otherwise, he said, would create an unacceptable situation in which his men would be guilty. Naturally, we were implicated. But so absurd was the allegation and without evidence for a prima facie case that we insisted on our brother's release or else we would abandon any work for security and report to the central authorities. Our brother was released, "But only for your sake." We left an improved but so precarious a situation that as we were leaving, people came running to tell us that seven of the educated who had assisted us in our work for peace had been arrested on suspicion of cooperation with the rebels. The officer had informed us the night before that they were to be arrested on purely disciplinary grounds, that they would be released shortly, and that we were not to worry about their safety. We tried to calm down a frightened people as we left to plead their case with the central authorities.

During our journey, two soldiers who were being transferred from Abyei requested to talk to my brother and myself in confidence. They told us that they had witnessed the shooting of our uncle. He was taken in the night, arm-bound from prison, to his house near Abyei.

His house was searched, and some medicines were found. These were thought to have been for the rebels, but our uncle explained that he had bought them in Khartoum for his chronically sick relative. The officer called him a liar, threatening him with a pistol. Our uncle said, "Kill me. The Government will ask for me. In any case, you will account to God for my death." Angered by this, the officer placed his pistol on our uncle's head and triggered several shots. He then commanded his soldiers to shoot into the air and later reported that the man had attempted to run and had been shot dead. The soldiers who spoke to us expressed great admiration for the man's courage, indignation at the officer's conduct, and willingness to testify—which they claimed military discipline forbade them to volunteer except in an inquiry. They told us a lot about the atrocities they had been forced to commit and how our arrival brought some relief ro themselves by minimizing further arrests and encouraging better treatment for those already in jail.

We met with the central authorities in the district, the province, and the capital to explain the situation, to present our findings, and to suggest measures for alleviating the crisis. Even before our contacts were completed, reports came from Abyei that seven people had been shot to death. They were others than those arrested in our presence.

The reaction of the central authorities was encouraging. In accordance with our recommendations, administrative and judicial powers were conferred on the Chief Elect, Abdalla Deng; the officer and his men were transferred from Abyei, an older and more experienced, although less educated, officer was sent to Abyei with a new regiment; and a commission of inquiry was set up to investigate the situation. Its report was never made public, but the officer was eventually exonerated.

It was then necessary for my brother and me to return to work abroad. Each day, we spent hours brooding over the catastrophe that had befallen our people. We recalled our childhood: the peace we had enjoyed, the games we had played, and the men of pride and dignity we had seen as we grew. We contrasted all that with what we had found on our return: children who had not seemed to understand the meaning of games, faces full of anguish and despair, people in subjection and subdued into indignities we had never imagined possible for a Dinka. As we listened to the Dinka songs I had tape recorded, we could still hear the dignity of the past in their voices, in the melody, and in the rhythm; but our minds and souls wandered into the devastations of change. Some songs expressed our grief and brought back memories of the life and the untimely death of that great and greatly needed man—our father, Chief Deng Majok. It was and remains uniquely moving to hear the voices of these uneducated men and women expressing their tragedy so simply, intelligently, humanly—even seeing its international dimensions:

> *How does the spoiling of the world come about?*
> *Our land is closed in a prison cell*
> *The Arabs have spoiled our land*
> *Spoiled our land with bearded guns*
> *Guns which thunder and then even sound beautiful*
> *Like the ancient drums with which buffaloes were charmed*
> *Until their horns were caught.*
> *Is the black color of skin such a thing*
> *That the Government should draw its guns?*
> *The police pacing up and down,*
> *Gunners causing dust to rise,*
> *Cowards surrendering to the arm?*
> *A country we took back from foreigners*
> *A country for which we fought together*
> *And the English left our country.*
> *Only to be attacked with bren-guns*
> *What a cieng!*

O what a cieng!
South of Deng, son of Kwol,
What the Government is doing
Is not a good thing;
Waving their bren-guns
Like frying sesame seeds,
Counting their shells
Then saying, "One million shots
Have not subdued the Ngok."
Our case is in Court
Our case is in the Court with the people above
The Court is convened between the clouds:
Acai of Pajok
And the Flesh of our flesh
Have a cause.
They seated the Court
And called God
Then said, "God, why are you doing this?
Don't you see what has become of the black skin?"
The Court adjourned,
Our maternal aunt came
With the divinities from above
And the Flesh,
They sat on the ground of the sons of Biong.
A storm of dust rose in Abyei
Cyclones reached the sky:
Family of Arob de Biong, nothing can be done
Who knows what the Government is pregnant with?
Even if they flatten us with bearded guns
Whom can we wish for?
This we shall always consider ...

While we pondered and speculated, encouraging news came from home. Abdalla was making notable progress in fitting into the shoes of our father and was becoming an effective representative and protector of his people. Being only twenty-seven years old and a successor to a uniquely great leader, he had not sufficiently developed his influence and control over the tribe and the security forces. Things were soon to worsen. The new officer was becoming even more atrocious than his predecessor. He arrested, tortured, and killed people whom the Chief thought innocent. He sought to confiscate and sell the cattle of all those he suspected. This he could not do legally without the authorization of the Chief's Court. That was often refused. Tensions and open conflicts developed between our brother and the new officer. Sometime at the end of August or the beginning of September 1970, the officer and his men attacked the cattle-camp of the Tuic Dinka from Bahr-el-Ghazal who were then grazing their cattle in Ngok territory. The attack was based on a false report that it was the camp of the rebel army, the *Anyanya*. They killed four men and took away about one hundred and fifty cows from the camp. The officer came to Abdalla's Court requesting sale authorization. Abdalla refused and told him that he would report the killing of the innocent men and the capture of their cattle to the central authorities and that he would request the Province Security Committee to visit Abyei and witness the activities of the security forces. As the two clashed publicly, the officer told Abdalla that he would never return to his Court for authorization and that if any violence occurred in Abyei, the first bullet he would fire would hit Abdalla. On September 17, 1970, as Abdalla, two brothers and three uncles were strolling on the fringes of the village, they were assassinated. Eyewitnesses identified the assassins as the officer and six of his men. The official report of the officer to the Province Headquarters and to Khartoum was that they had been killed by the rebels—a familiar alternative to being shot as a rebel. Under the title "How Six Sudanese Died: A Family

Massacre," Michael Wolfers wrote of these murders in the London Times of October 19, 1970. An excerpt from his article follows:

Mr. Joseph Garang, the Minister in the Sudanese revolutionary government responsible for Southern Sudan, has just announced a year's extension of the amnesty for Southerners who have been engaged in secessionist activity but wish to return to their own country.

The growth of their confidence may be seriously damaged by some new information on the recent killing of six members of one of the leading Dinka families (one of the main tribes in the Sudan) including the Paramount Chief of the Ngok Dinka. The critical point about these events is that they take place in a family which has traditionally favored cooperation between North and South, and at Abyei, in Kordofan Province, not on the southern borders of the country, but in the borderland between Northerners and Southerners. Kordofan is geographically in the North, but the Ngok Dinka are a part of the complex of Southern tribes.

The Government has since formed an investigation committee which highly impressed the Dinka with the way in which it conducted its work. Witnesses were made to take oath on the Sacred Chiefly Spears. This is done only in the most serious cases. Perjury after such oath is believed deadly. Thirty-six witnesses testified and all but one - who had already been implicated in the assassination plot - gave evidence against the officer and his men. As I write, the committee's report has not been made public. That it was formed several months after the incident and that no arrests have yet been made despite abundant evidence and the fact that the committee was authorized to arrest are serious shortcomings in a highly appreciated Government intervention.

Shocking as the foregoing incidents are, they do not fully reflect the magnitude of what prevails over the South. The diplomacy of Ngok Chiefs has kept their area more secure despite the present extension of the war into the area. As a military officer said during the investigations of the 1969 Abyei incidents, "When a man is transferred from the South to Abyei, we think he is going home to peace." The Abyei incidents only indicate what things must be farther South. But Abdalla's death marks a definite turning point in the history of Ngok leadership. Never before has the authority of a Ngok Chief been so questioned by, far less subject to, such a junior official. Indeed, when it is said that Ngok Chiefs have sought cooperation with various governments, it must be understood that they did so in consideration of government protection against outside subjection. The instrument of the modern state, which once reinforced the institution of chieftaincy, added to its traditional prominence, and made it pivotal, is now the instrument threatening its continuity. Chieftaincy being the backbone of Dinka society, its extinction also threatens the existence of that society. This is in essence the major crisis of the Ngok. They are a people molded to depend on individual leaders and on an institution that now exists only in doubtful form.

The image of the Paramount Chief of the Ngok is such that what happened to Abdalla and his relatives is the most demoralizing thing that could possibly have happened. The appropriate remedy should have been prompt, public, stringent measures against those responsible. That was not done. Exodus to Northern towns increased and continues. But some people refuse to leave. In determined and proud attachment to their country, they prefer to wait and see, perhaps to die and lie in the graves of the ancestral land they love.

Education

I have already pointed out that the British were not interested in developing the Dinka until much later in their half-century of colonial rule. Among the Ngok, the first school was opened in 1943; and the first government school for the Bahr el-Ghazal Dinka was opened in Tonj in 1944. All over Dinkaland, there was a great deal of controversy about sending children to school. Most people disapproved of the idea. Even in our family circles, there was much criticism of our father for sending all his sons to school, leaving no one to look after the cattle. Girls' education was especially abhorred because that implied turning them into town women, immoral and unsuited for marriage. Indeed, although our family pioneered Ngok male education, education for girls is still virtually nonexistent. The negative attitude toward the education of females is illustrated by the following song. The singer's husband, Mawir Rian (a Tuic Chief), wanted to send her only daughter to school. She opposed him; and after taking her complaint to the late Cyer Deng, "a man of God," her request was granted.

> *I am trailing Great Cyer to Anyaar,*
> *He said: "We shall meet early in the morning."*
> *I am a person tortured; I am a person bullied*
> *To give birth to a child now to be given away to the jur.*
> *O our tribe, where shall I go?*
> *O Dinka, where shall I go?*
> *An only child like the stand of a drum,*
> *How can I hear of her in town?*
> *I heard the name "Acol" and could not sleep.*
> *I could not sleep, but what could I do?*
> *Son of Rian, O Son of Rian,*
> *If you have left her for me,*

We shall be on good terms;
Mawir Ajingker, if you have left her for me,
We shall be on good terms.

Slowly the significance of the school began to make itself felt. Many school activities were geared toward changing the attitude of the people. Children were encouraged to influence their age-mates and elders to accept education. Social occasions were held in which parents and tribal leaders gathered to see children display their new skills and demonstrate their social responsibility and reverence for their parents, chiefs, and elders. Trips were organized around the tribe to bring the idea home to the people. Singing was particularly popular as a means of reaching the people and motivating the children. This is an example:

I am a small boy
But I am the gentleman of the future;
I am the goodness of my land
And I will do my best;
Teach me that my mind
May accept the word of learning;
Learning is power
Learning is the best.

So miraculous was writing and reading in the eyes of the Dinka that children with this accomplishment had cause to brag. The most popular game in our house, where there was always a crowd of tribesmen, was to ask some of us to write on the ground or on paper while others were escorted away and watched to make sure that they did not see what was written. To come back and read it accurately elicited loud laughter of astonishment. Whenever we read letters coming to our father from other chiefs about intertribal cases, it was common for the bearers to listen with utmost interest, then remark, "Exactly, that was what the Chief told his clerk to write," and an impressed audience would burst into admiring laughter. Nevertheless, acceptance of education was gradual. Some children were hard to keep in school. Many escaped and went home, only to be returned to school and ridiculed in song. Sometimes threats of imprisonment were used against uncooperative parents. It was not until people began to see the fruits of education that resistance began to wane. For the Dinka, who see a linkage between knowledge and mysticism, writing and reading came to assume a respected place in their system of values as sources of wisdom.

The initial motivation behind government education of the Dinka was to raise sons of Chiefs educated to take over the leadership of their tribes in accordance with the tradition-modernization principles of indirect rule. Tonj Primary School, to which we proceeded after Abyei, was almost exclusively for sons of Chiefs. It was governed by the principles of English public schools mixed with those of Dinka tribal life and crowned with an almost military-type discipline. The headmaster was an Englishman who had served in the British army. To keep up Dinka devotion to cattle as well as to provide the school with milk, parents sent cows to their sons in this school.

Residence was in "villages," each with four dormitories. Both the dormitories and the villages were headed by "chiefs" who formed a hierarchy, on top of which was the overall assembly of chiefs. The chiefs also sat in courts of various levels in the hierarchy, including a court of appeal. There were "policemen" to assist the chiefs. As these lines from a school song indicate, children were made to look forward to leadership:

> *Tonj school-boys*
> *Sons of Chiefs*
> *You will be the kings of the Sudan.*

Despite the attempt to bridge education and tradition, things fell apart and a source of conflict emerged from the kind of knowledge education entailed. While schoolchildren were disposed to respect parents, Chiefs, and elders, the content of the modernization which they often called upon their chiefs to introduce and accelerate undermined tradition. Because classroom education was not oriented to the child's living conditions, modern knowledge and wisdom eventually became acknowledged by both the traditionalists and the educated to be apart from traditional knowledge and wisdom. Education thus caused personal and cultural disparity in that only a few people obtained it and what they obtained was not oriented to the pre-existing culture. The cultures and the people who represented them were thus seen as opponents, with the educated attempting to change tradition and the traditionalists to maintain it. The traditionalists consider the educated their "eyes" because of their enlightenment in modern terms; but their radicalism is feared. It is not uncommon for the traditionalists to say with reference to the educated "We have not given birth," meaning that the educated do not reflect them. Their songs of self-exaltation weld a great deal of tradition with their novel pride: They see themselves as members of a special age-set, see their pens as spears, represent their tribes in competition, and regard their educational venture as a warfare. Yet, they express revolution.

> *Our junior age-set in white gathers at Abyei*
> *The school is convened*
> *The age-set in white knows the words of wisdom.*
> *I shall turn the land upside down,*
> *I shall change the land*
> *I am a small boy but I am a man;*
> *I sit in the place where words flow ...*
> *Our mothers all cry,*

"Our children have gone astray
The land has remained without a child."
Mother, I do not blame you
There is nothing you know,
Nothing you know
The word of the world is creeping on:
It comes crossing the lands beyond
In Khartoum, a child is born and goes.
Am I to appease you only with a cow
What about the white clothes and my pen?

Conflict with the chiefs is particularly striking. Opposition against the chiefs is usually spearheaded by the educated, who are felt to be the best equipped to confront the chiefs in front of national authorities. As I have already indicated, such attempts fail. The educated often find life in the tribe intolerable. Almost all the educated Ngok who had held jobs in Ngokland: schoolteachers, executive officers, agricultural officers, and accountants, left because of conflict with the chiefs. Many, of course, leave because of alienation from tribal life and culture—and primarily because education does not prepare them for any occupation in the tribe. While it is geared toward white-collar jobs, it is often insufficient to obtain them. Those who go on to higher levels of education get good jobs, but most have only elementary education; so they get low, sometimes demeaning, jobs; yet others remain unemployed under humiliating conditions.

The dimension of educational crises is now beyond interrelationships within the tribe. A generation has emerged which was educated along Western-Christian [British] lines and divergent from the Muslim-Arab culture. Post-colonial policies tried to reverse this trend, partly through education: hoping eventually to produce a pro-Arab Muslim mold in the South. They nationalized Southern schools to minimize Western-Christian influence and promote the

Muslim-Arab cause. But the politically enlightened Southerner had become too identified with Christianity and Western culture and too opposed to being molded into the image of the Arab. The alienation of this class from the tribes, their migration into the city, their confrontation with new obstacles on the national level, the attempt to subject them to Northern values and to deny them the leadership for which education had prepared them all combine to make them feel subjected by a new colonial master—the Arab. They turn into dissidents who must fight with arms or politics. They choose both. The civil war in turn frustrates education. Schools have been closed or are barely kept open. It was a sad sight to find our school at Abyei turned into barracks occupied by the security forces, for whom schoolboys had to become servants. What is more, Northern teachers fear to work in the South because of insecurity, and Southern teachers are even more frightened. After finding the condition our Abyei school was in, we tried to persuade Ngok Dinka teachers who were in the North to return home and take charge of the school. The Province Education Officer accepted our request to transfer them there if they were willing. All refused. They told instances of harassment, imprisonment, and torture by the security forces at Abyei. Some of them had narrowly escaped death. They would not return until the security problem was resolved. With a civil war, how could that be?

Thus, although Chiefs are part of a traditional institution and represent tradition whatever their education, the rise of younger literate chiefs and the intensification of the conflict with the Arabs is narrowing the gulf between the leaders of tradition and those of modernity, and uniting the Dinka against what they see as the common enemy. As a Dinka who had been arrested for accommodating rebels overnight and whom we had just rescued from the commanding officer put it: "What does the Arab think; are these not our own children?"

Religion

Turning back the clock by seventeen years, I recall an incident in my life which epitomizes disruptive religious change among the Dinka. It was an autumn evening. The moon was shining brightly in a cloudless sky. My father was sitting with tribal leaders and tribesmen in the open air, informally discussing tribal affairs. My brothers and I had just returned from a year's absence in school. "Father," one of us ventured to say, "we want our heads to be sprinkled with the water of God." That is to say, we wanted to be baptized. The company suddenly fell into deep silence. Our request was not purely out of filial piety; his consent was a legal requirement. There was nothing really new in the idea, for we had been learning Christianity for the last five years at school. As it was, Father held us close to him, rubbed our heads, and asked with a smiling face, "Why do you want your heads to be sprinkled with the water of God?" This gave us an opportunity to demonstrate our newly acquired wisdom. The Heaven which awaited Christians and the Hell to which non-believers were destined provided the theme of our argument. To this he had a further question: "Assuming that the Christians were to go to the home of God and the rest to the home of fire, would you be pleased to enjoy the home of God while the rest of the family burned in fire?" Father's question was natural, since in Dinka religion people face God not only as individuals but also as a family. Had we not considered our father's point in school? We had—or rather our religious instructors had. We were taught that on the day of "Major Judgment" everyone must stand for himself and only for himself. Thus, we hastened to dispel our father's skepticism. There was an awkward silence during which we could hear our cattle lowing in the byre and our women talking in their enclosure. Then, with a sign of resignation he consented, "Nothing is altogether bad; you will at least spare my cattle from many marriages." But in fact many people were to object to our conversion because they could not understand how we, being sons of the Chief, could be monogamous. That was the spiritual breaking point.

With few exceptions religion and education went hand in hand. Since education in the South was offered mostly by Christian missionaries, the educated became Christians and their denomination depended on that of the mission to which they went. Or, if the school was a government one, the children still became Christians, but their denomination was determined by the sphere of influence into which they fell. For the British allocated "spheres of influence," preferring that the South be left to the Christian missionaries to "civilize the natives."

The conflict between tradition and modernity was most striking in the religious field because children were conditioned to regard traditional religion as primitive, irreligious, and sinful. Snakes, which symbolize divinities among the Dinka, suddenly represented evil among the converts and were killed to the awe of the traditionalists who expected evil in consequence. The cures of a medicine man or the rituals of divination were refused and condemned by the converts who had been conditioned by the teachers and the missionaries. The meat of a sacrificial beast was regarded as spiritually polluted and avoided. Consistent with the use of social occasions for engineering change, the attitude these factors represented was displayed to the traditionalists not only in the family but also in songs, plays, and other school activities. The following are examples of songs that were aimed at promoting Christian education and degrading traditional religion.

> *The book is with those who write the word*
> *The ancient wisdom of the sons of Adam*
> *It's known to us the age-set in white who write.*
> *The lost child will not be looked for;*

The captured cow will not be looked for;
If they are looked for, it is we who write,
And what I write, the bearer will not read,
It will be seen only by him who reads,
Never by a pagan priest;
I do not honor your priests. I am a big man.

The Bishop is the one who orders the land;
Father, Master, the land is threatened by pagans;
The land is threatened by Mohammedans.
Oh what will the Christians do?
I turn this way and it is the evil spirit
And Mohammedans are facing East
They are facing where the sun comes from.
What misfortune, what misfortune?
We are tangled with bad spirits,
Some have evil eyes,
Some inflict evil spells,
Some are evil men who disturb the innocent,
The land is confused;
The land has its head in a knot.

Since the policy was minimum interference with tradition while "civilizing" through Christianity, the spiritual impact by far outweighed the economic advantages of modernization. In fact, there was hardly any material disposition in missionary education. The convert embraced Christianity but remained Dinka materially, usually drifting back into traditional economy. The missionaries in fact aimed at testing out spiritualism in the new world and wanted to avoid making the Dinka "materialistic."

One traditional Dinka institution that Protestant and Catholic missionaries alike used most effectively was singing. Every mass, low or high, and every occasion of prayer, night or day, was marked with singing. English and Latin hymns were translated, and many new ones were composed in Dinka, and by the Dinka, in the traditional music and rhythm. This way, Christianity was able to reach the depths of Dinka sentiments; and even when a man did not pray in the Western sense nor understand a Latin hymn, he simply prayed with the sound of music and song. Religious songs were even used as marching songs in competition between schools, sometimes on tribal bases.

The missionaries did a lot more than instill their faith in the Dinka. We have seen how education in the South was left to them for a long time. They provided health services even to remote areas of Dinkaland. They showed the Dinka movies of their land and played recorded Dinka songs for them. As the Dinka migrated to the North, the missionaries established for them and other Southerners social and literary clubs which, while introducing them to Christianity if they were not Christians already, helped them adjust to the social and economic environments of the towns.

Islam on the other hand was kept out of Dinkaland (by the British) until the policies of integration were enunciated. So, until after independence, Islamic proselytizing was not organized. Personal financial aid by interested Muslim merchants or religious personalities often did the job of conversion very well. Groups of Dinka tribesmen were convened, briefly persuaded to accept Islam, hurriedly clothed with jallabia and turbans (the national dress of the North), and ceremonially made to pronounce the words "There is no God but the God: I witness that Muhammad is the Prophet of God." Money poured in from excited merchants, the status of the converts suddenly rose to the envy of uncommitted pagans, and "submission" broadened. New Islamic names were assumed by the converts, and sometimes the father's pagan name was changed, even without his knowledge, just to complete the appearance of Islamization.

There was a brief period in which this process of Islamization was especially superficial. It even led to double conversion: For young boys leaving mission schools as Christians went to the North and found the fascinations of a second alien religion. Many tribesmen, literate and illiterate, were sent to Azhar (the classic Islamic institution in Cairo), not knowing a word of Arabic. They returned on holidays in glamorous suits out of harmony with their village atmosphere; they came with names impossible for the Dinka to pronounce; they went into the cattle market and upset the Dinka economy; in the streets they spoke, not only with an Egyptian accent, but in the classical Arabic of books, to the amazement and amusement of passersby. The people referred to them as "Sons of Egypt." Nevertheless, the display was often brief; many drifted back into traditional life. True, they no longer believed much in Dinka religion and culturally could never again fit perfectly into Dinka life; but Islam also lost, although its traces remained.

In order to foster national unity, the post-colonial educational system has been styled to encourage Arabic and Islam in the South. Mosques and Koranic and Muslim-oriented schools sprang up in the South. It became fashionable for chiefs and some government officials to convert and win the good will of local Arab officials and merchants. At the same time, the Government was eroding Christian influence in the South. In 1957 it nationalized all missionary schools in the South, but left those in the North undisturbed. It was thought that the missionaries in the South had encouraged and patronized the Southerners' growing hostilities toward the North. The Missionary Societies Act of 1962 not only virtually brought to a standstill the missionaries' religious activities, but also prohibited them from rendering social and health services. With the worsening of the political situation in the South, the Government decided in March 1964 to expel all foreign missionaries and priests from the South.

Inside the Catholic Cathedral at Wau. (Courtesy of the Sudan Government)

Religious experience in the South, past and present, shows that the South is deemed a vacuum to be filled by whomever is in power, whether his motive is separation or unification of the country. Today, the position of the Islamic mission is both advantageous and disadvantageous. Its influence is enhanced by the fact that it has been Government-sponsored. Yet, it is confronted with rising tensions of separatism in the South. Christianity also is losing and gaining. It is losing because of the Government's opposition to its foreign origin and agents. On the other hand, it has been swept into the country's internal political conflicts and is regarded as a "Southern" institution. Southerners have tended, and still tend, to look on Christian missionaries as guardians and allies. The present regime is not interested in promoting any religion, Islam included. Perhaps in this passive if not negative attitude it will find a common ground with the South. But this is only an aspect of a pervading conflict. The Government is Arab Nationalist. That identification is a sore point for the South, which cannot be soothed by the Government's religious indifference.

Health

Whether modern health services were provided by the missionaries or by the Government, the Dinka at first saw them as repugnant to spiritual wellbeing, and any medication or treatment was feared and rejected. Even during epidemics of diseases like smallpox, adults would literally run away from vaccina tion in sharp contrast to the bravery demanded by tradition. Sometimes they had to be forced by law to accept it. The diviners themselves encouraged rejection of modern medicine and saw any attempt to combine their efforts with those of missionaries or health officers as provocation against the spirits and the ancestors. Despite these initial reactions, the usefulness of modern medicine was admitted once the results were obvious. This, combined with the Dinka high regard for any genuinely religious man, whatever his religion, won the Christian mission aries much respect as "Men of God" and "healers." The missionaries, too, used this conception to make people join Christianity and abide by Christian dictates. But this strategy rarely, if ever, succeeded with uneducated Dinka. For them, to derive benefit from the spiritual powers of a person does not necessarily mean adopting his divinities or ancestral spirits—the entities that give real meaning to their concept of religion. Spiritual innovations, rather than causing doubt over their own religion, merely widened the gulf between the educated and the traditionalists. The former were dismissed in matters of religion as people who had been alienated and for whom their traditional elders were apologists in front of traditional powers. But the Dinka increasingly drew a distinction between modern medicine and imported religion, accepting the former and rejecting the latter. In the course of time, even the diviners began to profess that both they and the practitioners of modern medicine were interested in well-being, and it is now common for a diviner, as a curer, to administer his traditional cure and then advise his patient to see a doctor as well in order to achieve maximum effectiveness.

The problem for the Dinka today is not superstitious dependence on magico-religious concepts, but lack of modern medical facilities. To give one example, the Ngok are at least 200 miles from the nearest hospital. For six months the roads are closed. Even when opened, they are bad. The Ngok must therefore depend on a small, ill-equipped dispensary run by a medical assistant and dressers. Diseases that are easy to cure still kill.

The health problems of Dinka society are now made even more critical by the civil war. It has caused crowded settlements in search of security at a time when public sewers are totally lacking or outstandingly inadequate. And these same hazardous conditions of life make the traditional dietary supplements of the rivers and the forests no longer easily available. Even the man in the village no longer moves freely to hunt or fish. Starvation of all forms and degrees is apparent even in the faces of those who claim health. Crowning all this is the constant apprehension of death and the frequent sight of death itself.

Economy

Economic, but not developmental, changes have been even more rapid. In the past, the sale of cattle was considered shameful and going to work for cash in towns even more so. The colonial administration believed that since the Dinka were among the Sudan's richest in livestock and because livestock was among the main resources of the country, the Dinka were to be encouraged to sell it. Taxes and fines had to be paid in cash; and since there was no paid labor in the tribe, sale of cattle was mandatory. Traditionally, when people were short of grain for food, they went after wild grain and other products. They fished, hunted, or just depended on milk and meat from their cows. With the modern market, grain became available in the shops of Arab traders. All one needed was cash, obtainable only by the sale of cattle. Other things like clothes and salt were similarly available. Because the prices of livestock were low and those of goods exorbitant, one family might have to sell several cows to pay the taxes, survive a lean year, or obtain other necessities. This extended into Dinka trade: Soon after harvest, the Dinka who never seems to plan for the future would exchange grain for salt and other products, only to be sold the same grain when he ran short—and for excessive prices. In short, the Dinka have continued to lose their livestock and get little in return. Even Ngok livestock population has markedly decreased.

Migration

With decreased wealth came an increased need to migrate into the town or to rural Arab areas for work. Young men saw in the modern market an opportunity for independent wealth. Within the tribe, there was no paid labor; but more important, because of their intense pride, paid labor is seen as servility and is regarded as inappropriate for a gentleman: Therefore it must be done far away from Dinka girls and in a country where it does not matter. As the saying goes, "Dignity, remain, indignity, let us go," —which means pocketing pride in a foreign land where one is unknown. But, for the Dinka, the balance between the material advantage of the town and loss of the dignity in their traditional ways poses serious dilemmas and paradoxes:

> *O morning, come soon.*
> *My curve-horned Ox, Mading,*
> *The stream will be crossed,*
> *In towns, people cultivate with their ears;*
> *In towns, people depend on market grain.*
> *My Maker Majok,*
> *The riches that I hear of in towns;*
> *People live to old age buying and selling.*
> *They say, "Lend me two piasters* [24]
> *And at the end of the month*
> *I will return them to you."*
> *Then a millieme* [25] *is taken into the market.*
> *With it, salt and medicine will be bought,*

---

24 A monetary unit: There are 100 piasters in a Sudanese pound (approximately $3).

25 There are 10 milliemes in a piaster. Its use shows how ignorant about money the singer is.

Vegetables will be bought by a man, [26]
Cooking will be done by the couple together,
The family has lost its value;
Blood ties have been severed in the pockets,
Even a son of your maternal aunt
When you ask him for help
Will first invoke the name of God,
He will swear by his father,
"May I die, Brother, see my pocket
If you find a millieme, you are lucky."
In the town people dismiss one another:
"May I die, Brother,
If you find a millieme, you are lucky."
One hundred piasters go into trifles.
Then each man goes to his sleeping place.
In the towns people dance to the drums in their pockets
If one has nothing, one goes with nothing,
The drums are all alike as people of the same tongue
They are beaten on people's laps,
Bim ci ke ke bim!
Let me beat the drums,
The drums for which we will go astray to dance.

Dinka emigrants do such jobs as cultivating Arab fields, drawing and distributing water, and constructing roads and buildings. They leave their fields at home to be cultivated by a few who produce just enough for subsistence and sometimes less. The objective is always to make money fast and return home. Consequently, they work hard; eat little to avoid spending money; but drink much to bring some pleasure when there is none in their otherwise miserable, unhealthy,

---

26 Both the buying and cooking of food are traditionally done only by women.

and most degrading conditions. It is this illiterate group who, when they return, aim at buying cattle and controlling them independently of their families. But the marriages of their relatives or vicarious liability for such obligations as taxes or debts often dissipate their plans. Some, after a few such experiences, refuse to reurn to the tribe.

The migration of traditional youth is also abetted by the dwindling of the age-set system. As the warring activities of the youth become effectively curtailed, their vitality finds no outlet in the tribe. This is particularly so since the newly introduced working on the road, buildings, cultivations, and the like was abolished as forced labor. The warrior age-sets had come to regard it as part of their warrior activities in which the age-sets competed.

Recently, migration has affected girls and families. Women are generally employed in homes under more comfortable and respectable conditions, which permit them to adapt more easily to the new environment. But to the Dinka, the result is often not so respectable as it may seem. Dressed in Arab clothes and proficient in Arabic, superficially integrated into employing families and therefore lacking adequate supervision and cultural restraints, young girls grow up in an atmosphere of permissiveness and promiscuity. They came to acquire wealth to help their relatives subsist and maybe buy cattle, but they return worthless for marriage. Usually, there is "their kind" to marry them, but even then these are only "limping" marriages.

Migration has now become even more widespread as a result of the South-North hostilities. The motive is no longer economic as much as it is fear of death and an escape to the more secure towns of the North.

All these changes have had, and continue to have, serious repercussions on the family. An undercurrent is now wiping away the emphasis on the family as the fundamental unit of society and the cohesiveness, maybe the survival of Dinka society itself, is at stake. Children are going far away for education. But education is suddenly questioning the validity of the old assumption of age stratification. There are no jobs to bring the children home after they leave school. Traditional youths are going into the cities for jobs, but the modern and the traditional cultures are finding no encouragement for genuine integration, and the country is in a violent political upheaval.

Chapter Eleven

Conclusion

In this book, I have tried to paint a portrait of Dinka life, from birth to death; in tradition and in transition. Traditionally, Dinka life was (and is still) largely woven together around basic values, with procreation as the foundation and the yardstick for stratification. Since it aims at biological and social immortality through males, procreation gives the ancestors and their spiritual world supremacy over the mortal beings who are stratified according to age and sex, with male elders at the peak and women at the lower end. Procreation also classifies society along descent lines into commoners and the aristocrats who provide the chiefs.

But procreation is only a starting point into complex sets of values and institutions which balance one another and compensate for deprivation. In this complex, the deference values: affection, respect, rectitude, and the power of persuasiveness rank higher than the material values: wealth, scientific knowledge, technical skill, and physical health. At the core of the deferential values is *cieng*, the concept of ideal human relations. Whatever disrespect is implicit in the stratification of age, sex, or descent, the principles of cieng, reinforced by the ideals of human dignity expressed in dheeng, give every man not only the right to be esteemed but also alternative paths to dignity. The esthetics of cattle, the sensual values of singing and dancing, the admiration for physical strength and valor, and the expectation of everyone becoming an elder some day make youth aspire to the fruits of older age but content themselves with the pleasures of today. Women internalize the system of values, accept the stratifications, and glorify in their pride as wives and mothers to their men. Commoners and the poor see no gulf between them and the wealthy or the chiefs because the overriding value of social consciousness forecloses any indignities attaching to stratification. The Dinka do not have lords and serfs, masters and slaves: They have leaders among peers.

Traditional deprivations, of course, have their negative implications. Examples are the aggressiveness, the violence, and cattle-complex of youth and the jealousies, the divisiveness, and the "possession by spirits" of women. But these are only storms in teacups and, although they symbolize discontent, they never threaten the system or its equilibrium.

New forces have now intervened to threaten the foundations of the traditional society as the wind of change sweeps over Dinkaland. Change is not novel to the Dinka; they have been exposed to external influences for centuries and have so assimilated some of the cultural elements they have adopted that these elements have become an integral part of their culture and are no longer recognized as adopted. However, the first part of this century witnessed a combination of cultural preservation with intensification of alien influence and left the Dinka with striking features of both extremes. The effects in various aspects of the culture have not been uniform. While radical innovations have been introduced into some aspects, others have been only concomitantly affected. The people themselves have not been uniformly affected, for while a few have been almost transformed culturally, others have barely been touched, and the society has fallen into a sharp division between tradition and modernity.

Representing tradition are the Chiefs and the Elders, and on the modern side are the educated and the young who now go into the towns to work. But traditions die hard. Familial piety and respect for the fathers and the elders of the tribe still hold to forbid revolution within the system. The disposition of the educated youth toward more than they get, the intensity of the personality crises this provokes, the national dimension of their demands, and the raciocultural implications of the obstacles have extended dissidence far beyond the family and the tribe: in fact, onto the national scene.

Those on whom the burden of the decision rests face the challenge of integrating the past with the present and the projected future. For tradition and traditionals are as much a reality of today as the emergent modernity and moderns, even though the latter are stronger and more unrelenting than the former. To bring some calm into the turmoil, a system must be found which would elicit the support of the dynamic elements of both the traditional and modern groups and mobilize their latent or kinetic energies for constructive participation. The educated, the corporate warrior youth groups, and the women can now be integrated into the utilitarian roles of both tradition and modernity to help in reconstructing and promoting the new world of the Dinka. Even the values of immortality through worldly achievement, of unity and harmony, and of esthetic competitiveness can be utilized for development. Progress should be induced and made to give the society a dignity of self-realization and advancement, rather than made to appear as an imitation of previously disregarded mores of foreign origin.

But these are theories of peace; and the crucial issue for the Dinka today is no longer who gets what or should do what within their own system: It is how to survive the South-North conflict, a problem which has afflicted the Sudan with a 16-year-old civil war. Many hundreds of thousands, and some say over a million people have died; scores of thousands have fled their country, and the rest continue in constant apprehension of death in deprivation of their basic needs. The rebellious Southerners show determination to fight for what they first called "Federation" and now present as separation or self-determination. The ruling North finds that unacceptable and to suppress it, has used Islamization, Arabization, and coercion-all without success. Within the Sudanese system, the civilian Southerners work for peaceful change: some hoping to separate eventually, others waiting and hoping for a compromise with the Northern side—and yet others are merely striving for some security where there is none or little. While the insurgence and the ferments continue, many governments have come and gone on account of this problem. Some have given promises they did not fulfill, arguing that the disruptive conditions in the South must be normalized by the surrender of arms and the cessation of rebellion before reconstruction can begin. But the Southerner sees no change of heart to warrant his trusting the Northerner and wants visible signs of profound change as a necessary condition to the surrender of his arms. The vicious circle goes on.

It is the prediction and the hope of many that the Dinka will survive this internecine war. I share this optimism. Dinka determination and their genius of adaptation have saved them before from the ravages of unscrupulous human hunters. But the history of man has witnessed the survival of peoples only after devastating losses of lives or dehumanizing mutilation of personality and culture. This is the threat now facing the Dinka as they face problems of unprecedented dimensions far beyond their comprehension, much less their control.

Most of the responsibility for their decent survival must remain with the Dinka. They must now rise to meet the challenges of an integrating, although diverse and sometimes diversifying, world. But those with whom they integrate or interact must also be wise enough to meet them with respect and induce their cooperation in building a better world. This is the challenge facing the Arab in the Northern Sudan. The alternative is to question the heritage, the identity, and the dignity of the Dinka. That can only cause and has already caused, indignation and defeat is its end.

The challenge cannot be left to the Sudanese alone. It is a paradox that a world which is increasingly widening its concern for an all-embracing humanity can continue to ignore the plight of over four million people for 16 years. The peoples of the Sudan, including those who slam their doors on the world, are in desperate need of help. Diplomacy and mediation can restore some hope for peace and survival.

A hurricane has taken the Dinka by surprise. They are now adrift, struggling with the waves of a stormy sea and at the mercy of a superior order they do not know, cannot see, but call God. Their fate is also in the hand of man, and whatever the shortcomings of world brotherhood, a universal conscience is increasingly in the limelight. Isolationism has become anachronistic; responsible involvement is the call. There is much the world must desire in the dignity and the heritage of the people I have described, yet all is threatened with extinction. Should this come to pass, the humiliation, the suffering, the desolation, and the destruction of the Dinka will add to the heavy toll already afflicting the conscience of Man. It is not the dead who suffer, it is those who cause their death, and those who watch them die.

Chapter Twelve: Postscript, 1986
The Dinka of the Sudan Revisited [27]

~~~~~~~

Introduction

I n the first edition of this book, I wrote, "It is the prediction and the hope of many that the Dinka will survive this inter-necine [civil] war [between the South and the North]. I share this optimism. Dinka determination and their genius of adaptation have saved them before from the ravages of unscrupulous human hunters." [28] The same year the book was published, this prediction came true. A long process of negotiation in which many people were involved resulted in the Addis Ababa Accord which ended the war on February 27, 1972. Almost exactly a decade later, the Sudan was back in a state of war for virtually the same reasons.

While the case of the Sudan is undoubtedly extreme in degree, the fundamental issues involved tend to reflect patterns that are rather common to many countries in Africa.

---

27 Portions of this postscript appear in an article published in the Annual Report of the Rockefeller Brothers Fund, 1985. It is reproduced here with the permission of the Fund.

28 p. 166

What tends to be overlooked in the current concern with the problem of famine and the general economic deterioration in Africa is the extent to which policies and strategies, both domestic and foreign, have largely ignored and even undermined the resourcefulness of the Africans within the social and cultural setting of the traditional society. This has meant disregarding the identity of the ethnic or cultural groups as participating entities, dismantling the organizational structures that provided not only institutional support but also the human and material resources for getting things done, and invalidating the values that generated the inspiration, the motivation and indeed the energies for productive activity.

Geographically the largest in Africa, centrally located, with eight neighbors and Saudi Arabia across the Red Sea, and reflecting within its borders all the racial, ethnic, and cultural diversities of the continent, Sudan is justifiably considered the microcosm of Africa. Being Afro-Arab, it is also a vital link between Africa and the Middle East and therefore has a strategic significance that goes beyond the regional context. But, the experience of the Sudan is a good example of how disregard for diversities, combined with debilitating inequities in the racial, ethnic, religious and cultural structures of the state tends to undermine the resourcefulness of the people and may lead to tensions and conflicts that threaten the economy, the stability of the country and indeed the viability of the unitary state.

Anatomy of Traditional Society

In order to appreciate the potentials which are not being utilized in the process of nation building, it is necessary to have a closer understanding of how African traditional societies functioned before the formation of the nation-state.

As the portrait of Dinka society presented in this book illustrates, life in Africa traditionally centered around the family and the values of ancestral continuity through the lineage system. Despite the tensions and the rivalries which characterized the competitiveness of individual and group interests, unity, harmony and solidarity behind the ancestral ideals were emphasized and sanctioned through both secular and spiritual means. Authorized decisionmakers, Chiefs and elders, largely depended on persuasion rather than coercion, and only in extreme cases of wrongdoing, disobedience or insubordination did they resort to the coercive force of spiritual curse. Consensus was fostered behind these values by catering for the welfare of every individual and group as vital elements in the community. The society was, of course, stratified according to descent, sex and age, but whatever deprivations resulted from the inequities of such stratification, there were elaborate cultural ways and means for compensating the subordinated. For instance, while chiefs and elders were the authoritative decision makers in family and public affairs, male youth were organized into military regiments called age-sets whose role was to defend society from animal and human foes with the moral and sensuous encouragement of corresponding female age-sets. This role accorded them a high profile of respect, dignity, and self-assertiveness. Elders had a superior claim to the control of wealth, but wealth carried with it moral obligations toward the needy; young men and women indulged in the esthetics of cattle-complex; and married women exercised control over the management of agricultural produce, dairy products, and food in general.

Within the limited framework of subsistence, people depended on what they produced, supplemented by what was available in their natural environment. From time to time, areas faced natural disasters from floods or drought and had to turn to their less affected neighbors for survival, bartering whatever they had for whatever they needed, or otherwise depending on their generosity, knowing that their turn to extend a helping hand would come some day. While there was no conscious population policy, long periods of nursing, taboos on sexual relations during the nursing period, and an early termination of childbearing by a mother when her eldest child became of age combined with natural forces to maintain a demographic balance. Naturally, there were hazards and many negatives to the system. People produced just enough to live on and were often compelled to turn to the environment for natural supplements. There was a fatalistic attitude towards cause and effect, and while some lived to be very old, infant mortality was commonplace. And despite the compensational devices which ensured a measure of vested interest in the system and a high degree of conformity, the underprivileged members, especially women and youth, displayed attributes which ran counter to some of the ideals. Women were known for intrigues and divisiveness, which resulted directly from lack of open participation in decision making and the need to operate discreetly by influencing their husbands and sons. Male youth exaggerated violence and aggressiveness as martial qualities from which they derived their status and dignity, sharply contrasting with the persuasiveness of their elders, who wielded the established power of decision making.

But while inequities and grievances existed, and despite the paradoxes resulting from stratification, people were largely content, able to produce what they needed for a sustainable living and endowed with what they regarded as the ideal wealth—cattle. As one Dinka elder proudly expressed it, "We are the Dinka who inhabit this vast rich grassland, keepers of cattle." [29] Another elder went further:

> "It is for cattle that we are admired, we the Dinka. The government recognizes us because of our cattle wealth. All over the world, people look to us because of cattle. And when they say, "Sudan," it is not just because of our color; it is also because of our great wealth, and our wealth is cattle ... It is

---

29 Chief Giir Kiro (also known as Giir Thiik) in Deng, Dinka Cosmology, London, Ithaca Press, 1980, p. 46.

because of cattle that people of all the tribes look to us with envy." [30]

The consensus of expert opinion is that the Nilotics of the Sudan were a proud, ethnocentric and conservative people who, until recently, were unmotivated toward adopting the ways of those with whom they came in contact. Before independence brought about a more intense relationship with the outside world and opened doors to the allurements of the city, leaving the tribe was viewed as a reckless self-exile, while migrating into town was a shameful act that invited slanderous songs against both the person leaving and the remaining kith and kin.

The Paradoxes of the Nation State

The establishment of the state meant bringing together racial, ethnic, or cultural groups that had viewed one another as outsiders and had either been mutually isolated from one another or had coexisted and interacted as strangers and perhaps even enemies. In the case of the Sudan, the structures of the state grouped the wide ethnic and cultural diversities of the country into the Arab Muslim North, which constitutes two thirds in both land and population, and the remaining third in the South whose cultures and religious beliefs are more traditionally African, with a Christianized educated class.

But identification in the Sudan is a function of attitude resulting from a long history of racial and cultural stratification rather than a reflection of realities. The African Blacks occupied the lowest position, the Arab-Muslims a higher one, and the Europeans the highest. Since Islam and Arabism were flexible in assimilating others and thereby improving their status, it is easy to see why Northern

---

30 Chief Ayeny Aleu, id., p. 99.

Sudanese readily converted to Islam and identified themselves as Arabs even when racial or cultural realities might look different. For reasons of natural and man-made barriers, this assimilating trend did not affect the South whose only contact with the North was to provide a hunting ground for slaves and big game.

The framework of unity in diversity which the British established between the so-called Arab North and African South was modified by a separatist policy which insulated and isolated the South as "Closed Districts." While opportun ities for social and economic development were introduced to the North, and its Arab Islamic identity recognized, the South was left to evolve along indigenous African lines with some concession made for the Christian missionaries to proselytize and otherwise play a modest "civilizing" role. Independence left the country in a unitary system in which effective participation became dependent on cultural and religious considerations which subordinated Southerners, having been educated in a Christian, vernacular and English system contrasted with the Arabic Islamic system of the North.

Southern fear of Arab domination triggered in August 1955 a mutiny that began with a battalion but soon spread throughout the South, and eventually developed into a civil war that was to continue for seventeen years, until it was endowed by the Addis Ababa Accord of 1972, which gave the South regional autonomy within national unity. The rebel forces, the *Anyanya*, were absorbed into the national army and refugees and displaced people were resettled and rehabilitated with assistance from international organizations and friendly countries.

The stability which the Nimeri regime enjoyed for some 16 years was in no small measure due to this agreement which dramatically changed Southern attitudes from separatism to unity. The solution, undoubtedly the most significant of Nimeri's regime, gave the country a boost in international relations. Sudan improved relations with most of its neighbors, took or supported peace initiatives, and actively pursued development as a strategy for nation building which effectively took over from the war psychology. Building on those domestic achievements, Sudan used its foreign policy effectively to mobilize international cooperation in its development effort. With 200,000,000 acres of arable land, of which only ten percent was being utilized, Sudan was projected as the potential bread basket for Africa and the Middle East. Being Arab and with such potentials, the country was viewed as an ideal context for trilateral cooperation between Western technology and Arab financial resources.

But things began to go wrong. Sudan got carried away with borrowing at a time when the outside world was eager to lend money in order to circulate the rapidly accumulating petro-dollars, particularly to countries with such obvious development potentials. To compound the problem, however, the concept of development which the masses had in mind was not so much growth oriented as it was geared toward the provision of services and the establishment of schemes or projects with a visibility that promised and symbolized a significant economic take-off. The imagination of the nation was captured and engrossed in a grandiose and lavish notion of development that was more political than economic.

Then, debts began to mature, oil bills began to soar, the IMF began to impose economic measures, the gap between aspirations and realities became unbridgeable. Tensions began to rise, particularly in the worse off areas of the country of which the South was an extreme case. Ironically, all this occurred at a time when the Sudan had struck significant oil reserves, most of which was in the Southern part of the country. Even the oil find became a source of friction. In order to alleviate the heavy debt of the country, it was decided that oil be refined in those areas where the infrastructure would facilitate quick returns. This meant the North. Later, it was again decided that the crude be pipelined to the Red Sea for export.

These measures were viewed by the South as evidence of the North enriching itself at the expense of the South. The mammoth Jonglei Canal, which was aimed at saving the Nile waters from evaporation and retrieving valuable land from the swampy Sudd was also viewed with disfavor as benefitting the North and Egypt while destroying the natural environment and dislocating the human and animal life cycles of the areas.

The more the South began to assert itself as a separate culture entity and make demands for a more equitable share of power, national wealth, and development opportunities, the more the President saw its autonomy, with a constitutionally guaranteed liberal democracy, as an anathema in the context of the Presidential system which governed the Sudan. Internal political rivalries and ambitions for positions within the South also levied their toll. On the basis of alleged complaints of minority tribes against Dinka domination, President Nimeri decreed the division of the South into three regions and lowered the powers of the regional governments to be at part with the situation in the North.

Reading the restless mood in the South, the Government began to transfer the absorbed Southern forces to the North, ostensibly to consolidate the integration of the army, but presumably to weaken the capacity of the South to resort to military action against the government Southern policy. While some reluctantly obeyed the orders, one unit resisted, precipitating the Bor incident which triggered the renewal of organized hostilities. President Nimeri added fuel to the explosion when he decided to impose Islamic laws on the country, virtually turning the Sudan into an Islamic state in which the non-Muslim population would be inevitably relegated to the status of second class citizenship. The reaction was a spontaneous return to the conditions of the seventeen year civil war and the establishment of the Sudan People's Liberation Movement (SPLM), with its military wing, Sudan People's Liberation Army, (SPLA), both under the leadership of Colonel Dr. John Garang, an army officer with a Ph.D. in economics from the United States. With the sophistication of the arms now available to both sides and the level of outside support which the Southern movement was receiving from Ethiopia and Libya, the current war soon proved far more devastating than the Seventeen Year War. Work on both oil exploration and the Jonglei Canal was disrupted and terminated. With the devastations of the civil war, its implications on a deteriorating economy, compounded by drought in certain areas and the influx of refugees from a number of neighboring countries, and with the final stroke of the austerity measures imposed by the IMF, Sudan could not avert the popular uprising which brought Nimeri's downfall. Since Nimeri's fall, the equations have been slightly altered. Libya has shifted sides and relations between the Sudan and Ethiopia began to move in a more positive direction. But the war has continued unabated.

Developments on the utilization of the human and socio-economic resources of the traditional sector have also been painfully adverse. The detrimental effects of the dependency chain brought about by current externally oriented economic policies and especially by the disregard of the social and cultural resource base of traditional society have particularly hit the rural population and undermined their contribution to a sustainable economy. Massive influx into urban centers became the norm. Needless to say, it is not necessarily the utterly poor or the needy who leave tribal settings to seek opportunities in town. A young man of known social background, reasonable family wealth, and a respectable status may leave for town labor to seek personal sources to augment the family fortune or to establish an independent base that should enhance his autonomy in deciding his future over such matters as when and where to marry. Once he goes into the city, he is among the lowest of the urban low and his tribal emphasis on respect and dignity are sharply confronted with dehumanizing realities. But once they experience town life, it is difficult to settle back in the tribe and indeed, the logic of the system leaves nothing to be desired in the village. They begin to move to and fro between the tribe and the town, unable to integrate meaningfully into either.

The following lines from an ox song reveal the sentiments of a Dinka about the indignities of working conditions in the town. The singer comes from a family afflicted with infant mortality which had deprived them of girls, through whose marriages families normally acquire cattle. He had to migrate into town to labor for cash in order to buy cattle:

> *My grandmother, my grandmother, Aluel, the daughter of Chol,*
> *She came with a glory which God denied;*
> *A great lady who bore multitudes of children,*
> *But consumed her hoes digging their graves,*
> *Leaving my father a lonely bull of the buffalo;*
> *If he had sisters, we would be herding our cattle at home:*
> *And that is why I have become a slave,*
> *Laboring in a foreign land,*
> *Cracking my back-bones like the trap of a captured bird.*
> *I worked in the cotton field until my hair turned grey,*
> *It was not the grey of age;*
> *It was the bitter pain of the words in our heads,*
> *As we wasted away in foreign lands.*
> *O Marial, what I have found, I will not say ...*

From the perspective of the urban population, these masses from the rural areas, more than only a drain on the fragile services and the scarce resources of the city, are indeed a threat to urban security, especially as their dire poverty and reduced status fan a bitterness that sometimes expresses itself in such crimes of need and hostility as theft and robbery. Ironically, it was mostly the hands of non-Muslims which suffered amputation as a result of the imposition of Islamic law by Nimeri.

There was a time when the security authorities in Khartoum found themselves impelled to force masses of the so-called "homeless" migrants out of the city. People were unexpectingly apprehended, herded into football stadiums and trucked back to their rural areas, mostly in the South and West. This operation, known as *kesha*, ("raid,") was naturally resented by these regional communities who found considerable sympathy from the leaders of their constituencies, further aggravating the political problem of national unity and weakening the fabric of national security. So embittered by this action were the rural masses and so vocal were their leaders against it, some of whom were senior members of the government, that it was eventually abandoned. But much harm had already been done.

Abyei Project: A Case of Conflicting Perspectives

Let me now illustrate the problem I am attempting to describe and the remedy I am implicitly advocating by giving a brief account of a project with which I was personally involved and which clearly demonstrated the differences in the perspectives on African development. The people involved are the Ngok Dinka, whose headquarters is Abyei, from which the area now derives its name. Although the Ngok form part of the Southern ethnic and cultural complex, for historical reasons they have administratively been linked to Kordofan, one of the Provinces of the North. The area itself remains a crossroads for the pastoral Arab and Nilotic tribes in the North and the South, meeting there or alternating seasonally in search of water or to escape floods as the case might be. The peace and harmony that had prevailed between the Ngok Dinka and the Missiriya Arabs for generations had begun to be eroded by the civil war until in 1965 the area erupted with hostilities that sharply divided the people along the

North-South ethnic and cultural lines, forcing the people of Abyei even more into the war. That was the situation we witnessed in 1969 on our return home for the funeral of our father recounted in this book. During the Addis Ababa negotiations, Abyei was claimed by both sides. The Accord, which brought peace to the South, left the issue unresolved, supposedly to be decided by referendum. But although there was a popular call for joining the South by the people of Abyei, it soon became obvious that the problem was far more complex than that, for the stakes of the various interest groups in the area were, and remain, high.

That was when I came to the conclusion that instead of suffering the strains of a disputed territory, it would be more advantageous for the area to build on its positive history of linking the North and the South and the prevailing post-war climate of peace, unity, and reconciliation. I felt sure that if the grievances of the people of Abyei were addressed by granting them control over their local affairs and if, in addition, they were provided with basic services and a development program that would recognize and build on their distinctive features, their aspirations would be satisfied and they might become reconciled to the positives of their bridging situation. Their area could again become a peaceful border in which the neighboring tribes could meet and interact in a harmonious atmosphere, reinforcing national unity and integration.

The idea was well received in the relevant decision-making circles on the national level, including the President himself. The momentum reached its peak on both the national and international levels when President Nimeri reiterated in Kadugli, the provincial capital, in his Independence Day speech on January 1, 1977, the Government policy over the area, solemnly pledging his personal responsibility for the development of the Abyei area. Placing it in the context of the overall development of the Province, President Nimeri stated:

I would like development in this rich province to be comprehen-
sive and integrated and to promote the traditional sector, and in
particular, the contribution of the local population through self-help
efforts which we want to be an example for all the other prov-
inces. If this is what we want for your province, I want the area
of Abyei—where the great Dinka and Missiriya tribes meet and
co-exist—to be an example of the interaction of cultures. Abyei
is to the Sudan exactly what the Sudan is to Africa. This project
will be implemented under my personal supervision in cooperation
with all the institutions of the state, universities, and international
organizations.

My concern over the debilitating and dehumanizing trends of
change had already propelled me to embark on a graduate study
aimed at exploring ways and means of guiding development to be
more harmonious and less disruptive to traditional societies. The
outcome was my first book, *Tradition and Modernization: A Challenge
for Law Among the Dinka of the Sudan,* published by Yale University
Press in 1971. In that book I formulated in considerable detail the
theoretical bases and practical steps aimed at fostering the transitional
integration of the values, the institutions and the representative forces
of tradition and modernization, including elders, women, warrior
age-sets, corresponding female age-sets and the educated class. Well
received in scholarly circles, the book won the Herskovitz Award
in 1972 and was described by the Award Committee as "scholarly,
well-written, original and theoretically stimulating," which added to
my encouragement that the exercise had been more than a pursuit
of an academic degree.

With that comprehensive study of the social and cultural dimensions of development and a favorable political climate at home, I
began to look for international institutions which were qualified
to assist us in the implementation of the project. It was then that

the Harvard Institute for International Development, HIID, was brought to may attention as suited for such a research-action combination. I approached HIID in 1972 to undertake the implementation of the project, giving the political rationale as justification for the national support the project would receive and offering *Tradition and Modernization* as a theoretical model for experimentation. although their consideration of my request was to take some time, HIID eventually undertook the project in 1976 and became actively involved by 1977 with funding from the United States Agency for International Development—AID. By that time, I was back in the country in the position of Minister of State for Foreign Affairs, and could therefore lend a helping hand to the project from close quarters. And indeed, throughout the life of the project, I maintained very close association with those involved, both on the Sudanese side and from the United States.

HIID's approach to the development of Abyei turned out to be different from what I had envisaged. Using the argument that the financial and human resources available for the development of the Third World, especially such remote rural areas as Abyei, were scarce, their main objective was to experiment in search of the least expensive techniques that would work in such areas as agriculture, health, water supply, transport, construction, and animal husbandry.

But my main objective was not so much the modesty of the approach as its lack of a positive social and cultural orientation. Initially, the people of Abyei were asked to identify their needs, in many respects quite obvious; and that was the extent of their involvement. With considerable efforts, we succeeded in seconding to the project a group of fairly senior government officials from Abyei. But although they became a useful link with the people, in addition to their operational responsibilities, they were soon to express frustrations over lack of participation in decision-making, especially on matters of policy. Sharp differences began to develop between them and their American counterparts on a variety of issues.

One issue of disagreement on which the American field manager carried cultural insensitivity to an extreme was the use of cattle for animal traction. Anyone with the least idea of Dinka society would realize that cattle are central to their social, moral and spiritual values, in many respects far above the utilitarian value. They have seen their Arab neighbors use cattle as animals of burden for centuries but have never entertained the idea of subjecting their cattle to what they consider an indignity. The Dinka, including the educated, made it emphatically clear to HIID that such use of cattle was totally unacceptable on cultural grounds. The American field manager, dedicated to the idea of animal traction, threatened that he had the key to the money and that if the Dinka did not accept the use of cattle, the project would be terminated. This, of course, touched on Dinka pride and the calls for the termination of the project began to swamp me. The American field manager was eventually replaced by another American who succeeded in winning the confidence of the local people. But much damage had already been done.

Even the argument that the Dinka are too poor to sustain more than the most modest concept of development totally missed their proud self-image as wealthy cattle owners who, far from being pitied, are envied, and who, with their cattle and their labor, could indeed afford development, with appropriate guidance and channels for procuring equipment and expertise.

These words from a Dinka Chief are quite revealing, if only because of the self-confidence they convey:

> *Let me tell you what we have to do to improve ourselves. This wound you see on my hands is a wound from making roads. Ever since the government came my people have been building their own roads. I have always built the roads. Money has never come into my tribe to be paid for working on the*

roads. And if you need money for development, the cattle at home are all in your hands. Just show us what we can do with them. I collected money before I left and put it into a box. I came and asked, hoping that the government would secure for me a truck which I would buy and take to build my own area by myself. That is all I want. I just want a truck and I have the money. I don't want any help. I want a truck and I want tools ... And the thing that cultivates the ground for crops. When we cultivate the crops, part of the produce will be sold for cash and part will be eaten. Those are all the things I am asking for. And I have the money for them. [31]

After enumerating the institutions that he thought should be established, including schools and hospitals, another Chief posed and answered the question of financing:

And with what money will they be built? They will be built with the money of our people. The Chief must collect the money. The Chief must establish cooperatives. The Chief must hold meetings and ask his people to collect money and build houses and then say to the Government, "We want a doctor to be brought."

I am not suggesting for a moment that the Dinka are wealthy enough to afford their own development. I am merely stressing the issue of self-perception as an untapped resource for a broad-based development of the rural areas. There is something profoundly wrong with telling people with such a positive attitude that they are among the poorest of the poor who can therefore expect help.

There were, however, more problems to the project than HIID's

---

31 Chief Thon Wai, id., p. 170.

lack of social orientation. Indeed, apart from myself and the central government authorities, who shared my vision, most of the significant political elements in the area seemed unhappy with the project, largely because of its political connotations. Vocal elements of the educated youth of Abyei, who were politically militant, saw the project as a way of neutralizing pro-South nationalist movement in Abyei. Some of these differences reflected long standing rivalries between factions of the tribe. Beyond the Dinka, the Arab tribes and Kordofan authorities missed the main objective of the project, which was to serve the mutual interest of both the Dinka and the Arabs and saw it as a favoritism to the people of Abyei, a circumvention of Provincial authority, and perhaps a step toward ultimately severing Abyei from Kordofan and annexing it to the South. So entangled in the political conflicts did the project and the Institute become that absurd allegations were being made to the effect that the Dinka were receiving arms through the project. The outcome of the project turned out to be the exact opposite of its intended results. Political problems over Abyei and the project itself soon mounted, erupting into a series of violent conflicts between the Arabs and the Dinka and among the Dinka themselves. It was with the compounding of all these problems that USAID eventually decided in 1981 to terminate its funding and withdraw from the project. Harvard also left. The project was declared a failure.

In retrospect, the technological aspect on which HIID focused attention and the social and cultural aspect with which I was concerned are clearly complementary and in a way reflect our own respective cultural biases. Although I initially watched HIID experiment with various ideas, I eventually let my objections be known. I was candidly told that my approach would require an insight which could not be expected of outsiders. Quite apart from the fact that I would have preferred to be aware of that attitude from the beginning, it seems to me that the argument merely underscored the need for cooperation between outsiders and insiders in planning and implementing rural development projects rather than pinpointing the need to disregard social and cultural orientations of development.

Those of us who were closely involved on both sides share the view that it was a pity the project was terminated just as we were beginning to make significant adjustments towards each other's perspectives. All now seem to agree that much was learned from the failure. Indeed, a subsequent agreement between the people of Abyei and the Government of Kordofan included plans to reactivate the project under the auspices of the Province authorities and with the cooperation of international agencies. Problems connected with the general political and economic situation in the country have so far impeded the realization of this goal. It is, however, to be hoped that the area will once more be given the opportunity to benefit from this experience, to correct past mistakes, and to make another attempt at generating a socially and culturally oriented, technologically self-sustaining program of rural development.

Conclusion

In a study which I prepared under the auspices of the Yale Program of Law and Modernization in 1972, I wrote, commenting on the Addis Ababa Agreement which had just been concluded between the South and the North:

> With President Nimeri's granting of regional self-government to the southern provinces, the Sudan has just emerged from sixteen years of civil strife which characterized what is known as the Southern Problem. Peace has returned to the Sudan and the problem may be said to have ended. But its implications in terms of the future of the Sudan still pose questions to which the Sudanese must address themselves.

Foremost of these questions is whether the Sudanese can now foster a common integrated sense of identity which would guarantee a genuine and lasting national unity.[32]

In another context, I went on to say:

Issues of Sudanese identity linger on and may still prove a point of friction in the South-North relations of the future. Although regional self-rule is a short term solution to the South-North problems, it is hard to expect that the Southern Sudanese will be content with regional participation and not concerned with such major national and international issues as what Sudan's identification should be. One can only recommend a label that unites as opposed to one that divides. [33]

Some years later, I made the following evaluation of the agreement and the way it was functioning in practice.

The situation in reality today provides for both unity and separatism and it is precisely because it combines these seemingly opposed phenomena that it has such an appeal to the South and to at least the crucial elements of Northern leadership. According to the system, Southerners can participate on two levels, the regional and the national. The law governing this system is, as are all fundamental laws, phrased broadly enough to allow a margin of discretion. Ultimately, it largely depends on the national leadership, and particularly the President, whether regional autonomy is given wide or restricted operation. With the unquestioned support of the national leadership for the Southern cause, the present

---

32 *"Dynamics of Identification: A Basis for National Integration in the Sudan,"* Khartoum, Khartoum University Press, 1974, p. 1.

33 Ibid., p.102.

application of autonomy tends to be extensive, if only on matters not vital or sensitive to the character of the nation. Nonetheless, and by the same token, this implies a willing regional dependency on the center. Partly because of the centrifugal forces exerted by the President's authority and partly because of the importance of the center for crucial matters—such as handling international relations, on which depends much of the financial and technological input for development—regional participation is largely channeled through the controlling, though seemingly remote, hands of the center. For various reasons, this process is also characterized by Southern interpersonal or intergroup competition and sometimes by intrigues aimed at securing greater influence in the region and/ or the center.

A complex situation is thus created where unity is unanimously avowed and regionalism is conceived as conferring extensive powers; but paradoxically the regionalism is dependent on central support and therefore centrally controlled. This is likely to encourage subtle, central absorption of the autonomous South.[34]

Needless to say, the predictions have since become tragic realities. What prognosis can one now make in light of recent developments? Several alternatives come to mind. One alternative is that the North may choose to adopt a centralized system of government and use Islam and Arabism as tools of national unification. It is however difficult to see how the Nilotics, or for that matter, the Southern Sudanese in general, with their pride in their race and culture, could voluntarily accept a national unity based on such inequitable bases as one religion, Islam, one language, Arabic, and one racial and cultural identity, Arabism, all of which reflect only the North. What must be

---

34 *"Africans of Two Worlds: The Dinka in Afro-Arab Sudan,"* New Haven, Yale University Press, 1978, pp. 173-74.

recognized is that although Christianity and English are alien to the South, they have become adopted by the elite as modern symbols of identity that counterbalance the Islamic and Arabic identity of the North and guard against the dreaded assimilation and cultural annihilation. Northern symbols of identity can only become accepted as the basis of unity, uniformity, and integration through coercive imposition, which is nigh impossible. Another alternative is that the South may wish to separate from the North and establish itself as an independent state. But this too does not seem feasible, for quite apart from issues of economic viability and the threats of further disintegration along tribal lines, given the current almost dogmatic commitment of the Organization of African Unity and the world at large to maintaining national boundaries as the colonial powers left them, nothing short of a major transformation in African and global strategic thinking could make it possible.

A third alternative is to establish a diversified federal or autonomous system of Government which recognizes and preserves the current racial, ethnic, religious and cultural differences within an otherwise unified nation-state. While this appears to be the preference of most Southerners, it would seem to provide a fertile soil for continuing the stratifications and the inequities that generate divisive tensions and conflicts.

The fourth and last alternative that comes to mind as a promising ground for genuine unity is to build the national character on the bases of principles that unite and avoid those that tend to divide. This would mean combining a decentralized system of government which recognizes diversities with a national framework which positively reflects all the racial, ethnic, religious and cultural groups on equitable bases, fosters a sense of belonging and national pride in all the peoples of the Sudan, and permits the process of mutual national integration or assimilation to evolve in an atmosphere of unity and harmony. Cultural elements would then be adopted, retained, or discarded on the basis of their intrinsic merits or popular appeal. The ultimate outcome of the process would probably be a unique dynamic and mutually enriching Sudanese mold that defies such exclusive labels as "Arab" or "African."

Put in a nutshell, what the Sudan needs, it seems to me, is to build the unity of the country on the basis of religious neutrality—secularism, linguistic duality—Arabic and English, and a national cultural program that is genuinely Afro-Arab. Indeed, even in its foreign relations, Sudan can best realize its postulated role as the microcosm of Africa and a link between the Continent and the Middle East by taking full advantage of the dynamics of its dualistic identity as African and Arab, which it cannot do without the full participation of the non-Arab population of the South, the West, the East, and indeed the North, and at all levels, local, national, regional and international.

Recommended Readings

DENG, FRANCIS MADING (1971), *Tradition and Modernization: A Challenge for Law among the Dinka of the Sudan*. New Haven, Conn. and London: Yale University Press.

With some emphasis on law, this book is a comprehensive study of tradition and modernity in Dinka society and the need for balancing them in a program of guided change.

(1972), *The Dinka through Their Songs*. Oxford, Britain: Clarendon Press.

A comprehensive coverage of Dinka songs (texts and translations) with a sociological introduction of about one quarter of the book.

HOWELL, PAUL P. (1951), *The Ngok Dinka of Western Kordofan*, Vol. 32 of Sudan Notes and Records, 239.

An analytic description of the Ngok Dinka: their history, their social and political structure, and their law.

IBRAHIM, EFFENDI BEDRI (1939), *Notes on Dinka Religious Beliefs in Their Chiefs and Rainmakers*, Vol. 22 of Sudan Notes and Records, 125-131.

A short account of the Dinka's religious beliefs in the divine prerogative of their hereditary Chiefs and other religious functionaries.

(1948), *More Notes on the Padang Dinka,* Vol. 29 of Sudan Notes and Records, 40-57.

A general survey of the Padang Dinka of Upper Nile Province, focusing on their history, divine leadership, and religious beliefs.

LIENHARDT, GODFREY (1961), *Divinity and Experience: The Religion of the Dinka.* Oxford, Britain: Clarendon Press.

With religion as its starting point, this book covers a wide range of Dinka life and culture.

(1958), *The Western Dinka, Tribes Without Rulers* (Eds., J. Middleton and D. Tait.) London: Routledge & Kegan Paul, 97-135.

An examination of the association between the political structure and the kinship system of the Dinka and of the religious undertones permeating them.

MACHRELL, J. E. C. (1942), *The Dinka Oath on Ashes,* Vol. 25 of Sudan Notes and Records, 132-134.

An account of the ceremony and the significance of oath among the Dinka.

NEBEL, A. (1954), *Dinka Dictionary.* Verona, Italy: Verona Fathers.

A short dictionary of the Western Dinka dialects.

(1948), *Dinka Grammar.* Verona, Italy: Verona Fathers.

A book of Rek and Malual Dinka grammar, with texts and translations of folk lore and vocabulary.

O'SULLIVAN, H. (1910), "Dinka Law," *Journal of the Royal Anthropological Institute,* 40: 171-191.

A short account of Dinka substantive law with an introduction by E. S. Hartland.

SELIGMAN, C. G., and B. Z. SELIGMAN (1932), *Pagan Tribes of the Nilotic Sudan.* London: G. Routledge & Sons, Ltd.

A compilation of information on many Southern Sudanese peoples, including the Dinka, and surveying various aspects of each with emphasis on their regulations of public life, kinship, and family (including marriage), indigenous religion, and finally death and funeral rites.

STUBBS, J. N. and C. G. T. MORRISON (1938), *Land and Agriculture of the Western Dinka*, Vol. 21 of Sudan Notes and Records, 251-265.

A demonstration of the agricultural occupation of the Dinka (which is often overlooked in favor of their preoccupation with cattle). Also discusses Dinka land in general and its connection with Dinka social and political organization.

TITHERINGTON, MAJOR G. W. (1927), *The Raik Dinka of Bahr el-Ghazal Province*, Vol. 10 of Sudan Notes and Records, 159-209.

A general survey of the Dinka: their history, their physical characteristics, their outlook, their culture, and their means of livelihood.

TREATT, MAJOR C. COURT (1931), *Out of the Beaten Track*. New York: E. P. Dutton & Co., Inc.

An account of Major Treatt's hunting trips in East Africa and his experiences with various peoples, including the Dinka, in the early part of this century.

Glossary

As a prelude to the glossary of Dinka terms used in this book a few guiding principles of orthography and pronunciation are included below.

1. All vowels have Latin (new pronunciation) values.
2. The letter "c" is always pronounced as "ch" in "change," never as in "care."
3. The nearest English letter to the Dinka letter "dh" is "th." But in the Dinka letter the tongue is drawn farther back than in the English "th."
4. The letter "ŋ" and "y" were added to the Roman alphabet by Christian missionaries who developed written Dinka. "ŋ" equals the English "ng" when it occurs at the end of an English word. "y" has no equivalent in English, but approximates the English "h" with the middle of one's tongue pressing the middle of his upper jaw, leaving a much smaller space for air than is the case in the sound of the letter "h." Here, "ng" and "gh" are used to represent "ŋ" and "y."
5. The letters "ny" are pronounced as in the Italian "gn" [gnocchi, for example], never as in the English "many," as in Latin.
6. When a vowel is doubled, the sound is an elongation of the vowel: "oo" is pronounced something like the "oa" in "goal" and

not as in "pool"; "ee" is pronounced like the "a" in "scale"; "ii" is pronounced like the "ee" in "geese"; "aa" is pronounced as in "car"; "uu" is pronounced as in "pool."

7. The letter "g" is always pronounced as in "gain," never as in "George."

8. The single vowel "a" is pronounced as in "car"; "e" approximates the "e's" in "every"; "i" is pronounced as in "kill"; "o" is pronounced as in "poll"; "u" is pronounced as in "bull."

§

Abaar: Orphan. But unlike its English equivalent, abaar is applied by the Dinka to adults as well as to children.

Aci boot: Eaten by ants and termites (literally). Generally used as a metaphor meaning that a person is dead.

Acituck: Dinka field hockey.

Adheng: As applied to a man: noble, handsome, elegant, charming, graceful, gentle, hospitable, generous, well mannered, kind, or of marked esthetic attributes. Also used to mean a gentleman and an initiated man as opposed to a "boy." See *Dheeng* for the noun forms of adheng.

Agamlong: The acceptor of speech (literally). A man who repeats in a high-pitched voice the whole or part of each sentence said in court, prayer, or any public speech. At an official function, no one can speak without the agamlong's acceptance.

AGE-GROUP: An unorganized group of people about the same age. Although without a corporate identity as Westerners would see it, age-grouping has important social consequences in Dinka values and etiquette.

AGE-MATES: Members of the same age-set.

AGE-SET: A group of people—male or female—of about the same age who are formally organized, initiated together into adulthood and continue as a corporate unit throughout their lives.

AGNATES: Persons related through the male line.

AGNATIC: Pertaining to a relationship reckoned through the male line.

Agoor: Food given by a woman to her husband, son, or any other male relative in private as opposed to the food normally served in the presence of visitors or other companions. The practice is publicly denounced, but is nevertheless expected of every wife.

Aguen: An affectionate term applied to small children by women. The English word closest to it is "darling."

Akeeth: Incest. Also a skin disease that affects pigmentation and is associated with incest or stepping on the grave of a maternal uncle.

Aleeng: Conversation or joking (literally). Used to mean the stage of courtship when the couple is intimate enough to sleep together although not necessarily to indulge in sexual intercourse.

Alueeth: Liar. Also applied to vanity or show offishness—not always in a derogatory sense, sometimes indeed quite the opposite.

Amiyok: A plant.

Anyat: Members of a newly initiated group who are almost too young for their age-set.

Anyoic: The period immediately following the end of the rains when crops are ripe and the cattle begin to graze further away from the villages.

Anyanya: The military wing of the Southern Sudanese movement.

Aril: "Chills," applied both to a difficult delivery and what Dinkas believe a baby suffers from when not given the warm bath which is considered an important part of infant care.

ACEPHALOUS: Adjective that refers to societies in which power is exercised through the lineage system without overall central authority.

Awec: Payment made to a wronged person, not so much to indemnify him materially as to appease and reconcile him.

Ayic: A tiny fish with delicate fins and soft bones.

Ayur: The opposite of adheng.

Baai (plural *bai*): Family, home, village, tribe, country, or people, according to the context in which it is used.

Baggara: Nomadic Arab tribes in Kordofan Province, one of the provinces of the Northern Sudan.

Beeny: Chieftaincy. Also used generally to connote nobility or aristocracy.

Beny: A Chief. Also applied generally to anyone who is a descendant of a chiefly lineage or clan.

Biook: An institutionalized fight between the last initiated age-set and that immediately senior to it. These usually occur over competition for the age-set of girls corresponding to the youngest male age-set.

BRIDEWEALTH: Wealth paid by the bridegroom and his kin group to the relatives of the bride who, among the Dinka, are also expected to make a reverse payment equivalent to about one third of the bridewealth. This reverse payment must be paid from the wealth of the bride's relatives and not from what they receive as bridewealth.

BLOODWEALTH: Wealth paid in compensation for a victim of homicide. But the Dinka apply the same term to compensation for bodily injuries.

Cak dit: To create a song, (literally); that is, to compose.

Cak wel: To create words (literally); In other words, to tell a lie.

CATTLE BYRE: Large huts twice or more the size of normal huts—used for keeping livestock at night during the rainy season.

CATTLE-CAMP: Anywhere other than within the normal residential compound, in which cattle are temporarily kept. Usually, young men and women take cattle to camps far away from permanent residences in order to search for better pastures or, sometimes to get away from the controls of their elders.

CATTLE-HEARTH: A fire-place, usually in the center of the area where cattle are fettered, around which the male members of the group sit. The same term is applied to the lineage and the clan (*gol or dhien*), since they symbolize the male line.

Cien: A dying declaration usually expressing the last will of a person. *Cien* or *acien* also means a curse, whether intentionally inflicted by a wronged person or automatically resulting from a wrongdoing. Although the curse may be effective in the lifetime of the wronged person, *cien* usually implies punishment by the spirit of a dead person and may be transmitted onto the cursed one's posterity. It is probably because of the spiritual dangers believed to result from failure to fulfill the last wishes of a dead person that the same term is used for both will and curse.

Cieng: As a verb: to look after, to order, to rule, to inhabit, to treat [a person], and to relate to a person. As a noun: human relations, conduct, behavior, habit, personality, custom, law, rule, way of life, culture, essence, and nature. The Dinka concept of ideal human relations.

CLAN: A group of persons who believe themselves related through a common ancestor, although they may not in fact be able to trace their genealogies to the common ancestor.

COMPOUND FAMILIES: Polygynous, usually large, families.

Cot: Literally, "calling [a girl]." A term used for courtship visits in which a man is expected to stand a distance from the girl's house in respect to her relatives and "call" her, first by indicating his presence and then, when attended to, by asking for her.

CO-WIVES: Wives of the same husband.

Dhieth: Birth.

Dheck: A game of tag.

Diet: Birds (literally). But in most Dinka dialects this term is used to mean twins.

DIVINATION: A skill whereby a person induces in himself the necessary conditions for acquiring divine enlightenment and insight into the spiritual causes of illness and mishap; and sometimes into the meaning of dreams. Divination is often followed by suggestion of appropriate measures to be taken to remedy the situation.

DIVINER: The person who performs divination.

Dor: A special type of a war-song in which a solo, followed by the chorus, excites peace or 'war demonstrations.

ELEMENTARY FAMILY: A family consisting of a man, his wife, and their children.

EVIL-EYED: A practioner of black magic who harms his victim with his evil eyes.

EXOGAMY: The practice of marrying outside certain degrees of blood or marriage affinities. (The opposite is endogamy.) While the Dinka are exogamous, they are ethnically endogamous in the sense that they object to marriage outside their ethnic groups, and in particular with respect to their women.

FULL SIBLINGS: Persons of either sex who have the same father and mother.

Geem: The acceptor [of a baby] (literally); in other words, a midwife.

GHOST-MARRIAGE: An institution whereby relatives of a dead man marry a wife for his spirit and select one amongst themselves to cohabit with her and beget children to the name of the dead relative.

Goor: A ballet in which people run and jump, holding spears in a throwing position, and appear to be dodging spears—all in imitation of spear-fighting.

Gur: "To hatch" a baby. This is done through having sexual intercourse with a pregnant woman because the Dinka believe it aids the development of the baby.

HALF-KIN: Used here to include people related through the same father but different mothers.

Homr: A tribe of the Baggara who neighbor the Ngok Dinka to the North.

INITIATION: A ceremony by which youth are turned into full-fledged adults.

Jak (singular jok): Spirits associated with illness and other forms of misfortune.

Jur (plural *juur*): The Dinka word for non-Dinkas [excepting the Nuer whom they designate as "Nuer"]. Normally used by the Ngok to mean "Arab."

Ka rac (singular *ke rac*): Literally, "bad things"; also, the Ngok word for snakes. In some dialects, snakes are referred to as *ka piiny* (the things of the ground). Most snakes also represent clan totems and therefore "relatives" who must not be harmed just as they too must not harm their relatives. This is perhaps the Dinka way of pacifying the dangerous creatures with which they must live in their natural environment.

Kei: Roots of water lilies.

Ker: The season from May to early July—a wet season.

Ket: Insulting through songs. Also applied to the singing and dancing custom by which a senior age-set attempts to disparage the immediately younger age-set by singing about shameful incidents involving members of this younger age-set, then presenting the songs in a dance that is usually performed only by females and thus associating the younger age-set with female attributes.

Kic: Commoners.

KIN: A group of people who trace their relationship through parent-child or sibling relations for recognized social purposes.

KINSHIP: Relationship actually or putatively traced through parent-child or sibling relations and recognized for social purposes.

Kooc e nhom: Literally, "standing the head." Immortality through procreation.

Koor: A lion normally, but is also used to mean "fairy-tale" because lions figure very prominently in Dinka fairy-tales.

LEVIRATE: The institution whereby a relative of a dead man co-habits with his widow to beget children to the name of the dead man. The Dinka term for it is *la ghot*: literally, "entering the hut."

LINEAGE: A group of people who can trace their relationship to a common ancestor, reckoned by the Dinka through the male line.

Lir: High-jumping.

Loor: Drum. Also used to mean "dance."

Luk: Lawsuit or court action. Also means persuasion, or an appeal to anyone for any purpose. Can also be used as a verb.

Luny: Release. Termination of the status of new initiates and the commencement over their status as full-fledged adults.

MAGIC: The use of symbolic action to manipulate persons and things for good or evil purposes. The Dinka respect only the spiritual power that people possess by virtue of being human beings and the special power of divine leaders which is hereditary. Newly acquired "magic," the power of the Evil-Eye, and all forms of what might be called "Black Magic" is loathed by the Dinka.

Mai: The season from February to May—a dry season.

MATERNAL: Pertaining to the mother.

MENOPAUSE: The age when a woman is physiologically no longer able to bear children.

Micar ageer: Black bulls with wide-spread horns (literally). A rather comic way of referring to the commoners, to indicate their powerlessness. A bull of such horns does not fight as powerfully as a bull with upward and pointed horns.

Mioc: A short poetic utterance about one's Ox or a significant incident in one's life. Used in dance, in war, hunting or fishing when one has hit, or to express any emotion [usually of anger].

MONOGAMY: A mutually exclusive marriage of one man and one woman.

Monyjang: Literally, "The lord (or the husband) of all Peoples": the Dinka word for themselves. The term "Dinka" is a foreign term.

Naar: Maternal kin. Derived from the word for maternal uncle.

Ngok: A small, but dangerous, fish with sharp fins which the Dinka liken to horns.

It may be that the Ngok Dinka were named after this fish.

Nguoth: A term used when a person has speared an enemy, an animal, or a fish. Also said by a group when sprayed by a Chief or a holy man with holy water.

Nhialic: God. Occasionally applied to lesser divinities, but understood that they are one with the Supreme force.

NILOTIC PEOPLE: A group of tall, slender, black people found in the Southern Sudan and Uganda. In the Sudan, they include the Dinka, the Nuer, the Shilluk, and the Anuak.

Nyal rot: A chant of special verses by which intimate friends crown their laughter. An expression of their gratification in the mutuality of their sentiments or under standing in particular situations. Usually associated with gossip, chitchat, or raillery.

Paan: The possessive form of *baai* (see above); that is, as belonging to a named person.

Paar: To tell a fairy-tale. The word *paar* has a connotation of uncertainty that is lacking in the English expression "to tell a story."

PARAMOUNT CHIEF: The supreme authority in the tribe. The Ngok Dinka has nine subtribes, each with its chief and junior chiefs. On top of all these chiefs are two chiefs whose power extends over the whole tribe. Then, on top of these two chiefs and all the other chiefs, is the Paramount Chief.

PATERNAL: Pertaining to the father.

PATRIARCHAL: Pertaining to the patriarch—the father or any other male ascendant as the head of the family.

PAYMENT OF APPEASEMENT: See the Dinka term.

Peeth: Evil-Eye.

Por: A type of porridge made of milk. Usually prepared by children or (in larger quantities) by wives as a special delicacy for their husbands.

PERSONALITY-OX: A favorite ox which a man acquires by virtue of his ownership of a particular color-pattern that is determined by his status in the family. In polygynous families this depends on his mother's order of marriage and his own order of birth. Actual ownership of oxen accrues on initiation, after which a person is given a metaphorical name based on the color-pattern of his ox and is in many other ways fully identified with his ox. At this point in his life he then decorates it and displays it for esthetic pleasure and recognition.

POLYGYNY: The form of polygamy in which one man marries more than one wife. The other form of polygamy is polyandry, in which one woman marries more than one husband. This last form is unknown in Africa.

Prima Facie: A legal term meaning sufficient liability on first impression, pending further investigation.

PROPITIATION: Appeasement through a gift of property, usually livestock.

REVERSE PAYMENT: See bridewealth (above).

Riar: To perish (literally). This term is applied to mean "death" (or dying) when one does not have male issue to continue one's name.

Ril wei: To freeze. Also applied to what the Dinka believe will happen to a baby to whom the customary hot bath is not administered. The idea of the bath is not so much to warm up the baby as it is to aid its physical development.

Ring: Literally "meat" or "flesh," but also the divinity Ring (also called "Flesh"), who is the source of the divine power and enlightenment of chiefly clans.

RITES OF ATONEMENT: Practices by which a wrong is corrected and reconciliation achieved.

RITES OF PURIFICATION: Symbolic actions by which a person is cleansed of a wrong.

Ruaath: An initiation in which men dance with older women, especially the mothers of newly initiated youth. The only Dinka dance in which bodies (and then, only legs) touch.

Ruel: The season from July to October - a wet season.

Rut: The season extending from November to February—a dry season.

SELF-HELP: An institutionalized practice whereby people, usually young men, take law into their hands either to enforce their own rights or to facilitate the administration of justice in front of the Chiefs and Elders.

SPIRITUAL CONTAMINATION: The effect of a curse usually resulting from wrong-doing—either by one's self or one's kin. It manifests itself in misfortune, illness, and even death.

STEP-KIN: Used here in the same way as half-kin: persons related through the same father but with different mothers.

Theel: Drum sticks.

Thiang: A children's disease believed to be caused by violation of the taboo against sexual intercourse with a nursing woman. It is also believed to be contagious.

Thiou: Various stomach troubles. Also applied to guinea worm and the swelling it causes its victims.

Thooc: Literally, "elevating the throne [of a chief]," a term applied to the burial of a chief. The term "burial" itself is not used in the case of a chief.

Toc: Lying down (literally). A custom by which young men go to distant cattle-camps for two or three months, gorge themselves with milk and meat, move as little as possible, get fat, and compose songs about matters of serious concern to them—usually marriage.

Toc, pronounced differently, also means swampy savannah land used for dry season cattle-camps.

Waak: Literally, "bathing." Applied to songs composed during the period of *toc* (above).

Wal: Evil medicine usually supposed to be in a bundle of plants or other symbolic objects.

WEANING: The termination of breast-feeding the child. Among the Dinka it takes place after two or three years or whenever the mother dries up.

Weer: Racing.

Weeth: Children's diseases. Also applied to certain chronic adult diseases.

Wiel: A general symbolic practice designed to bring death or other misfortune to whomever it is directed against. Always understood as evil and loathed.

Yeth (singular *yath*): Clan divinities (beneficial as opposed to *jak*).

Yuur: The opposite of *dheeng* for which, see this glossary above.

About the Author

Dr. Francis Mading Deng is a diplomat, statesman, author, and scholar from what was then the Republic of the Sudan, now divided into Sudan and South Sudan. He was South Sudan's first Ambassador and Permanent Representative to the United Nations from 2012 to 2016. Most recently, he has served as Deputy Rapporteur of the National Dialogue and a member of the Revitalized Peace Process in the category of Eminent Persons. He is now Co-Chairperson of the Governance Working Committee as well as a member of the Constitution making Working Committee, both of the Revitalized Joint Monitoring and Evaluation Committee, R-JMEC.

Francis Deng was born in 1938 at Noong in the Abyei area of the Ngok Dinka at the border of Sudan and South Sudan, of which his father, the late Deng Majok, was the Paramount Chief. He received his early education in both South and North Sudan and joined the University of Khartoum in 1958, where he obtained his LL.B (Honors) in 1962. First in his class, he was appointed 'Tutor' and sent abroad for post graduate studies. He received his LL.M. in 1965 and J.S.D. (Doctor of Juridical Science in 1968, making him the first South Sudanese to receive a doctorate in any field. He also attended post-graduate courses in London University, but before graduating, he was accused of masterminding and leading the anti-government activities in Europe and was recalled. He refused to return, resigned his position on the Faculty and went to the United States on a Senior Fellowship from Yale University Law School.

Deng has devoted his professional life to public service. He first joined the United Nations in 1967, when he was appointed as a Human Rights Officer in the Division of Human Rights in New York. In 1972, he joined Sudan foreign service, following the Addis Ababa Agreement that ended the 17 year civil war. He served as Ambassador to the Nordic countries of Canada, Denmark, Finland, Norway, Sweden, and the United States of America, and as Minister of State for Foreign Affairs. In 1983 he resigned after turning down an assignment as Ambassador to Ethiopia, as that would have pitted him against the SPLM/A, which had just rebelled against the Government, triggering the civil war that was ended by the Comprehensive Peace Agreement of 2005.

Following his resignation from Sudan foreign service, Dr. Deng was appointed the first Distinguished Fellow of the Rockefeller Brothers Fund. He subsequently joined the Woodrow Wilson International Center for Scholars, initially as a Guest Scholar and then as a Senior Research Associate. While at The Wilson Center, he was appointed one of the first Jennings Randolph Distinguished Fellows of the newly established United States Institute of Peace. He then joined the Brookings Institution as a Senior Fellow, where he founded and directed the Africa Project. During the 12 years he spent at Brookings, he served concurrently as Representative of the U.N. Secretary-General on Internally Displaced Persons (IDPs). At Brookings, he co-directed the Brookings Project on Internal Displacement with Roberta Cohen, to support his U.N. mandate.

In 2001, he left Brookings and accepted appointment in a tenured position as Distinguished Professor at the Graduate Center of the City University of New York (CUNY). Several years later, he decided to go back to Washington where he accepted the position of Research Professor of International Politics, Law and Society at Johns Hopkins University School of Advanced International Studies (SAIS). During this period, he continued his U.N. service on Internal Displacement and co-directorship of the Brookings Project on Internal Displacement until his mandate ended in 2004 in accordance with the newly introduced term limit for the Special Procedures mandates of the Commission of Human Rights.

At the end of his U.N. service on IDPs in 2004, Deng left SAIS to become a Distinguished Visiting Scholar at the John Kluge Center of the Library of Congress, after which he became a Wilhelm Fellow at the Center for International Studies of the Massachusetts Institute of Technology (MIT). In May, 2007, United Nations Secretary-General, Ban Ki-moon, appointed him Special Advisor on the Prevention of Genocide, on a full-time basis and at the level of Under-Secretary-General. At the end of his UN mandate in 2012, he became the first Permanent Representative of South Sudan to the United Nations.

In his national and international service, Deng focused on the crises of national identity as the underlying cause of conflicts and related mass atrocities, in some cases amounting to genocide. The conflicts emanate not from the mere difference, but from the mismanagement of the differences These crises usually dichotomize countries into the in-groups, whose members enjoy the rights of citizenship, and out-groups, who are generally discriminated, marginalized, excluded and denied their human dignity. The strategy of constructive management of diversity, which Deng advocated for addressing the crises of national identity, aims at promoting exclusivity, equality, dignity, and the enjoyment of all human rights, without any discrimination based on race, nationality, ethnicity, religion, culture or gender.

In pursuing his U.N. mandates, Deng travelled extensively throughout the world, and engaged in constructive dialogue with

Governments and other actors. To avert concerns over national sovereignty, Deng stipulated the concept of Sovereignty as Responsibility, which he and his colleagues developed at Brookings. Rather than be viewed negatively as a barricade against international involvement, should be understood as placing the primary responsibility for protecting and assisting, if necessary, with the support of the international community.

Deng, however, argued that if a state manifestly fails to discharge its national responsibility, and does not call on the international community for assistance, with the result that masses of people become exposed to severe suffering and the threat of death, the international community is duty-bound to step in and fill the vacuum. The best way to protect national sovereignty is therefore to discharge the responsibility of sovereignty, and call on the international community to assist, if necessary. Sovereignty as Responsibility has since evolved into the Responsibility to Protect, (RtoP) with the same pillars of shared responsibility. But because RtoP, as it is popularly known, is generally perceived as posing a threat of international military intervention, it has generated considerable controversy, and a degree of resistance from Governments. The principles Deng applied in his work however proved to be useful a building block in discharging very difficult U.N. mandates. His efforts aimed at bridging idealism with realism to make what seems impossible possible.

Dr. Deng has documented his ideas in his numerous publications, having authored and edited over forty books on a wide variety of subjects, including in the fields of law, conflict resolution, internal displacement, genocide prevention, human rights, anthropology, politics, history, and folklore, including two novels on the theme of the crisis of national identity in the Sudan. Deng has received numerous national and international awards and honors for his public service and his scholarly and literary contributions.

Index

Deng xvi, xix, xx, xxi, 14, 38, 44, 66, 116, 133, 137, 167, 181, 192, 205-7, 210, 219-220, 226-7, 232, 234-9, 244-5, 249, 276

Dheeng xiv, 31, 36, 39, 41, 102, 300

Dhiendior 66

Dietary 70

Digging 217

Dinka ix, x, xi, xii, xii, xiv, xv, xvi, xvi, xix, xx, xxi, xxi, xxi, 3-36, 38-40, 42-5, 47-65, 67-74, 77, 79-80, 82-6, 88, 90-3, 95, 97-100, 102, 106-114, 118-121, 123-131, 134, 138-9, 141-151, 155-7, 159-163, 165-6, 168, 170-6, 178-180, 183-9, 191-3, 195-8, 200-210, 212-6, 219, 221, 223-8, 230-6, 238, 240-1, 244, 246-251, 254-9, 261-6, 268-274, 276, 280, 282-3, 285, 287-9, 292, 295-7, 299-300, 302-310

Dinkaland 6, 10, 13, 15, 35, 49, 69, 108, 175, 211, 249, 258, 269

Dinkas 18, 28, 41, 118, 156, 205, 237, 301

Diplomacy 272

Divination 304

Divinity 206-207, 296

Doctorate xx

Dongbek 216-217

Dongolawi 226

Drags 152

Dun 57

Dung 87

Dutton 4, 37, 297

Early 114

East 257, 274, 279, 294, 297

Economic 263

Egypt 224, 259, 280

Egyptian 259

England xix

English 43, 82, 210, 244, 251, 258, 278, 293-4, 299-301, 307

Englishman 251

Equatorian xv

Eternity 213

Ethnic xii

European xxi, 204-5

Europeans 28, 205, 277

Evil 310

Exodus 248

Faculty xix

Filial 194

Fishing 176

Folkways xiv

Foremost 153, 291

Francis xvi, xix, xx

Frictions 73

Garang x, xi, 220, 228, 247, 281

Gentleman 33

Gentlemen 226

George xxi

Giir 276

www.ingramcontent.com/pod-product-compliance
Lightning Source LLC
Chambersburg PA
CBHW021849020426
42334CB00013B/243